MODERN GOVERNANCE

MODERN GOVERNANCE

New Government-Society Interactions

Edited by
Jan Kooiman

SAGE Publications
London · Thousand Oaks · New Delhi

First Published 1993, Reprinted 1994

SAGE Publications Ltd
6 Bonhill Street
London EC2A 4PU

SAGE Publications Inc
2455 Teller Road
Thousand Oaks, California 91320

SAGE Publications India Pvt Ltd
32, M-Block Market
Greater Kailash – I
New Delhi 110 048

ISBN 0-8039-8890-7
ISBN 0-8039-8891-5 pbk

Printed in Great Britain by The Cromwell Press
Broughton Gifford, Wiltshire

CONTENTS

1. Social-Political Governance: Introduction
    Jan Kooiman (Erasmus University Rotterdam, The
    Netherlands)   1

I. CONCEPTUALIZATIONS

2. Governing Failures and the Problem of Governability:
    Some Comments on a Theoretical Paradigm
    Renate Mayntz (Max-Planck-Institute, Köln, Germany)   9

3. Modes of Governance
    Andrew Dunsire (University of York, Great Britain)   21

4. Governance and Governability: Using Complexity,
    Dynamics and Diversity
    Jan Kooiman (Erasmus University Rotterdam, The
    Netherlands)   35

II. PREDICAMENTS

5. Lost Opportunity: The Case of Labour Market Manage-
    ment in the Republic of Ireland
    Frédéric Royall (University of Limerick, Ireland)   51

6. Public Policy Planning and the Problem of Governance:
    The Question of Education in Finland
    Kirsti Stenvall (University of Tampere, Finland)   63

7. Women's Emancipation as a Question of Governance:
    Actors, Institutions and the Room for Manoeuvre
    Marijke Prins (Humanistic University, Utrecht, The
    Netherlands)   75

III. EXPERIENCES

8. The Governance of Data Protection
    Charles Raab (University of Edinburgh, Scotland)   89

9. Environmental Regulation of Business: Options and
    Constraints for Communicative Governance
    Martijn van Vliet (Erasmus University Rotterdam, The
    Netherlands)   105

10. Public-Private Partnership: A Model for the Management
    of Public-Private Cooperation
    Vincent Kouwenhoven (Private consultant, Amsterdam,
    The Netherlands)   119

11. Dynamics and Room for Manoeuvre in Governance: The
    Channel Tunnel Decision in France and Britain
    Michèle Breuillard (Université de Lille II, France)   131

12. Governance between Legitimacy and Efficiency: Citizen
    Participation in the Belgian Fire Services
    Geert Bouckaert (Catholic University Leuven, Belgium)   145

13. Governance in Interaction: Public Tasks and Private
    Organisations
    Herman Aquina (University of Nijmegen, The Nether-
    lands) and *Hans Bekke* (University of Leiden, The
    Netherlands)   159

IV. PROSPECTS FOR REFORM

14. Public Management; from Imitation to Innovation
    Les Metcalfe (European Institute for Public
    Administration, Maastricht, The Netherlands)   173

15. Complexity, Governance and Dynamics: Conceptual
    Explorations of Public Network management
    Walter Kickert (Erasmus University Rotterdam, The
    Netherlands)   191

16. Governance and the Problem of Representation in Public
    Administration: The Case of Finland
    Kyösti Pekonen (University of Jyväskyla, Finland)   205

17. Modes of Governance and Administrative Change
    Torben Beck Jørgensen (University of Copenhagen,
    Denmark)   219

V. EVALUATIONS

18. The Governance of Education: Britain and France
   Roger Duclaud-Williams (University of Warwick, Great
   Britain)   235

19. Findings, Speculations and Recommendations
   Jan Kooiman (Erasmus University Rotterdam, The
   Netherlands)   249

   ABOUT THE AUTHORS   263

   BIBLIOGRAPHY   267

SOCIAL-POLITICAL GOVERNANCE: INTRODUCTION

JAN KOOIMAN

Background

Collaboration on this book started with an ECPR Workshop titled: 'GOVERNANCE: new patterns of interaction between government and society', in Essex, England, in April 1991. The purpose for which Prof.dr. Jan Kooiman convened this Workshop was to see whether changes taking place in more traditional patterns of governing and governance in The Netherlands, can also be found in other West-European countries.

In many countries the main tendency in recent years has been to shift the balance between government and society away from the public sector and more towards the private sector. Partly, this added up to privatization and sometimes to deregulation. But there are also efforts to shift the balance towards a sharing of tasks and responsibilities; towards doing things together instead of doing them alone (either by the 'state' or by the 'market').

New patterns of interaction between government and society can be observed in areas such as social welfare, environmental protection, education and physical planning. These new patterns are apparently aimed at discovering other ways of coping with new problems or of creating new possibilities for governing.

Examples show experiments with co-regulation, co-steering, co-production, cooperative management and public-private partnerships on national, regional and local levels. We regard these examples as concrete, often new, ways of governing on the borderline between government and society; as non-traditional mixtures of the public and private sector.

More generally, there are many indications that the governing capacity of political/administrative systems (by which we mean all those institutions, authorities, groups or individuals who separately or together perform governing actions) either has crossed the threshold of the law of diminishing returns or is quite close to such a boundary. In those situations, actors, either as parts of governing systems, or separately, or in a combination, not only try to reduce the need for governing (let problems solve themselves) but also rephrase their capacities (let others help). Such changes do not take place in a vacuum. They may be the expression of a change in preference of ways of governance. One could say that they have to do with efforts to deal with matters of governability. In other words, the discussion about new patterns of interaction between government and society takes place on two (analytically) distinguishable levels. On a concrete governing level there is the search for new models of governing in terms of 'co' such as co-steering, co-managing, co-producing and co-allocating. Such changes can be empirically observed in several sectors and in different countries. But one can also observe changes in terms of patterns of governance: broader and maybe more pervasive efforts to come to grips with fundamental developments and structural characteristics of the societies we live in. These are what we would like to call changes taking place on the governance level (or even 'meta governance level'). In the conceptualization we try to develop in this book, we use concepts such as 'dynamics', 'complexity' and 'diversity'. These concepts play an important role in trying to understand the purpose of the changes at the governance level.

In terms of working definitions: by governing we mean all those activities of social, political and administrative actors that can be seen as purposeful efforts to guide, steer, control or manage (sectors or facets of) societies. To distinguish these new or modern interactive forms from others, we call them social-political governing and governance in this study. Social-political forms of governing are forms in which public or private actors do not act separately but in conjunction, together, in combination, that is to say in 'co' arrangements. The interactive aspects of these forms are quite important. By 'governance' we mean the patterns that emerge from governing activities of social, political and administrative actors. These patterns form the 'emerging' outcome as well as a more abstract (higher level) framework for day-to-day efforts at governing. Modes of social-political governance are, in our opinion, always an outcome of public and private interaction. Governability of a social-political system can be seen in terms of a balancing process. It is not something static, but a constant process of coming to grips with the tension between governing needs on the one hand (problem situations or the grasp of opportunities) and governing capacities (creating patterns of solutions or developing strategies) on the other hand. We consider sectors of societies to be appropriate empirical levels to study and analyze governing, governance and governability.

These new ways of governing and governance may have reached a phase in which (broad) evaluations can be developed. Against this background the convener of the Workshop asked for contributions which focus on particular forms of social-political interaction as expressions of social, economic, technological and cultural forces that are complex and dynamic and have to do with 'primary processes' in sectors of society. Secondly, contributions might deal with the ways these (new) patterns of interactions are organized, for example in partly public, partly private inter-organizational networks. Thirdly, contributors might show new forms of interactive steering, managing, controlling or guiding in certain sectors of society. Finally, reports might have a more conceptual nature, dealing with matters such as governing needs, governing capacities, questions of governability and conceptualizations of aspects of social-political governance and governing.

In all categories of invited studies contributions were made, albeit not in the same amount. On the basis of the scope of participation in the Workshop, the convener invited a few others to participate in the project after the meeting in Essex. The contributors to the present volume came together for a second meeting in The Netherlands, February 1992. At this meeting general conceptual issues and suggestions about rephrasing individual chapters were discussed.

Aim

The aim of the project, of which this book is an expression, is to explore the possibilities of developing conceptual frameworks for analysis and (practical) applications of new ways of interaction between government and society in terms of patterns of governance and governing. Interactive social-political governance means setting the tone; creating the social-political conditions for the development of new models of interactive governing in terms of co-management, co-steering and co-guidance. Social-political governance and governing are not primarily looked upon as acts of governments, but as more or less continuous processes of interaction between social actors, groups and forces and public or semi public organizations, institutions or authorities. There is a division of labour between them, which may shift during the interaction. This is their strength, yet also their weakness. The possibilities and limitations of the interactional qualities of these forms of social-political governing and governance may become apparent in those new ways of governing and governance.

In a theoretical perspective our explorations contain elements of systems-theory, of theories of inter-organizational networks, of theories of public administration and public management, of communication theory and of theories of the state. In trying to come to grips with the tendencies we do not (yet) pretend to form a new theory. Partly, we take issue with existing theoretical notions, partly we develop some new notions ourselves. We are convinced that both our conceptualizations and the empirical illustrations we show, point in the same direction. This direction is partly defined by the recognition of new patterns of governance related to basic changes taking place in the societies we live in and look at. Changes we do not see as temporary but as structural. Changes we try to conceptualize under the heading of growing 'complexity', 'dynamics' and 'diversity'. As we will show more explicitly in the final chapter, differences of opinion do exist within our group, not on these changes as such, but on the degree of their pervasiveness. However, these are questions of either conceptualization or of empirical substantiation. We all agree on the need to make serious efforts to work on the two levels we have distinguished: on the governance and on the governing level; and to do this against the background of more stringent conceptualizations in three areas: firstly in the area of interactions between government and society;

secondly in the area of complexity, dynamics and diversity of our societies and the problems and opportunities these qualities create, and thirdly in the area of governance, governability and governing. These three areas in conceptual terms and in terms of empirical illustrations, are the main subject of this book. In this introduction we will indicate concisely what we mean by them. The following chapters will show more detailed aspects of them. In the final chapter we will bring the results together and sketch the outlines of a potential theory of social-political governance.

Interaction

There seems to be a shift away from more traditional patterns in which governing was basically seen as 'one-way traffic' from those governing to those governed, towards a 'two-way traffic' model in which aspects, qualities, problems and opportunities of both the governing system and the system to be governed are taken into consideration.

Besides varieties such as shifts to the private in terms of deregulation and privatization other forms of more systemic interaction are being tried out. These new forms can still be put under headings such as management, control, steering and guiding but the emphasis is not on the uni-lateral but on the bi-lateral or even multi-lateral aspects of these models of governing. This means that the place of boundaries between state and society changes, but also that the boundaries themselves change in character. One could say they are becoming more permeable. Where government begins and society ends, or the other way around, becomes more diffuse. The borderline between public and private responsibilities itself becomes object of interaction. These are basic matters of governance. These interactions are often themselves based on the recognition of (inter)dependencies. No single actor, public or private, has all knowledge and information required to solve complex, dynamic and diversified problems; no actor has sufficient overview to make the application of needed instruments effective; no single actor has sufficient action potential to dominate uni-laterally in a particular governing model. These are basically matters of the relation between governance and governing.

Some decades ago Chandler promoted 'structure to follow strategy'. This is directly opposed to the traditional view of the way in which the public sector works where strategy usually follows structure. It seems that finally Chandler's advice is being followed now. In other words: it seems as if in contrast to, or at least somewhat different from the usual, the emphasis is less on formalization and structuring (as in (neo) corporatist models), but more on putting a central focus on problems or opportunities (in all their aspects). By doing so the structural components follow as part of the outcome of interactions. 'Let us do something together (for example: try to approach a complex problem situation), later we will worry about the form in which we do this' seems to be the message. These are basically matters of governing.

We call such approaches interactive social-political forms of governing. The (macro) conditions under which these models develop within complete sectors or within even broader societal contexts, form what we call (interactive) social-political governance.

Social-political Governing

We look upon social-political governing as a collection of rather specific models of interaction between the public and private sector in terms of co-managing, co-steering, co-guiding of actors (individuals, authorities, organizations) with public as well as with private responsibilities . We are not primarily interested in these actors themselves, but in their governing activities in conjunction with each other. This makes the 'who' somewhat less tangible, but we expect to gain in terms of insights in the more systemic aspects of these sectors and the way they are governed. How do interactions develop, what kinds of forces do they express? How are interdependencies translated into decision-processes? What kinds of positive and negative feedback processes and loops can be determined?

We presume that these new ways of governing have reached a phase in which more systematic conceptualizations are needed to evaluate, underpin and analyze them: to explain why these new forms of governing are being developed; why more traditional ways of doing (maybe the same) things no longer work in terms of steering, management and control, and why these new forms might do better.

A first hypothesis might be that such interactive forms of governing can not be explained from an 'official policies' point of view. It might be exactly dissatisfaction with or ineffectiveness of approaches such as 'the administrative politics of policies' that lead to the search for other - more interactive - governing models. Social-political governing must be seen as a continuous process of interaction between public and non-public actors. The division of labour between them and the sharing of responsibilities are all part of the same process. Their connection (probably based on perceptions of mutual dependencies) seems to be their essence. In other words, structure, process and substance, interrelated in dealing with complex, dynamic and divers problem situations and the creation of new ways for solutions, are their specific characteristics.

In our opinion, we need other conceptualizations of these new ways of governing. More traditional policy models or arrangements seem to be either too government-oriented or too limited in scope. Our endeavour is more in line with theoretical efforts such as developed by the 'Bielefeld' Project (Kaufmann et al.) which itself builds on earlier work by Dahl/ Lindblom, Etzioni, Deutsch and others.

Social-political Governance

In this book we want to develop the argument that for a conceptual (and empirical) understanding of new forms of interaction of government and society in different new models of governing, it might help to pay systematic attention to questions/aspects/conceptualizations of governance and especially to social-political governance in terms of coping with the complexity, dynamics and diversity of modern societies.

It seems as if in these new developments more basic characteristics of modern societies are finally beginning to emerge. By this we mean that the growing complexity, dynamics and diversity of our societies, as 'caused by social, technological and scientific developments', puts governing systems under such new challenges that new conceptions of governance are needed. So far these developments have been taken for granted, or just considered to be nasty and difficult. Why not take them seriously and put them in the centre of new ways of thinking about how to govern, steer, manage, control and use them?

A second hypothesis we could phrase here is that changing patterns of governance might be connected to the growing recognition on the part of social and political actors of the complexity, dynamics and diversity of social-political systems.

What social-political governance is about is expressed - for the time being - in words, concepts and images such as conditions, qualities and opportunities for more concrete governing models such as co-managing, co-steering and co-guidance. As a starting point we consider these conditions as specific to a certain sector. Different mixtures of complexity, dynamics and diversity show differences between and within sectors of societies. Different realizations of them will lead towards inter-sectoral and inter-cultural differences. At the moment we do not have worked-out theoretical concepts or concrete data on the level of social-political governance. This means that what we want to show in this book about social-political governance and about its relations to more specific governing models will still be predominantly pre-theoretical in nature. However, we are confident that what we have to offer in this project may be the beginning of a more profound way of looking at the many shortcomings of more traditional models of governing against the background of more traditional modes of governance on the one hand and the first signals of new ways of governing against the background of new modes of social-political governance on the other hand. We realize that we will probably raise more questions than we will be able to answer and that there is a certain element of normativeness in what we are doing. In the final chapter we will return to matters such as these in a somewhat more systematic way, after having presented our theoretical notions and having looked at empirical illustrations to indicate what we are talking about.

INTRODUCTION TO PART I

CONCEPTUALIZATIONS

The first part of the book contains three chapters of a predominantly conceptual nature. Although the argumentation in these chapters partly is to be seen against the background of discussions and experiences in the countries the authors come from (Renate Mayntz from Germany, Andrew Dunsire from the UK and Jan Kooiman from The Netherlands), the scope of their argumentation is such that these contributions set the tone for the conceptions developed in the book.

In the first chapter Renate Mayntz uses the concept of steering - and the debate as carried on in Germany about this concept - for at least two purposes. In the first place she argues that we should make the problem of what (un)governability is, as clear as possible. Too often a remedy for failures is suggested which is a normative preference rather than a good problem analysis. Secondly, she shows that problems of governability are related to the dynamic and complex character of (sectors of) modern society and actual power distributions in them rather than to the so-called 'auto-poetic' character of social subsystems. Forms of social-political steering are necessary, but forms that differ from the more traditional 'state-oriented' ones.

In chapter 2 Andrew Dunsire argues that in situations of high complexity, dynamics and diversity, the role of government is one of what he calls 'collibration': steering by making use of opposing forces. Traditional forms such as regulation and central control are no longer adequate. He considers collaboration as such as a new way of interactive governing, using complexity, dynamics and diversity, rather than reducing them in inappropriate ways.

In the last chapter of this section, Jan Kooiman places complexity, dynamics and diversity as 'basic characteristics' which call for new modes of governance, in the centre of the conceptual discussion. He argues that instead of seeing complexity, dynamics and diversity as contributing to ungovernability, they can be seen as useful to enhance governability. This line of thought requires a new theoretical approach. As a starting point of such an approach he develops a concept of governability, consisting of the balancing between social-political needs and social-political capacities.

In the light of the discussion on different forms of governing, the three chapters show some possibilities and limitations of social-political governance and governing. In their approaches they use the concepts of complexity, dynamics and diversity to indicate their importance for the outline of a conceptualization of governance and governing which makes a systematic use of those central societal characteristics.

2

GOVERNING FAILURES AND THE PROBLEM OF GOVERNABILITY: SOME COMMENTS ON A THEORETICAL PARADIGM[1]

RENATE MAYNTZ

Starting Point: Governing Failures

For some twenty years now we have spoken of the, at least partial, failure of the modern state to perform its duties. Three areas of concern can be distinguished in the debate, each related to one of the main functions of the central state: regulation, welfare, and development. Especially in the 1970s the discussion about regulation focused on the imminent ungovernability of Western democracies. Central to the second discussion, which started in the 1960s and still continues today, is the so-called crisis of the welfare state. In the third discussion the scale and causes of governing failures play an important role. Although the three discussions overlap in terms of the problems addressed, three different theoretical lines of thought can be distinguished.

The issue of ungovernability stresses problems related to the acceptance of political leadership, a lack of conformity and a decreasing level of compliance. Ungovernability becomes manifest in political radicalism, a turn away from the party system, the emergence of new social movements and unorthodox forms of protest, increasing crime rates and a move to re-privatization of force. Explanations have been sought in societal factors (e.g. failure of socialization, loss of traditional values), political factors (failure of party system to represent popular will and to bring about consensus) and in the government system (inability to decide and to prevent popular distrust in and disagreement with the state.

The crisis of the welfare state appears mainly as a financial crisis. The problem is not so much whether a comprehensive welfare system is desirable or not, but whether it can be financed in a situation of increasing demands. Furthermore, the comprehensive welfare state emphatically shows problems deriving from bureaucratization: deficits of efficiency and legitimacy, the latter manifested in the critique of overregulation.

Although the debate about the welfare state has not been concluded yet, in Germany the theme of governing failures is particularly popular.

---

[1] Translated, with revisions especially in section 2, from: Politische Steuerung und gesellschaftliche Steuerungsprobleme - Anmerkungen zu einem theoretischen Paradigma. In: Jahrbuch zur Staats- und Verwaltungswissenschaft, volume 1, 1987. Baden-Baden: Nomos.

The assertion basically is that the state, because of the inherent short-comings of its traditional instruments, is not able (any more) to solve the economic and social problems it has identified. Since the state is not able to steer social development in a preferred direction, in order to prevent unwanted developments it is either necessary to look for alternative instruments or to lower the aspirations of central-state control. In this connection, alternatives to law as well as alternative legal instruments are considered.

The following observations deal with the paradigm of governing failures, and more in particular focus on the presumed relation between the causes of these failures and the particularities of the suggested solutions. It may be obvious that in the realm of governing one cannot sensibly speak of possible therapies if there is no diagnosis. The main alternatives that are presently suggested - decentralization and a change of political instruments - should match the presumed causes for governing failures. However, in the debate to suggest new ways of societal guidance, the methodological principle that a proper diagnosis of problems precedes the formulation of solutions seems to be widely neglected. In practice we see the well-known habit of jumping to conclusions. No doubt every solution that has been suggested implies a certain problem diagnosis. However, when the relation between diagnosis and solution remains implicit or is not scrutinized itself, there is a danger that the theoretical assumptions underlying a reform proposal are used uncritically to justify an essentially normative preference, for instance for decentralization. In other words: we should also question whether the search for alternatives (such as decentralization) to the more traditional mode of political guidance is really primarily based on the experience of governing failures. As long as a relation between reform strategy and problem analysis has not been clearly established, a possible reform effort will almost automatically lead to disappointments. Before I will address the presumed causes of governing failures, a conceptional clarification may be useful.

On Governing and Governance

The German-language debate on the effectiveness or failures of political control - or governing, in the definition used by Kooiman - is couched in the terminology of 'Steuerung' (steering), a term that became increasingly popular in the 1970s and 80s. The concept of 'Steuerung', when it first appeared in German macro-sociology, was probably the translation of the Anglo-Saxon term 'control'. In German micro-sociology, 'soziale Kontrolle' had been used as a translation for 'social control'. However, the German 'Kontrolle' is a much narrower concept than 'control', which is more properly rendered by the word 'Steuerung'. Thus, Parsons' control hierarchy is translated into German as 'Steuerungshierarchie'; similarly one speaks of 'Steuerungsmedien'.

In German political science, 'Steuerung' was first used to refer to the ability of political authorities to mould their social environments, i.e. in the sense of governing. Later, the concept was also used as a synonym for governance. Here the German debate closely followed the Anglo-American one, in which the Market was first added to Politics, followed by Solidarity and finally by Association. In Germany similarly, the market as an alternative mode of 'Steuerung' came first into the centre of attention (e.g. Gretschmann, 1981), soon followed by Community or Solidarity (e.g. Hegner, 1986). The concept of 'soziale Steuerung' has been further broadened by Kaufmann (1985) to cover the 'successful coordination of behaviour' in general.

However, the concept of 'Steuerung' loses its analytical sharpness when it is used both in the sense of governing and of governance. This double meaning of the German term follows from its being rooted in systems theory as well as in action theory. Thus 'Steuerung' is sometimes conceived of as a way of acting, sometimes as a process, and sometimes as a functional aspect of systems.

The English language (which, in contrast to German, is also able to distinguish between politics and policy) offers the opportunity to avoid the conceptual haziness resulting from this mixture of different meanings by setting off governing as an action from governance as a mode of social coordination, or order (see the definitions by Kooiman in the final chapter). Governing presupposes a subject (an actor). In the social sciences only persons or social collectives that are able to act can be governing subjects. The 'market' or 'solidarity' is no actor, but market principles as well as community ties can be used as governing instruments to reach specific objectives.

Governing typically involves not just singular actions, but is a process in which often several actors may participate. Especially when the governing subject is a social collective, governing - similar to decision-making - is a matter of division of labour. Being linked to actors, the perspective of governing is consciously selective, meaning that complex patterns of interaction are observed from the vantage point of the actor whose governing activity is being studied. From this perspective, the activities of the object of the governing efforts appear as reactive (adaptation, avoidance, counter strategy, etc.) irrespective as to whether the object sees itself as an object or primarily as a subject in its own right. It is this selective perspective which makes it possible to distinguish governing from governance (as a mode of social coordination), but one should remain sensitive to the limitations that accompany such a selective perspective.

As an action, governing - as the more technical 'steering' - not only means the exertion of goal-directed influence but more generally it means bringing a system from one state into another. The concept of governing thus presupposes that the object of governing efforts has an autonomous existence, that is to say that it will develop further on its own in absence of external interventions. To put it differently, the object is itself a system. By governing, its autonomous dynamics should be purposefully changed, be it that a certain structure will be protected against existing tendencies to change, a spontaneous change process will be re-directed, or a structure that would remain stable if left alone will be modified.

Besides a subject and an object, the concept of governing also includes the notion of an intention, for example a goal (in general a certain change of the state of the system which functions as object). Furthermore, it includes the application of measures to achieve the goal, and as a precondition for the choice of measures it also includes a conception of the causal nexus between governing activities and their results. Explicitly excluded from the proposed concept of governing is the notion that it will be successful, in other words that the goal should be reached. Even in the boundary case that purposeful interventions have barely any effect at all, one can still speak of governing (as action). This means that one should systematically distinguish between governing as an activity, and its effects. To use the concept without recognizing this distinction is overlooking the problem that is central to governing, which is the very precarious relation between action and result.

Limits of Governing

The growing interest in the topic of governing reflects the increased claim of political guidance, which first manifested itself in the 1960s in a growing orientation of political decision-makers towards planning and the use of planning techniques. Had there not been the ambition to steer social and economic processes according to plan, people would not have been conscious of and accordingly disappointed by the experience that intended reforms, attempts at problem-solving, and even efforts to cope with acute crisis so often fail. After all, the individual as well as the collective experience of being powerless and unable to fully control one's destiny is as old as mankind itself; the present time has only given it a special accent because of the awareness of our increased technical capabilities to destroy.

On the other hand, the claim that the human race or national communities should be able to shape their own destiny is not new either. In modern Europe this claim has existed at least from the Age of Enlightenment. After the end of the Second World War, certain events may have fostered the belief that it is indeed possible to collectively steer national and international developments. In Germany the so-called 'economic miracle', which very soon was presented not as a miracle but as a man-made success, contributed to such a belief, as well as the enlightened restraint practised by the Western Allies, and the successful process of political stabilization of the new democracy. The disappointment was therefore only the greater when it was realized that the prosperous time of the 'economic miracle' was just a short interval, the result of an unrepeatable combination of very special factors. Similarly brief was the phase of a planning euphoria with its attendant expectation of lasting social harmony.

Against this background of disappointment, governing became an issue among scholars, and the search for the causes of what against the back-grounds of earlier hopes was identified as failures of political control quite rapidly initiated the search for more successful alternative political instruments. Critics first argued against the ideal of all-encompassing planning, the ideal of deterministic control as in a command model, and therefore also against centrally established regulative norms. Surely this criticism was partially based more on normative preferences than on efficiency arguments, as evidenced by the simultaneous and quite vocal emancipation and self-determination claims. But the observation that the political instruments that had been used did not have the intended results, was not therefore inconsequential; in fact it influenced the choice of strategies to overcome the experienced shortcomings.

When governing by means of regulatory policies fails to meet its goals, this can be attributed to several causes. Firstly, regulatory policies can fail because they cannot be implemented, be it because of the fact that the executive authorities are unable to enforce the norms (implementation problem) or because the target groups are not willing to comply (motivation problem). A completely different set of problems occurs when, even if the rules are being complied with, the original problem does not disappear, or when in the process of implementation all kinds of unwanted side-effects appear. This may be due to the lawmaker's deficient knowledge of causal relationships that are of relevance to reaching a given goal (knowledge problem), or to the impossibility to intervene in a goal-directed way in certain system processes by means of the instruments that are available to central authorities (governability problem). In the discussion about potential solutions for the failures of political control, the - often implicit - diagnosis of problem causes has shifted several times; presently the emphasis seems to be on governability.

In West Germany during the late 1960s and early 1970s, when planning units, planning procedures and information systems for political decision-makers were being developed, it was hoped that the policy process could become more effective and that, as it was formulated then, 'the intelligence of the apparatus' could be increased. Thus the deficit was diagnosed as a 'knowledge problem', which could presumably be solved by more information and a greater information-processing capacity. The root of the problem thus seemed to lie with the political actor, and not with the object of his governing efforts.

As the experience was gained that even well planned and effectiveness-oriented reforms could fail, the problem diagnosis next shifted to 'implementation deficits'. The discussion about environmental politics can serve as an example of this. Research on the implementation of environmental laws for the Council of Environmental Experts drew attention to problems that occurred in the execution of laws (Mayntz et al., 1978). In the second half of the 1970s, implementation research boomed and indicated among other things that the governing subject is in fact a complex multi-level actor system. Those responsible for the execution of policy measures do not function as docile and neutral instruments but engage in governing themselves as they use the discretion conceded to them or manipulate and even circumvent the rules. Therefore, the implementation process itself should become an object of governing for the sake of an effective goal attainment. An administrative strategy responding to this analysis will not necessarily try to maximize the instrumentalization of the implementation agencies. On the contrary, it became apparent that granting the subordinate agencies more discretionary action space can improve their adaptation to situational requirements, which might subsequently lead to more effectiveness in the fulfilment of tasks. Partial decentralization to lower level agencies is an alternative strategy to solve the knowledge problem: not through better conceived central norms, but by means of a stepwise concretization of general norms so that the local knowledge of implementation authorities can be utilized. A partial decentralization along these lines will mean some loss of governing capacity for central authorities, not however the general lowering of control over the behavior of the target group.

The implementation research of the 1970s has not only drawn attention to implementation problems as such, but also to problems of motivation that affect the effectiveness of regulatory policy. The resistance of target groups to norms that restrict their behavior has been noted time and again. At present, the growth of regulatory interventions and the growing insistence on self-determination may well increase this resistance. It has become particularly clear that regulatory norms cannot motivate behavior that depends on personal initiative, innovation and positive engagement. Therefore, alternative forms of governing such as positive and negative financial incentives, information and persuasion were recommended. In accordance with the practice possibly started by Luhmann (1981) to treat money - and later also information - as alternative governing instruments, these efforts to overcome policy failures concentrate on the choice of alternatives to law (for a critical comment see Mayntz, 1985). At any rate, it is primarily the motivation problem on the side of the target population that is addressed.

The choice of alternative legal instruments seems to be a reaction to solve the recurring knowledge problem, but particularly problems of governability. The origin of both these problems is no longer primarily seen - and that is a new problem diagnosis - in insufficient intelligence of the bureaucracy, in the lack of the government's ability to make decisions or in a choice of wrong instruments, but in the particular character of the objects of governing attempts. These objects, moreover, are no longer conceived of as particular categories of persons, households or organizations, but as societal subsystems such as economy, science, health etc. The internal dynamics of those societal subsystems seems to make them impenetrable for outsiders in a double sense, both cognitively as well as in terms of the possibility to be purposefully influenced. According to

Teubner and Willke (1984: 5), 'self-reference and internal dynamics of differentiated societal subsystems make centralized political control in the traditional juridical way more and more difficult, if not impossible'. If, however, political guidance through control over target-group behavior cannot be achieved in principle, because there is no direct and discernible relation between such behavior and desired systems or (macro) effects, then motivation or unwillingness to comply is no longer the real problem. At the same time, the knowledge problem becomes almost insolvable for the central actor, as it is impossible under conditions of high complexity to make general and long-term forecasts of the kind of behavior of specific actors that would solve a particular problem at the system level. Under such circumstances, a strategy which aims only at improving the knowledge base of central state intervention, is a priori doomed to failure. Therefore, the new legal instruments which are suggested to solve the governing problem, in particular procedural rules (Wiethölter, 1982) and reflexive law (Teubner, 1982), aim to enhance the independent adaptive, reactive, and problem-solving capacities of societal actors, which means to motivate and to enable them to react purposefully at any moment to changing conditions. For the advocates of this strategy this does not mean to revert to the classical Nightwatch State. Autonomy is not left to societal subsystems because it is impossible to do otherwise. Quite on the contrary, it appears as a positive value as it is conceived as protecting against the destructive consequences of ignorant state intervention (Teubner/Willke, 1984). Nevertheless, there is a serious danger that a program of 'help to self-help' will result in the devolution of central state control to societal actors, and thus a return to liberal laissez-faire. This can only be avoided if one may assume, or can assure in fact, that through societal self-organization it becomes possible to achieve what the central political authorities have failed to reach: effective problem-solving. It is quite clear that such assumptions play a role in the strategies for deregulation and privatization, which have been popular in so many countries. These strategies rely on the well-known market forces, the carrot (and stick) of competition, and the rationality of large organizations which in their own long-term interest will not neglect the interests of the larger system they are part of. Here the advocates of new legal instruments are less optimistic (or less unrealistic). They are of the opinion that the state needs to be involved in contextual control through the setting of legal norms that can secure the success of collective societal problem-solving by self-regulation and horizontal co-ordination. True enough, so far it has remained unclear how this can be brought about. Procedural rules, aimed at bringing conflicting societal actors to an ordered settling of their differences, without having influence on the substantive results, may indeed diminish the sharpness of conflicts by working out compromises. However, they do not assure that the system problems that produce the conflicts will be adequately dealt with. The concept of reflexive law seems to be related to conceptions of global planning through framework prescriptions, which function similar to persuasion and incentive programs, except that they do not refer to a specific target group behavior, but to the achievement of general goals that are defined at the macro level. To devise such framework prescriptions, however, one would need the very knowledge previously defined as unavailable.

Autonomization and Governability of Societal Subsystems

In this situation, it may be worthwhile to take a closer look at the premises of these alternative solutions. In particular we want to elaborate on the question whether a growing self-referential closure of societal subsystems will indeed make obsolete efforts of central political control, because the processes within the subsystems become increasingly impenetrable and thus impervious to interventions from outside. In doing so, we must carefully distinguish between the asserted situation and its presumed causes.

It is beyond argument that with the emergence of today's highly differentiated societies and their functional subsystems, the complexity of functional interdependencies and causal networks has grown immensely. This results in unpredictable direct and indirect effects which originate in wide-ranging output-input relations between many actors. Moreover, cumulation and aggregation processes occur which, above a certain threshold level, may have undesirable and even contra-intuitive consequences. Many of these are not new per se, as can, for instance, be illustrated by environmental pollution, but they stayed under a critical level for a long time. The quantitative increase in certain human activities and the greater technical potential thus contribute to the fact that the autonomous social dynamics appear dangerous and no longer transparent. The network character of social systems also presents evident cognitive and manipulative problems (Vester, 1983). We are beginning to understand these cognitive difficulties and the way human actors react to them (Dörner et al., 1983). Social science, too, begins to respond to these problems, but we are still not able to say that we fully understand the dynamics of these systems. The theory of self-referential and autopoietic systems, used by the advocates of 'new' legal instruments offers little assistance here; in fact, this theory seems to lead to a wrong diagnosis of the real governability problems.

The operational closure implied in the 'basic circularity' of self-reproduction is, at least in the perspective developed above, not really a problem for governing. At most it defines a limit to claims of purposeful construction of social units and processes. But such an 'omnipotency' claim even the most ambitious politicians have hardly ever made. Governing means no more than to intervene in self-reproductive processes when their (desired) functioning seems to be endangered or when the way these processes function has problematic consequences. This is only seemingly impeded by the 'basic circularity', in which for example payments produce further payments, juridical acts further juridical acts, and scholarly communication scholarly communication (which makes for the operational closure of the economic, legal, and science systems). Only a kind of sociology that amputates social systems to mere communication and thereby takes away their material substratum and all driving forces, can state that it is really communication of a certain kind that produces communication of that same kind. Those who (with von Foerster, 1984) emphasize the 'energetic' dimension of system processes in addition to their communicative aspects, will agree that, for example, scholarly communication may be inspired and its content more or less determined by other scholarly communication, but they will hold that such communication is produced by social actors in a process resting on a series of preconditions. The discernible preconditions for payments to be actually followed by other payments and juridical acts by further juridical acts, will show where it may be possible to intervene in the processes in order to direct and redirect them. Since human beings are able to 'speak' the 'language' of several subsystems, there is no fundamental barrier to inter-system communication as a result of incompatible media. Payments, for instance, 'are' not scholarly communication, but through the researcher who has been paid or will be paid, they influence no doubt whether certain scientific statements can or will be made or not.

This is not to deny that social subsystems under certain conditions are able to define their own boundaries, and to actively protect themselves against external interventions. Also, social subsystems will be inclined to place self-preservation, growth, and the preservation of their own resources above the production of services for others. These phenomena are known not only from organization sociology, but also from the analysis of political institutions (and not in the last place from our own experiences in the scientific field). With reference to the performance expected of social subsystems, these phenomena, certainly when they surpass critical threshold levels, are experienced as dysfunctional and even as perversions. However, the tendencies towards autonomization are the product of recognizable strategies of identifiable actors, who act or react in particularly structured situations. The undoubtedly existing resistance of social subsystems against political control should thus be attributed to the growing power resources and capacity for collective action characteristic of highly organized societal sectors, and not to their self-referential closure which makes effective intervention impossible because of the basic incompatibility between different modes of communication.

At this point of the argument the question should be asked whether highly institutionalized and organized social subsystems indeed and under all circumstances resist central political control. With the institutional consolidation of social subsystems, and especially with the emergence of multi-level structures including actors of a higher order (organizations, umbrella organizations, associations, peak associations etc.), their ability of self-regulation or at least self-organization increases. The superior action capacity of powerful and articulate corporate actors means that the negative externalities and threatening aggregate effects which are unavoidable in complex systems, are not only recognized by those negatively affected, but countermeasures can be initiated. Understood in this way, self-organization and the capacity for horizontal coordination with other similarly organized societal subsystems should not necessarily diminish political governability but, quite on the contrary, could enhance it.

Thus Kaufmann (1985) points to the fact that social interaction in larger and internally differentiated organizations is more amenable to legal regulation than other kinds of interaction. Furthermore, the fact that formal organizations, because of appropriate structural and procedural arrangements, tend to behave more rationally and predictably compared to the cumulative result of aggregated individual acts, increases the opportunities for external control. Also very important are the better chances for articulation which organizations have, compared to a mass public of individuals. The better chances of organized interests to have their voice heard in the development of political programs, have long been observed. Implementation research has confirmed this finding also for the phase of program execution. The modification of central political impulses in the course of program implementation, can be demonstrated particularly well in the interaction between public authorities and large companies (Klitzsch, 1985). Such bargaining leads to more complicate, and at least sometimes to better decisions. Direct contacts and especially direct bargaining are quite rare where individuals or households instead of organizations constitute the target group, as this would rapidly increase the number of those to be addressed by a particular authority. Therefore also in the implementation phase, the specific rationality of highly organized social subsystems can enhance governability.

A positive relation between a societal subsystem's ability to organize, its capacity to act and its governability is the basis for neo-corporatist forms of governance. These forms are considered highly successful, at least with respect to certain economic goals. Wilensky (1983: 57) also points to this relation when he remarks that precisely those welfare states '... with more corporatist bargaining structures have been able to combine good economic performance and high levels of taxing and social spending with relatively little political uproar ...'. This does not simply mean to replace political control by private government, the earlier-mentioned fourth type of social order (besides hierarchy, market and solidarity), as has been emphasized by Traxler and Vobruba (1985: 19), when they state that the special capacity of organized social partnerships to make binding regulations and to solve problems is based on a 'complex mutual resource transfer between state and associations in the framework of their cooperation. The unburdening of the state in its regulatory duties concurs with the assistance of the state in solving organizational problems of the associations. 'The dichotomy between self-regulation and state intervention, which is often made in the discussion on political order, becomes obsolete'. It should be added that this form of governing can also be distinguished from 'reflexive law' (Teubner/Willke, 1984), which focuses on the legal framework for subsystems that are otherwise left to their own devices. On the other hand, there is a link with 'negotiation systems', as propagated earlier by Willke (1983).

Not all policy sectors have the character of more or less well-organized subsystems. Compared to the relatively tightly coupled neo-corporatist structures or the 'iron triangles', the consensus and decision-making capacity in policy fields characterized by open and fragmented 'issue networks' is less-developed, although even there some large organizations may assert themselves as corporate actors. In this perspective it is consequent of central political authorities to embark upon a governing strategy of building better structured policy networks of public and private organizations, as has been observed by Sharpe (1985) for Britain. The existence of a few advocacy organizations as, for example, in youth or family politics does not provide a policy area with the kind of consolidated structure to be found in the education, research or economy subsystem. In these cases, therefore, negotiation and mutual adjustment do not seem to be an effective strategy. Quite in line with this, Tyrell (1979) considers the family system difficult to direct politically because of its loose structure. The same holds true for policy areas that are structured as 'aree di movimento' (in the terminology of Melucci, 1984), i. e. extensive networks consisting of some institutions (such as service centres), small informal groups and loose interweavings of personal acquaintances fostered by meeting in certain places. Such social networks oscillate between latency and activism and they will organize themselves to become collective actors only occasionally and will fall apart again afterwards.

A high degree of formal organization is of course not the only precondition of governability; other factors should be added. Depending on the specific situational conditions, a high degree of organization can also hamper the governability of a policy area. A simple inversion of the general thesis that highly organized policy areas will resist governing attempts more strongly would be as wrong as the thesis itself. The effective organization of sectoral interests can of course be used as veto power, and block solutions to societal problems, and even if negotiations take place the corporate actors can fail to reach consensus or to take decisions that will solve the problem. Schmitter himself recognizes this when he states that exchange relations in an associative-corporatist order can be quite instable (1984), while Traxler and Vobruba (1986) more specifically point at the dilemma that with this form of governance the preconditions of problem-solving and of creating commitment are in competition with each other: decisions that are easily accepted by the participating societal actors will hardly solve public problems, while decisions that would solve public problems are difficult to accept.

The actual state of theory does not allow to make general statements about the structural preconditions on which the governability of a social subsystem rests. Factors that are of relevance certainly include the degree of centralization, the existence or lack of communication channels, and the polarization or normal distribution of preferences among the main actors; these dimensions have been developed by Knoke and Lauman

(1982) to describe the structure of policy sectors. Important might also be the 'technicality' or the degree of professionalization in a policy area, factors to which Scott and Meyer (1982) have pointed. Furthermore, it is definitely important for the governability of a subsystem that the available organizations, which will function both as targets and as bargaining partners in the political process, give expression to the basic cleavages and communication relationships that are central to its autonomous dynamics. If, for example, diffuse scientific communities, loose networks of researchers in a specific discipline, are crucial for the progress in science, this will be a barrier to purposeful intervention in a research policy that is based on the dialogue with large research organizations not organized on the basis of disciplinary differentiation (such as the German Max-Planck-Society or Research Council DFG).

To summarize, it has been argued that the undisputable governability problems have less to do with the basic autopoietic character of social subsystems, but rather with (1) the special dynamics of complex modern societies and (2) with the capacity of highly organized policy fields to resist political guidance. However, under specific conditions the very capacity of societal actors to act in an organized way can facilitate governing and the solution of problems that originate from social complexity. Therefore, it is not so much the kind of governing instruments that is crucial, but a special form of organizing the policy process to secure that in the decision-making process not only information about the needs and fears of actors in the policy field is taken into account, but more importantly also indications of side effects, interdependencies and emerging problems. Organized societal actors function in this respect as a network of sensors or look-out stations; at least in part the availability of the necessary systems knowledge may therefore be an organizational problem rather than a problem of good theory.

If the cognitive as well as the power conditions of the successful implementation of problem solutions can be found in the structural characteristics of policy sectors, their structural differences become not only a practical but also a theoretical problem. Highly organized, loosely coupled, and very fragmented policy sectors do not only call for quite different modes of governing; they also offer quite different chances of political intervention. Therefore, the recent shift in the debate about political failures is very fruitful because it brings into focus the preconditions of and barriers to state action, implicit in the systems characteristics of policy fields.

3

MODES OF GOVERNANCE

ANDREW DUNSIRE

Introduction

The thesis of this book is that the pace of social change at the end of the twentieth century is increasing. Change in technology, in communications, in lifestyles and fashions, comes faster than it used to - which may be recognised as common experience even by the relatively young, especially in the rich countries. Things get ever more interrelated, there is more and more to be known, and less and less time in which to react.

This, of course, has been happening since the dawn of human life. But, like a graph plotting the speed of human transport through the ages (Doxiadis 1968: 146), until the nineteenth century the dynamic of social change was relatively slow, the line on the graph hardly moving from the horizontal; but then it began to curve upwards and at the end of the twentieth century is not far off the vertical: change is not only frequent but fast. Society is highly volatile.

Society is also becoming ever more diverse. The political world, once composed of a handful of empires, and counting at the end of the second world war a hundred and fifty or so nation-states, now must come to terms with a relative plethora of significant ethnic/linguistic/religious communities each claiming separate statehood; and the doctrine of subsidiarity (as well as the so-called *democratic deficit*) will increase devolution of responsibilities even in the supra-national communities that have also emerged. The British and other civil services *executivise* their former monolithic structures in like manner, de-emphasizing accountability. Massive multinational corporations which a decade ago centralised economic power to their headquarters across national boundaries now dissipate it again to their peripheries. Not only are there now few command economies on the East European pattern, there are few command corporations(a phrase I owe to Professor Nigel Harris). The typical large company sees itself as a network (or in another metaphor a *flotilla*), where the boundaries between itself and its environment are hazy and not all that important, and where the relationship between its own parts is not hierarchical, but hovers between competition and collaboration, not a polity and not quite either a market or a community. In the third or voluntary sector, more and more organisations spring up for more and more purposes, so that in the developed countries at least, each of us belongs to many groups and associations.

How we see society is also changing. The relationships between individuals and their organic groupings bound by family and ethnic ties, and between those and their functional associations for economic production, for defence and public order, for religious, eleemosynary, cultural, and purely leisure activities, become ever more interpenetrative and inseparable with each advance in ease and speed of communication, and with the increased awareness of shared as well as conflicting values that it brings. Yet instantaneous mass communication also enables a comprehension of all this that is more holistic than was ever possible before - and global satellite broadcasting erodes national conceptions of what human society means. Just as the same stock of money can produce a low or a high GNP according to its rate of circulation, so the same set of social values can produce a placid or a turbulent society according to the degree of intermixing. Today's societies tend to have very high complexity: that is, the number of different ways in which people can be linked together, and the number of different combinations of shared and conflicting values that could actually be found, are each several orders of magnitude higher than was the case in, say, the early twentieth century, let alone any earlier period.

A society that has become highly-differentiated - using many one-purpose products, all roles clearly demarcated and professionalised, technocratically-ruled - can deliver great benefits to consumers, so long as nothing goes wrong. But as in manufacturing, the higher the technology the lower the substitutability of each part, and therefore the higher the criticality of the whole - the more likely is the failure of one part to cripple it, and perhaps render it dangerous, or set off a chain reaction of failed parts. A high-tech society where the machines need too much maintenance, where demarcations have begun to crumble and hierarchical authority has lost its magic, is one vulnerable to crises: a tiny event may trigger a catastrophe - urban riots in India, a Black Friday on the world's stock exchanges, a Chernobyl. Such a tiny event is perhaps no more likely to occur than it ever was, but if it does, the consequences can be infinitely more severe than they used to be. A long plank across a shallow stream is less of a hazard to the drunk wanderer than a short plank across a chasm. This is what high criticality entails.

Some analysts call this kind of society postmodern (Lyotard, 1984; Clegg, 1990). The modern period in history ushered in the Enlightenment, scientific reason, the eliciting of the order in the Universe -and with that, industrialisation, specialisation, professionalization, and bureaucracy- all processes of ever-increasing differentiation. Lash (1988) bases his understanding of postmodernity on the reverse process - *de-differentiation*: the blurring of boundaries and distinctions, the questioning of established values, and hence the spread of cynicism, the elevation of the image over the substance.

All social change disturbs existing gradients of social power to some degree. The apocalyptic question is whether social change at an ever-increasing rate, towards ever-increasing complexity, diversity and criticality, can be accommodated by the arrangements societies now make to keep disturbances within bounds and to steer change away from undesired and towards desired directions - which is the writer's own definition of governance: or whether - in no long distant future - some random fluctuation in turbulence will produce a catastrophic decline in compliance, in governability, leading to social chaos. Chaos theory teaches that once the threshold of turbulence has been crossed, but change-inducing energy continues to flow through a system, a new kind of structuring may emerge - order out of chaos (Prigogine and Stengers, 1984; Gleick, 1988). But perhaps, at the social level, it is unconscionable just to wait in hope of that.

It can be argued that this apocalyptic question goes over the top- is in a form too extreme to represent reality today. After all, the arrangements societies have made in the way of self-government have always been fluid, and have altered over the past two centuries almost as rapidly as societies have changed. What we are tempted to call *traditional methods*, in the way of taxation, government regulations, public ownership, and so on, may have their antiquarian roots in ancient times, but the dominant form of modern government, bureaucracy as we know it, really only ages with the railway and the telegraph. Maybe that very argument, however, is an own goal. The point may be that we shall simply not cope with social change now, let alone in the future, if we rely on the railway for transport, the telegraph for communications, and bureaucracy for government.

Kooiman (this volume) asks: "how can a dynamic, complex and diverse socio-political world be governed in a dynamic, complex and diverse way?" Echoing Ashby's first law of cybernetics (Ashby, 1957; Conant and Ashby, 1970) - only variety can cope with variety, every good regulator of a system is also a good model of that system - he says: "Not only does this mean that we have to know about the dynamic, complex and diverse qualities of these objects [to be governed] and their relations but also what those qualities of governance should be. These two have to fit". Renate Mayntz (this volume) adds another infinite complication: "... it is not so much the kind of governing instruments that is crucial but a special form of organizing the policy process to secure that in the decision-making process not only information about the needs and fears of actors in the policy fields is taken into account, but more importantly also indications of side effects, interdependencies and emerging problems."

If that is the way governance of a dynamic, complex and diverse socio-political world has to develop (more dynamic, complex and diverse models of it first), then indeed we have overload problems. As other writers put it (Van der Zouwen and Geyer, 1986: 208): "... the need to steer processes like the arms race and the ecology has certainly not diminished - to the contrary. But our experience demonstrates that in these cases governability is hardly or not at all increased by expanding and differentiating our models regarding these processes ... What is especially needed, in our opinion, is a reflection on the meaning of the concept of controllability itself, in the context of its application to social systems and processes."

It is such a reflection that this chapter seeks to present.

The next section discusses the relationship between policy and enforcement, in two cybernetic modes, steering and self-steering or self-regulation. The third section explains the theory of a third mode, Nature's own mode, which can be called conflict of opposed forces, or more briefly, competition. The fourth section describes how this third mode is already used in government, and the final section explores its import for the governance of social systems high in complexity, volatility, diversity and criticality.

Government by Regulation

There is an assumption implicit in much of our thinking about governance, because implicit in the democratic process as we have evolved it, that government acts by making and implementing policies for change. Social interaction is conventionally parcelled out in policy fields or sectors, and you have more and more policy initiatives because that is how politicians get their rewards, just as you have more and more powerful drugs or scanners because you have medical researchers, bigger and better missiles because you have a military-industrial complex. Politicians show what they are made of by having new laws in their knapsacks. The urge to seize the reins, to take charge, and use legislative action to change things to how you want them, is strong. This corresponds to the first of three modes of governance in cybernetic theory, which is usually named steering or regulating: receiving a set datum or norm or desired course, and then using power to correct deviations from it, in a linear model.

But that mode is implementation-intensive and enforcement-expensive. There is no need now to labour the point that implementing a policy is often difficult. The burden of all the policy implementation and evaluation studies that ever were is that the disturbing factors, whether within the bureaucracy or in the society between output and outcome, are commonly so many and so strong as to render nugatory the assumptions of policy-makers about what is being achieved -or even what it would be reasonable to expect to achieve. Linear remedies do not cope with non-linear cases.

Apart from that, some critics say implementation of government policies can be harmful. The dysfunctions of bureaucracy are age-old and legion: doctor-spread illness: patients in hospitals contract diseases they did not go in with, making regulations simply induces a search for ways around them, creating the need for more regulations to stop up the loopholes; and courts spread wrongdoing, by sentencing policies that fill prisons to overflowing, producing riots and creating crime schools for young minor offenders.

A whole industry of thought provides remedies. Leave it to the market is currently the most prominent. Another school blames top/down policy making and implementation, as not only illusory but undesirable in principle; bottom/up policy-making, street-level networking and point-of-trans-action selection of treatment is not only what happens anyway but a much more effective way of attaining given ends with given resources. Other schools attack over-specialism, or sheer size, or an authoritarian managerial *culture*; and so on.

What is common to many of these doctrines, from the present point of view, is that they are asking for less steering and more self-steering or self-regulation.

The paradigm of steering as a mode of governance is (of course) the helmsman on a ship, who corrects any discrepancy between his set course and the ship's actual heading by turning his helm (provided he has *steerage way*, i.e. energy converted into forward motion). The paradigm of self-regulation is James Watt's steam-engine governor, or its ancient hydraulic servo-mechanism precursors. The governor's whirling brass balls fly outwards as the speed of the drive-shaft increases (for whatever reason), the movement being fed back to close the steam-inlet a little, and vice versa if the speed drops, thus keeping the output of the engine within predetermined limits without human intervention. The resulting effect is called homoeostasis -the condition in which a system successfully keeps the values of some of its essential variables constant, or at least within acceptable limits.

Homoeostasis is the outcome of negative feedback, feedback with the sign changed. Positive feedback, or reinforcement, is what makes amplifiers work; it leads to the familiar vicious cycle, but also to learning. Self-regulation is less implementation-heavy than regulation. But moving from steering to homoeostasis is not abandoning governance; the standards to be achieved, the limits to be observed are still set from above, or outside. But it is usually felt as a relaxation of control.

For example: to move from parental financing item by item to a pocket money allowance is to move from regulation to self-regulation. Payment-by-results or performance measurement or management-by-objectives, and variants, as compared with direct supervision and inspection of operations, are self-regulatory in effect. Governance in this mode is not necessarily via simple servomechanisms, or by restoration of a previous state. If the object system is in process of rapid positional or even structural change, for example, feedbacks and corrections can be incorporated to ensure that each new state lies within preferred parameters - the concept of the autopilot. Some state-of-the-art airplanes are so inherently unstable that they cannot be flown manually by their pilots at all, even in crisis; the pilots can only set values on the state-sensing computers. Similarly, in a political crisis, a gram of ideological commitment implanted deep in the actors is worth a tonne of commissar supervision. Illustrations proliferate, and could be categorized if need be (see Kickert in this volume).

In any complex system, however, both in practice and in theory, there is less distinction between the first and second modes of system governance than this argument might convey; both are based on linear models. Let me take an example. Steering your car on a winding road follows the same formula as the classic paradigm of the steersman on a ship, except that the course you are given to steer (the direction the car ought to be going in) changes every fraction of a second. The criticality is higher. To cope with that you have to keep your wits about you more than does the helmsman: the speed of your reaction must match the rate at which the situation is changing, or you crash. But you might crash anyway, if your steering system was not reliable. What does that mean - not reliable? Well, it reminds us that a modern car is an incredibly complex machine, which can be driven and steered by one person only because homoeostasis is being maintained in a large number of subsystems. Even if each of the subsystems is separate every subsystem will itself comprise a host of sub-sub-systems which are quite self-regulating, yet on whose proper functioning the driver relies, in order to move, to stop, to steer, to see and be seen. Few cars now have ignition-advance levers on the steering wheel; it's all done automatically, like a hundred other such adjustments, servo-mechanisms within servo-mechanisms, in a hierarchy of self-government.

It is not different in organisations, or in the society at large. It is a totally general feature of government in complex systems. A social system is steerable from outside, or self-steerable from within - moving in a chosen direction, or kept within laid down limits on any number of dimensions - only if it can make use of its major component systems as effectors of correcting action; and each major component is a useable effector (*"is reliable"*) only if its own variability is being kept within bounds, i.e., if it is self-regulating. Each major component can be so only if it can in turn rely on each of its own component structures to cope with its own internal fluctuations; each such structure similarly must delegate managerial capacity to branch management - and so on, down the line. Governance has to be hierarchical, systems-within-systems; the whole is only steerable if it is able to harness the government being maintained level by level, function by function, attribute by attribute, throughout the complex. Complex self-governing structures are fractious: the shapes of adaptability are copied and multiplied level by level.

Governments could never govern if the people - in their organisations, their families, their groupings of all kinds - were not self-governing. Consider the use of law. It is a fairly commonplace notion that if you call a command a Law - that is, in British terms, if it passes Hart's (1961) second order test by having three readings in each House of Parliament and receiving the Royal Assent - most people will comply with it because it is the Law. That is, you do not have to enforce their compliance; they will adjust their behaviour themselves.

Enforcement is only required for the minority; and by and large, the larger the minority, the higher the enforcement costs. So you have to be careful with what you arrange to be called a Law, even if you have the necessary power, or else you will depreciate this currency of trust; to the extent that people lose their readiness to comply merely because it is the Law, your steering problems increase.

This conclusion supports Kickert's understanding of the reality of public governance in its context of democracy and legal state: it is a process of co-directing in a network of many separate actors with different and opposing interests and more or less independent positions (this volume); and also Kooiman's two-way traffic between governors and governed. But from the present point of view, this has nothing to do with democracy, or with participation. That is a quite distinct value. It is just cybernetic fact of life.

Governance without a Governor

Wishing to steer a social system in accordance with one's own objectives, or to damp down some unwelcome disturbance, are reasons for attempting to govern it at a particular time and place. But it would be foolish to believe that if a social system did not receive such government constantly, catastrophe or disaster would certainly ensue. We do not really imagine that social stability is so fragile that the government must monitor it and adjust it minute by minute night and day in every particular. Except in circumstances of overwhelming external turbulence, a social system remains identifiably the same system, with the same parts in recognisably the same relationship within much the same boundaries, even if the government is on holiday or paying no attention to most of it. System persistence is more likely than system collapse, with or without steering.

Yet the concept of social self-steering, through feedbacks and voluntary self-correction, only partially explains this result. For that would imply constant return to a preferred state, or during change, agreed selection of one among the possible future states. But we all know that such agreed preferences in a social system of even the smallest size are likely over only an extremely narrow range of subject matter, concerning the basic survival of the system; and then only in crisis situations - attack from without, natural disaster, and so on. The normal situation would entail disagreement and conflict precisely over whether a former state of affairs should be restored or a change made to a projected improved state of affairs. What we want to show is that it is just that normal situation, of opposition and conflict over alternative possible states, which provides the rest of the explanation of social governance without governors.

Many non-social systems meet this specification of dynamic constancy without governors. No one can steer the weather, or even predict with any certainty what it will be at some point on the earth's surface at some date in the not-distant future. Global weather is always restless, because of the diurnal rotation of the earth (and some small man-made inputs), even if seasonal patterns can persist regionally. What we experience as our weather is merely the local effects of regional gradients in the three related variables of temperature, humidity, and barometric pressure, for which there are no set values or equilibrium state; yet there are observable limits to the values any one of the variables can take up before triggering off violent correction within the system. Because it is non-periodic, it is not predictable; but it is not out of control.

More surprisingly perhaps (except to biologists), governance within the human body is almost entirely of this same kind - not steering, not homoeostasis, but the outcome of conflict of opposed forces. For instance, the motive power of bodily movement is mediated by sets of muscles with contrary functions, pushing and pulling; every time we decide to move a finger, we execute the act by chemically inhibiting one set in favour of the other, in a number of different places. The two autonomic nervous systems are also opposed in the same way: one for ever trying to speed things up, the other to slow them down: their mutual hostility varies the heartbeat, the breathing rate, and other life rhythms to suit changing circumstances. This yoking of incompatibles, the mutual battle of opposing tendencies, or simply competition, is Nature's typical mechanism of governance. For a technical term, we can use isostasy: equilibrium brought about by equal pressures (or suctions, or tensions).

The principle is far from unknown in the realm of human societies. Montesquieu's (1748) principle of the separation of powers is an elegant and very subtle appreciation of multiple coupled positive feedbacks, which would repay detailed technical analysis. The American political system is permeated throughout by the idea of *checks and balances*; not only explicitly as in the Constitution, and in federal-state-local competition, but implicitly in such theoretical constructions as Lindblom's (1965) mutual partisan adjustment model of the polity, in the concept of adversarial bureaucracies, in the game-theoretic approach to bureaucratic politics, and much else.

And this is all before we mention economics, and the enormously fertile model of perfect competition in a free market. And so on. All of these illustrations have points of difference from one another, in closer analysis. But the idea of competing forces, even if we call it isostasy or tension between opposed maximisers or coupled positive feedbacks, is hardly a new idea.

Why, then, do I highlight it here, as if indeed it had just been discovered? Well, firstly, because I do not know that the identity of this ubiquitous device through all these different contexts has been sufficiently recognised. The cybernetic approach in that regard offers a unified theory of what is going on in a wide variety of milieux. And, secondly, it is not simply a recognition of the ubiquity of competition as a mode of governance that I am concerned with here: it is also a recognition that the mechanism, like homoeostasis, can be manipulated, the effect harnessed to the purposes of the policy maker, to provide a mode of governance that may not normally come to mind as an alternative.

In the human body, the brain routinely manipulates the opposed tensor/extensor muscles in order to engineer bodily movement, by inhibiting one set and allowing the other to *win* temporarily (in the same way as you make use of one of the springs of a Terry Anglepoise lamp to help you move the shade to a new position - but when you take your hand away, the other spring re-establishes the balance and the lamp stays where you put it). The feeling of thirst is a bodily appeal for external assistance in an internal water-balance struggle it can no longer cope with. Less routinely, if our sugar balance is at a dangerous level (because the body is running out of effector capacity) we can put our finger on the scale, or come to the assistance of the weakening adversary, by taking medicine.

In administrative engineering, something similar can be found. I have elsewhere outlined the way I conceive that any bureaucracy works (1978; 1986). A bureaucratic organization exists to accommodate (i) high specialism of function (both horizontally and vertically) with (ii) managerial hierarchical command. But these are antithetical. Top people are often unable to issue instructions to subordinates on substantive matters; they do not know enough about them, unless advised by these same subordinates. But they can enjoin on decision-makers a handful of procedural criteria simultaneously, often mutually incompatible, such as speed and accuracy, probity and legality, equity and prudence, economy and conformity to agreed conditions of work; and use performance on these criteria in structural sanctions over appointments, promotions, rewards and punishments. The organization typically maintains functional controllers with authority to monitor decisions in all these procedural dimensions, all metaphorically looking over the decision-maker's shoulders in all substantive work. The decision-maker must prioritise, but in the anxious knowledge that an explanation may be required for (in effect) not maximising all procedural goals all the time.

Having two mutually-exclusive goals puts a decision maker in dilemma; having several potentially competing constraints can be called polylemma. The decision environment thus corresponds to isostasy, multiple conflicting tensions, and rule over specialised decision-makers in a bureaucracy is maintained by selective crackdowns on one goal at a time, steering the equilibrium- without ever acknowledging that tightening up on one criterion implies slackening off on another.

This type of system, of which the static paradigm is the anglepoise lamp, Christopher Hood has called interpolable balance (1986: 765ff), a great improvement on my own earlier selective inhibition of opposed maximisers (1978: 209). What we are both saying is that under certain circumstances, although you may not know what the point of balance between rival forces is likely to be or should be, you may be able to bias that location to suit yourself, within limits, by intervening in the equilibration process. There isn't a technical term for this idea. Compensation and redressing the balance convey the idea: but like all balance metaphors, they are almost inextricably linked with only two opposing forces or weights, like the see-saw. Counterpoise and counterweight are the same. None quite conveys the idea of strengthening one force or weakening another in a polydynamic arena so as to alter the outcome without superseding the tensions altogether. Rigging (as in rigging the market) uses an appropriate metaphor and has the exact meaning, but it has a somewhat pejorative connotation. To avoid connotations one falls back on a neologism or a hi-jacking. To find the weight of a letter, you put weights in the scale pan until the balance librates- swings gently. There is an Oxford Dictionary word *collibrate*, meaning to weigh together or compare. I use it here to mean to join in the process of equilibration: to manage *isostasy*.

If we aspire to collibrate with Nature, and intervene in our own interest, we have to be sure we know what we are doing. Argument raged in the 1960s about whether the deliberate spreading of the rabbit disease myxamatosis was wise. At the present time, it seems to be clear that through ignorance we have succeeded in disturbing the ozone balance in the upper atmosphere, but it is not clear how we restore it; and we have been loading the scales against marine mammals for some time by polluting the seas with PCBs [polychlorinated biphenyls]. On the other hand, the mechanisms of beta blockers and many other recent drugs are absolutely consciously-designed collibrations, intervening in specific reactions in bodily biochemistry; as are the introductions of predator species in agricultural pest control, as an alternative to poisons.

The idea of maintaining stability through an exploitation of rival forces is far from strange in the study of human societies. Aristotle's discussion of the best form of government is even explicitly collibrative: "It is plain, then, that the most perfect political community must be amongst those who are in the middle rank, and those states are best instituted wherein these are a larger and more respectable part, if possible, than both the other; or, if that cannot be, at least than either of them separate; so that being thrown into the balance it may prevent either scale from preponderating." (*Politics*, Bk IV, chap XI (1295b)).

Spinoza's design for a state (1677) is full of such ideas for harnessing ambition and turning natural conflict to the common benefit: "Men should be governed in such a way that they do not regard themselves as being governed, but as following their own bent and their own free choice in their manner of life; in such a way, then, that they are restrained only by love of freedom, desire to increase their possessions, and the hope of obtaining offices of state." (1677, X.8.; 1958: 435-37.)

To these ends, army officers would receive no wages but remunerate them-selves from booty (having first had to win the battle); senators, on the other hand, would have an interest in preserving peace, since their remuneration came from a duty on imports and exports. If cities quarrel amongst themselves, that tends to ensure that no one city dominates. Let the rich, if they cannot be thrifty, be at any rate greedy for gain; and make public office attractive to them, so that they will increase their wealth only by honourable means for fear of disgrace.

It has to be questioned, however, whether isostasy in human society - stability owed to a balancing of multiple forces - is a natural phenomenon, as one might predicate of an ecological system, or whether, on the contrary, it is more like the ship's mast, in which isostasy has to be brought about and subsequently maintained through management.

Now that question, as distinct from the terms, is not new either, in the practice of politics. It is overt in the history of the idea of balance of power in international relations. In Hobbes, the balance between powers is a natural process, just the way the world works; by the nineteenth century, it is a goal of policy, to be brought about by shifting alliances. Democratic pluralism exhibits something of the same evolution (Richardson and Jordan, 1979).

But the concept is also implicit in the age-old statecraft maxim divide and rule; or in the activities of an Iago. Skilled manipulators have always known how to tip a balance with a word in the right ear, or how to set two sides at each's throats in order to slip something past while attentions are distracted, or how to rig a market. Yet as we may see in the next section governments are using this technique all the time; they just have not set it into a coherent (and respectable) theory of intervention.

If it be granted that social isostasy exists, that a degree of social stability or *firmness* or near-equilibrium results from the constant pulling of rival social forces against one another, each inhibited from maximising its own interests by being locked with others in a complex of positive-feedback cycles, then it may be allowed that, along with the social system's capacities for negative feedback self-steering, it provides sufficient explanation for the observable phenomenon of the persistence of social systems without endemic governmental helmsmanship. But there is more. The management of social isostasy, intervention to stabilise in the longer run by controlled local destabilising in the short run, the deliberate tipping of the balance of one conflict or another, the rigging of a market whether economic or political or some other kind, the manipulation of group desires and energies -this kind of activity, dignified here by the term collibration to provide the missing respectability, furnishes a mechanism for guiding, influencing, biasing, loading, or otherwise affecting the course or outcome of a conflict in the interests of the governors; in other words, a steering mechanism.

Collibration in Practice

The provision of information is one of the most cost-effective modes of government intervention in an already contested field. The British government in 1981 began publishing what, on the basis of a number of social indicators like proportion of school children, mileage of roads, and so on, would be a reasonable level of expenditure for each individual local authority, in each area of expenditure; and urged voters to compare their own local authority's proposed charge for services with the calculated charge for a standard level of service. The central government was putting its thumb on the local political scales, intending to tip the balance in favour of one of the local sides.

Requiring commercial companies to publish and deposit their annual accounts, including sample information such as the emoluments of the (unnamed) highest-paid employee, is of the same nature. So is the publication of applications for planning consent, urban development, mineral extraction, and so on. This is intended to elicit what objections there may be, to stimulate the discovery of contrary facts and reasoning, to create local adversarial controversy and participation, and to put government in the role of adjudicating between the sides. In the environmental protection arena: "Around 60 per cent of packaging is used for food, and this gives the manufacturers a big corner to defend. The organisation set up to do that is INCPEN, the Industry Council for Packaging and the Environment.

In the other corner, not so wealthy but a lot noisier, stand the environmentalists, stabbing their fingers angrily at packagers and shops alike. The Government, in the meantime, is showing some signs of joining the fray against the industry." (Liv O'Hanlon, *The Guardian* 9-10 May 1992).

There are thousands of *self-help* groups in any modern society, enthusiasts for or fellow-sufferers from almost anything you can think of, many of them with national headquarters and networks or federations of local branches: societies for steam-railways, natterjack toads, Esperanto; friends of a hospital, a theatre, a prison; mutual aid groups for poliomyelitis sufferers, road victims, immigrants; and so on. Any of these can mutate into another kind of interest group, the protective associations for e.g. children, animals, pensioners, when their interests appear to be in danger; or become pressure groups like the peace movements, noise abatement societies, or anti-smoking groups, should they mobilise to act upon public opinion towards some change in law or policy. Thus, whether or not originally social-conflict-oriented, their existence makes them a potential side when a question of the governance, or self-governance, of their interest arises. And of their nature, they gather and circulate information about their interests, and so can be made partners in this kind of intervention, without significant implementation costs, if government wishes to avert turbulence in that area without regulating it.

Freedom of Information Acts are another intervention on the side of the perceived weaker contestant; the legislature seeks to keep the executive within limits by making life slightly more difficult for the bureaucrats, slightly easier for the enquiring citizen, the press and mass media. A really liberal government might even assist groups protesting against their own proposals, by offering documents and facilities. It is a vexed problem, how to offer succour and support to whistle-blowers, whose actions may uncover scandals in government to the general benefit, but whose personal lives are often ruined in the process.

The second most cost-effective way of intervening in a contested area is by fiscal and financial means. One widespread method is the loading of a less socially-desirable product with a tax, or the relieving from tax of a desirable one. This is intervention in the market, certainly, but not by regulating it. Probably all governments use grants and loans in a similar way. Subsidising consumer advice bodies weights the scales slightly more in the individual consumer's favour than would leaving her to the mercy of caveat emptor; by stimulating the production of comparative information, and facilitating the taking up cudgels on her behalf with refractory retailers or manufacturers - without the government itself getting involved. Other areas often subject to government support at arm's length but not regulation are culture and the arts, where some contestants would survive in a pure market but others would not.

These are in no way novel but very familiar types of government action, of which many more illustrations could be given. The only thing that may be new is the recognition that they form a distinct category, a method of achieving government objectives that may not have the same leverage as passing laws and policing them, but is much less subject to the enforcement costs and other drawbacks of legislating and regulating.

On the Concept of Controllability

How, then, can a volatile, complex, diverse and crisis-prone socio-political world be governed in a requisitely matching way? Only by a reflection on the meaning of the concept of controllability itself, in the context of its application to social systems and processes (Van der Zouwen and Geyer, 1986: 208, quoted above).

The first step in such a reflection is to appreciate that social systems by their nature are in a constant state of relative turmoil, because they comprise independent actors (individual, group, or corporate) seeking their own interests and in so doing coming into conflict with other independent actors seeking different interests. There is no possible state of social affairs all could agree to aim at or return to. From time to time, some actor or coalition will accumulate power; but no one individual, group or coalition will dominate for long, since that will create a temporary common interest for a number of other actors in returning to a more opportune situation, where they can all again pursue interests currently stifled. Thus the most likely state in which a social system is to be found is a relatively stable arena of opposing forces, which can persist as such without internal management by any super-actor (government or state), so long as the external environment is benign and nutritive.

Whether one thinks of this condition of relatively stable turmoil as being self-government or anarchy, as a system under control because not running away to death or destruction or as a jungle because no one is controlling it, is a matter of choice of words and model.

Now and again, some actor or group of actors may sufficiently dislike the configuration the internal equilibrium has taken up to wish to alter it; and, again simply because it is a social system, one amongst other social systems, the external environment will not always be sufficiently benign and nutritive. In such circumstances, a government may want to intervene in the equilibration and to impose order (i.e. a different order or pattern), to take command, to regulate or control. The traditional understanding of how this is done involves the establishment of a monopoly of legitimate physical force, and issuing directives, with feedbacks and corrections sanctioned by that monopoly.

Such methods are efficacious enough in stable, simple and homogeneous societies. As a society becomes more volatile, complex and diverse, they become self-defeating. The regulating apparatus gets more oppressive than the ills it is meant to avert. In the extreme, it may so damp down the underlying conflicts in a society as to negate the systemic equilibrating forces and risk social stagnation or explosion.

What this chapter suggests is that a government trying to steer the social equilibrium to a certain position, or to manage it in specific ways, has an instrument to use which depends but little on the government's legitimate monopoly of physical force; an instrument well adapted to a postmodern society (where traditional boundaries and distinctions no longer provide a handle or leverage for government action as formerly) because it is essentially empirical in operation, using what it finds; an instrument which runs with the systemic stabilising forces and not against them, except minimally, thus enroling in the public interest the natural conflict of private interests in a generalisation of Adam Smith's hidden hand - though by active management, not *laissez-faire*; an instrument which in fact is in frequent use today, just seldom recognised as such. The government may intervene in such a private conflict not only (as T.H. Green had it - 1895) to be the *hindrance of hindrances*, or (in modern parlance) to establish a level playing field, but positively to help one side against another.

Collibration - participating in the conflict of forces - as a technique is only an additional alternative to government by other means; it is certainly not advocacy of no government. It is the opposite of Spencer's philosophical radicalism: it by no means holds that all will be for the best in the best of all possible worlds if forces in contention are left to fight it out, or that the survival of the fittest in the market-place is the only golden rule.

The essence of collibration as a tool of governance is to identify, in any area of interest, what antagonistic forces already operate, what isostasy or stand-off configuration presently obtains, and what intervention would help create a more desirable position - not by calling in the matter for central decision, or committing oneself to laying down a standard or a prohibition (which will conventionally then apply to other situations unforeseen), but by giving that degree of ad hoc support to the side which needs it as will do the trick. Just as a child at the fulcrum of a see-saw can by moving a foot raise an adult on one end and lower one on the other, so government with a minimum use of power and resources may shift a little weight, and in a time-honoured and ubiquitous but surprisingly untheorised way, steer the equilibrium.

4

GOVERNANCE AND GOVERNABILITY: USING COMPLEXITY, DYNAMICS AND DIVERSITY

JAN KOOIMAN

New Forms of Governance?

In this chapter I will try to argue that recent changes in patterns of interactions between the public and the private sector may have to do with the growing realization of the complex, dynamic and diverse nature of the world we live in. Others in this volume (Dunsire, Kickert among others) develop the same kinds of ideas but in a somewhat different way.

Empirically we see around us that capacities of political/administrative governing systems either have crossed the threshold of diminishing returns (policies cancelling each other's effects) or are quite close to these boundary (implementation difficulties). In this situation governing systems try to reduce the need for governing (e.g. by deregulation) or shift the need (e.g. by privatization). But a third way seems to be developed and not in terms of more 'neo-corporatist arrangements'. These also seem to be victim of boundaries as the ones just mentioned. In the new forms of governance one can see a shift from unilateral (government or society separately) to an interactionist focus (government with society). The growing realization of interdependencies may lie behind such efforts. In a more theoretical perspective one could speculate that in these new forms of governing and governance - which we call social-political as stated earlier - more fundamental characteristics of modern societies are (finally?) being taken somewhat more serious. By this I mean that the growing realization of the enormous complexity, dynamics and diversity of social-political sub-systems (such as health care, education, transportation, environmental protection and social welfare) should not be left alone but somehow and in some respects have to be 'governed'. Even a profound neo-liberal like Hayeck was of this opinion.

What makes these new forms distinct from more traditional ones seems to be that they take complexity, dynamics and diversity much more seriously than their predecessors who often regarded these characteristics as nasty side effects, which unfortunately did not fit in the applied models. In other words in these new forms of governance the complex, dynamic and varied qualities of social-political systems may find a better and more profound expression than in most traditional political/ administrative models of governing.

The shift seems to be away from 'one-way steering and control' to 'two- or multi-way designs' in which (dis)qualities of social-political systems and their governance are viewed from the perspective of the recognition of mutual needs and capacities. In these efforts the higher complexity, faster dynamics and greater diversity of (major) social-political problems we want to tackle comes to life.

Looking at Dynamics, Complexity and Diversity

Dynamics, complexity and diversity (we reserve variety for the more technical sense it is used in cybernetics - Ashby and others -) are the kinds of concepts every scientific discipline has to come to terms with. How do we make something systematic and fruitful out of a world of phenomena which are fundamentally complex, dynamic and diverse? In the terms of this study: how can dynamic, complex and diverse social-political systems be governed in a democratic and effective way? The first answer is that governing and governance itself should be dynamic, complex and varied.

These qualities not only apply to the objects to be governed, but also to those who govern and by necessity to the relation between them. That is to say: governing, governance and governability themselves have (highly) dynamic, complex and diverse qualities of their own and (probably) should have these qualities. The lack of insight in this might be one of the major reasons why so much governance seems to be ineffective. An insight Etzioni already formulated some twenty years ago. (Etzioni, 1968) A simple example: the dynamics of many sociotechnical processes are such that the matching governance practices seem to be continuously 'out of breath': they have been overtaken by the developments, because the developments are dynamic and the governing is not dynamic (enough). The same kinds of examples for complexity and diversity are given by others in this book.

Apparently the dynamics, complexity and diversity of phenomena to be studied and of subjects to be handled is very difficult. Recent developments in physics indicate that the systematic realization of this can bring about fundamental discussions as to the nature of science itself (Prigogine, 1984).

Everything in nature is liable to changing and maintaining forces; in other words nature is basically dynamic. Even the smallest physical and biological particles consist of even smaller elements which cohere in manyfold ways; that is to say they are complex. And all phenomena in biological and social life show an immense and fundamentally uncomprehensible scope of differentiation and variability. In other words: they are basically diverse. The difficulties we have in coping with these qualities might have to do with these qualities themselves, with our methods to cope with them or with the lack of position to observe them. In my opinion this means that fundamental aspects of the physical, natural and social world we live in and which we use are not only 'in the eye of the beholder' but also belong to the reality out there, whatever our theoretical or applied capacity to understand or to handle them may be.

In the scope of this study the notions of dynamics, complexity and diversity apply to such social-political phenomena and the concepts by which we try to understand them such as: actors, interactions, problems, solutions, steering, management, control, needs and capacities. These are all parts of social-political systems, their governing, governance and governability.

It is the lack of tradition in looking at and working with complexity, dynamics and diversity in disciplines such as public administration and political science (somewhat less so in sociology and international relations) which makes that hardly any analytical tool or operationalization of them is available. I will try to develop a few of them in this chapter. To begin with I will say some more general things about dynamics, complexity and diversity.

Dynamics

Dynamics can bee seen as a composition of forces resulting in non-linear or (exceptionally) linear cause and effect patterns. Dynamics in reality is about systems going from one state or place to another: pushed, drawn or in other ways influenced by natural, technological or social forces. Recent developments in the natural sciences have stimulated the interest of social science in the usefulness of concepts such as (neg)entropy, non-equilibrium dynamics, chaos and dissipative structures for the explanation of social phenomena. (Mayntz, 1990) Especially since some important natural science scholars themselves (Varela and Maturana, Prigogine) established links between biological or physical theories and their application to the social world, interest in phenomena such as non-equilibrium dynamics has grown rapidly (see also in this volume Dunsire and Kickert).

For my particular purpose the reading of this (non technical) literature stimulated me greatly to emphasize the importance of dynamics as a basic phenomenon (variable category) in a governance theory. This literature shows that from the point of view of energy production and consumption (and analogously also information production and consumption) all systems, also social systems, are dynamic. It is a mutual tension of forces (such as entropic and negentropic) which forms the basic dynamics of systems. Boulding sees entropy also in terms of potential: that is to say a potential for change which is not being used. Negentropy is the realization of the potential for change (1978, p. 10). Entropy is the movement (a tendency always present in a system) which leaves the potential for change unused (equilibrium), which means in the long run disintegration and even disappearance. In most social-political systems such entropic states of (final) equilibrium will (fortunately) never be reached. However, irresponsible dealing with natural and ecological systems 'for human production and consumption' has brought us close to some of such states. Besides anything else this is already an important argument to pay more serious attention to the fundamental dynamics of modern societies and their natural environments.

In the social sciences dynamics related to different forces working at the same time has been conceptualized in quite different ways. A few examples follow. Atkinson sees the dynamics of human behaviour always as the result of three forces working together and at the same time (1970). Mayntz speaks of internal 'Eigendynamik' or external dynamic forces (1987). Zijderveld distinguishes centripetal and centrifugal dynamical forces (1985), and in the polemological literature one often finds the distinction between conflicting or harmonious dynamics. According to Boulding dynamics can be evolutionary or revolutionary (1970); Sorokin makes a distinction between rhythmic or arhythmic dynamics (1941, esp. vol IV). In spite of these differences all authors agree in some sense that there is always at the same time strive or tension between on the one hand some kind of will to preserve the existing state and on the other hand the causation of change of that state. It can be presumed that in social-political systems many of these different tensions will exercise their influences at the same time.

Dynamics (of social-political systems) cannot be understood without an insight in interactions. Dynamics always imply interactions. An interaction is inherently dynamic. Interactions may explain macro processes such as differentiation and integration, but also processes of cooperation and conflict on the micro- and meso level. Interactions are as it were the primary operationalizations of the dynamic forces in societies. Every interaction consists of three elements: an action level, a structural level and the level of the units between which the interactions take place. Within and between these three elements all kinds of tensions take place. These tensions or forces together form the dynamics of social systems on the micro-, the meso- and the macro level. It may be clarifying for a theory of governance to distinguish different sorts of interactions. I distinguish between interferences, interplays and interventions. Interferences are the (dynamic) basis of natural and human life (Kooiman, 1988). Whitehead, in developing a process philosophy, even extends these basic dynamics to the interactions between physical entities. He calls these basic patterns of interactions (in my terms interferences) nexuses (Sherbourne, 1966). Within the of scope governance these interferences can often be considered to be operating between primary objects: families, schools and firms. In modern societies there is a second type of interaction which is important; I call them interplays. They are usually highly organized and take place in formalized patterns. From the point of governing and governance these structural arrangements (such as organizations of interferences with common characteristics or inter-organizational networks) are important because they have (inter)dynamics of their own. And, thirdly, interactions might be organized and directed. These I call interventions. In many of these, although certainly not in all interventions, public (political and administrative) actors play a role. Interventions - as we know - also have dynamics of their own. Interferences, interplays and interventions have in common that they basically are dynamic relations between two or more actors. The difference is mainly in the form of organization and the degree of direction. For governance it is of great importance to get theoretical and empirical insight into the many forms interactions can assume. Insight in the dynamic qualities of interactions and the systems they are part of enables governance to make use of these qualities. The same - of course - applies to complexity and diversity.

Complexity

Complexity - again - is a concept which is used quite easily, but more often than not its use does not mean anything more than that an issue, a situation or a problem, is difficult to understand or complicated to handle. In my view however, complexity is more than that: it is a basic aspect of the phenomena we deal with.

A review of the literature offers three major ways to use complexity in terms of usefulness for the development of a theory of governance and governability: reduction and selection (Luhmann, 1970), structuring (Simon, 1969) and operationalization (La Porte et al., 1975).

Luhmann develops, at great length but in a highly abstract manner, the thesis that the fundamental problem of all social systems is to reduce complexity. In his opinion, complexity does not have to do with the number or variety of subsystems, but with the way they interact. Selecting and ordering interactions is the essence of coping with complexity. He and others have used this theoretical approach to analyze broad developments of systems, such as education and the judicial system, on a macro level and in a historical perspective.

In 'The architecture of complexity', Simon gives numerous examples for his assertion that most complex systems have some kind of hierarchical structure: a structure within a structure, within a structure. Simon argues that complexity can best be analyzed by applying the principle of 'nearly-decomposability' which means that, in practice, some parts in systems are more closely related than others (1969).

A third way to handle complexity is to see it as an operational problem. Different approaches have been used to do this. I can mention studies like Laporte et al. with conceptualizations and case-studies on different social levels. Most of the approaches mentioned share the basic notion that complexity has to do with manyfold interactions of many parts within a system; a characteristic certainly applicable to the social-political systems we are interested in. Secondly, from these approaches it can be derived that complexity always has to do with parts and wholes. No understanding of complexity is possible by leaving out interactions between parts and talk about wholes, or by looking at wholes without taking the interactions of parts into consideration. Thirdly, one can say that these studies underline the fact that there is no single way to cope with complexity; it is probably best to make a reasoned selection of different forms of decomposition depending on the problem at hand. Criteria might be aspects such as centrality, intensity and scope of the interactions between the parts of the systems involved.

The distinction in three forms of interactions I made earlier, may help here. The distinction itself is a way of reducing the complexity of interactions I was confronted with in terms of their usefulness from the point of view of governing and governance problems. Interferences are interactions of and around the basic - primary processes taking place in certain systems: caring for the sick and disabled, producing material objects, moving objects from one place to another or transmitting values in terms of education or religion. All these interferences have their own complexities, which are quite different from other basic interferences. To forget this, or not recognize this, probably means false reductions. The same applies to interplays and interventions. Network configurations in 'industrial systems' have types of complexities differing from those in social affairs. Interventions without governments (self-interventions from a public point of view) or with governments, differ considerably in their complexities, depending on the centrality or intensiveness of governments taking parts as actors in these forms of interactions. Distinguishing between such forms and types of complexities is a necessary step in the development of a theory of social-political governance.

Diversity

Diversity as a basic concept has to do with the great and growing individualization, differentiation, specialization and variety of the modern world. Some see diversity as an element of complexity; the greater diversity or variety, the higher complexity. I have defined complexity in terms of relations and diversity addresses the components of these relationships. Systems may have a great diversity of components but relatively simple relations between parts (most technical systems). They are probably complicated but usually not complex. But systems may also consist of elements with relatively small differences, but highly differentiated relations (a faculty). Then I would presume them to be complex.

However, my main argument to make diversity a third basic characteristic of social-political systems (and their governance) is the growing importance of diversity within those systems. By means of the concept of diversity we draw attention to the actors in those systems. By means of the concept of complexity we examine structures and by means of diversity we examine aspects of the system itself, such as goals, intentions and powers. As Wilden puts it: "The combination of diversity that creates complexity is a qualitative process. In contrast, a combination of variety may be simply quantitative." (1987: 173) We could hypothesize that diversity implies that all variations, differentiations and specializations are possible; some, however, are more probable than others. This is what, in a somewhat different way, recent work in evolutionary theory draws attention to.

Growing diversity is a characteristic of our time, with its emphasis on individual opportunities and responsibilities on the micro (individuals), the meso (organization and management) and the macro (regions) level. This a social-political datum which has to be taken seriously. The neglect of diversity as a special and important characteristic of social-political systems is probably at the root of many governance and governability problems.

Diversity is of special importance in relation to dynamics and complexity. Neither dynamics nor complexity by themselves contain objective criteria to decide whether an interaction is going in a certain direction or to decide whether a certain interaction still belongs to a (sub)system or not. Diversity is the conceptual denominator to introduce such substantive criteria. It opens possibilities for substantive analysis of social-political systems; an analysis which otherwise could only be abstract and formal. In the context of theorizing on social-political governance, it shifts disciplines such as public administration and political science in the direction of interdisciplinarity. Other fields, such as economics, sociology and ecology, are needed to uncover and interpret the diversity of social-political actors with their goals, intentions, purposes, norms and powers. This means a theory of governance which takes complexity, dynamics and diversity seriously, has to be interdisciplinary, with all its problems and opportunities.

Governance and Dynamics, Complexity and Diversity

Social-political governing takes place in interactions between actors on micro, meso and macro levels of social-political aggregation. These interactions not only reflect the basic complexity, dynamics and diversity of our societies, they are themselves complex, dynamic and diverse. That is to say: they are connected in complex patterns, they move and change on the basis of dynamically working forces and they refer to different kinds of substances. In complexity the structural substances, in dynamics the changing substances and in diversity the different substances of mutual interdependencies of social-political systems are expressed. And in these, the relations between the complexity, dynamics and diversity of interactions also become apparent. Social-political governing and governance has to take these qualities into consideration. One cannot say that in traditional approaches these basic characteristics are not taken into consideration at all, but usually only piecemeal, unsystematic and often accidental. As Wilden puts it: the last fifty years show a revolution against simplicity (1987).

In social-political governance the three qualities are not only considered to be central, but also essential for effective governance.
A dynamic approach to governance emphasizes the process and change aspects of interactions. It pays systematic attention to the forces which bring about movements and it tries to influence these patterns of change and their consequences. It manipulates aspects of the dynamics of interferences, interplays and interventions. Centripetal interferences require other

forms of governing than centrifugal interferences, competing interplays other forms of interventions than consensual or cooperative interplays. And 'new' interventions can be different from ones having to reckon with already existing forms of interventions. The dynamics of governance refer to the intentional dynamics of the basic interactions. The patterns of relationships between these interactions in terms of complexity enhance or limit the structural (im)possibilities of specific governing actions or longer-term patterns of governance.

All this is expressed in, for instance, the handling of problems. If we define problems in terms of disturbances in equilibrium or disequilibrium states of a certain (sub)system, then problems will always be part of a field of tension. In public administration and political science many of the widely-used models presume reversibility of dynamics, or at least, if not reversibility, they often assume continuity, linearity and predictability. (Mayntz in this volume) However, in a real problem situation these kinds of dynamics will probably only occur as an exception to the rule. Presuppositions such as these reflect the limited capacity to conceptualize and handle dynamics as many forces on a subject at the same time. As Dunsire conceptualizes in his use of 'collibration', this is exactly what the manipulation of dynamics could be: do not consider it as a nasty side-effect of basically linear, stable and predictable models, but use it explicitly (Dunsire in this volume). Or as Kickert states: bring networks in a state of (extreme) disequilibrium to provoke opportunities for governing and governance (Kickert in this volume). To start with, we could use insights from cybernetics much more systematically. Concepts such as negative feedback, but certainly also positive feedback, can be explored much more thoroughly than we have done sofar. Steering, managing and even control and coordination can be seen as much more dynamic forms of governing than has been done traditionally. One could even say that in practice these forms of governing are often quite dynamic but we have not been able to conceptualize them and to make them part of modern theories of social-political intervention in that way.

The same could be said of making use of complexity. With very few exceptions, there are hardly any theoretical insights available on how to 'decompose' and 'compose' complex social-political systems in terms of their 'nearly-(de)composability' (Simon's approach), or in terms of the reduction and selection of central patterns of interaction within systems or between systems and their environment (Luhmann's approach), or even in terms of trying to operationalize complexity in simple terms such as number, intensity and different forms of interactions between parts of systems and parts and wholes of social-political systems. Again, there are exceptions, but they have hardly become part of the central body of political-administrative literature.

From the angle of diversity, traditional governing becomes really quite problematic. As it was recently stated in a newspaper article: every citizen his or her own civil servant.

But still, the quite well-known 'law' stated by the cybernetic scholar Ashby, holds: variety can only be destroyed by variety. This confronts governance with severe dilemma's from which simple escapes seem not be readily available. One direction might be more and more thorough representation (Pekonen, this volume). But we know from literature and from practical experience that representation in the classical sense has its own quite severe limitations because of large-scale reductions which must be made when large numbers are involved or when large interests are at stake. One important step might be to start from the assumption that most problem and opportunity complexes in the societies of today are indeed of a social-political nature. And in that case, the representation of the basic dynamic, complex and diverse nature of their (basic) interaction patterns should be the starting point for governing and governance and not a 'closing entry' at the end of a problem-solving or opportunity-creating process. Regarding such processes as social-political governance, instead of social or political governing, might already be quite an important step. This is an important challenge for the development of a theory of governing and governance which focuses on the complexity, dynamics and diversity of modern society, its problems and its opportunities.

Governance and Governability

There are hardly any theories available which regard governance systematically in terms of interaction between government and society. More than two decades ago (1968), Etzioni came closest with 'Active Society' and more recently the Bielefeld project (Kaufmann et al., 1986) came close. Neo-corporatist theories and what has been labelled 'private interest government', have some common ground (the interaction element) but they are more directed towards a theory of social order. The same applies to the so-called ASD (actorsystems dynamics) approach by Burns et al. (1985). I propose that the concept of governability, which can be seen as the permanent balancing process between governing needs on the one hand and governing capacities on the other, is central in this approach. The theory is considered to be dynamic itself because it will make systematical use of dynamic concepts such as 'balancing'; it will be complex in the sense that it will distinguish different levels of governing and governance and it will be diverse in the sense that it starts from problem situations and problem complexes and carefully represents the diversity of the actors (intentions, goals, powers) involved. To put it somewhat differently: this theory will have as its distinguishing characteristic the view of social-political governance not only as interaction between government and society, but also of governability as an expression of governance in terms of effective and legitimate adjustment of governing needs to capacities and capacities to needs. It distinguishes itself from others by not regarding needs as something in society and capacity as something of governments. No, needs and capacities in their tensions (dynamics of interactions), patterns (complexities of interdependencies) and actors (diversity of meanings and interpretations) should be seen at the same time as being social and political, public and private, state and society in their mutual interdependencies.

In my opinion such an approach might offer some new insights and perspectives not only for theory development but also in helping to answer some practical and nasty questions. An example might be the strange paradox that governments seem to need more, or at least other, capacities to diminish their own governing capacities. Efforts in this direction seem to be rather fruitless as long as they remain within the traditional and rigid patterns of divisions between public and private in the classical sense.

That such an interactive approach itself will create problems is self-evident. This is inherent in a perspective which regards governing interactions as complex, dynamic and diverse expressions of problem formulations and at the same time problem solutions as interactions. Every 'solution' creates its own 'problems'. So does this solution. However, this solution can be expected to open up some new ways of thinking on aspects of interactions which have been neglected so far; and in that sense it offers opportunities for governance more in tune with the demands of the world we live in.

Governing Needs

Every social-political problem (past, present or future) can be seen as a potential need. But a problem is only a problem in governing terms when it has been articulated as such. The articulation of a problem implicates the wish for a solution, public, private or mixed. In this sense every need (physical, social, emotional) can be expressed as the wish of a system to be governed in the direction of satisfaction. In the development of needs as parts of governance, a thorough understanding of the system concerned is essential.

Every system moves as a result of (at least) two opposing forces, one that tries to move it away from the existing state and one that tries to keep it in the existing state (in thermodynamics the tension between entropy and negentropy). If complexity is not kept in check the system will develop in the direction of chaos. If dynamics is not kept in check this will lead to disorientation. If diversity is not kept in check this will lead to disintegration. This all has to do with entropic processes. But social- political systems show, because of the same complexities, dynamics and diversity (in other combinations), tendencies to escape from entropy in terms of negentropy. These tendencies are constitutive for basal needs of every (social-political) system: the boundlessness of the (natural) need to prevent chaos, disorientation and disintegration.

On the social level we see that these basal needs, in what Vroon has called the opposite demands, are put before the development of societies. On the one hand there are the needs for planning, ordering, steering and coordination; needs which are reinforced by growing (technological) possibilities to control processes. On the other hand there are the needs for individual freedom, autonomy, growth and influence; needs which are also reinforced by technological, economic and social developments. After a period in which much of the coming to terms with these 'opposing need ways' have been put on the public plate, there are movements now to roll back these collective demands. By so heavily emphasizing the role of governments in this coping process, one might forget that the vast majority of these need-balancing processes has always been private on all social levels; even in the social-political systems which we used to call 'people's republics'. Still an overwhelming number of needs is satisfied on a self-regulating and self-steering basis (autopoiesis). However, the continuous process towards higher dynamics, greater complexity and increasing diversity might threaten the balance here. In my opinion, the over-all management of the tendencies towards chaos, disintegration and disorientation on the systems level (and these in practice will be sectorwise) is at the heart of the social-political formulation of needs. Recently this need has been increasing. Partly, this has to do with the 'polarization' between the public and the private sector. Both (basically interdependent) parts of societies have become - as it were - opposing forces, competitors, rather separate (conglomerates of) actors, instead of complementary ones. In the view of a large part of the private sector the public sector has become foreign and vice versa. In my conception this lies at the root of problems at the 'need'-level.

Governing Capacity

The interactional context prepares the way or creates a potential for social-political governing: purposeful and planned interventions. Interplays and interventions are both forms of governing interactions between the public and the private, between government and society. In interplays parts of government are inter-actors just like social organizations. These interactions have a tremendous governing capacity. They form, as it were, the potential on which interventions are based. Werlin (1988) calls this 'elasticity' when he discusses bridging the micro and macro dimension in administrative theory. In my terms: elasticity of interplays enhances social-political governing capacity under the umbrella of the ultimate governance responsibility shared by social-political leadership in terms of interventions. This should be understood in process as well as organizational terms. In fact, "the structural and organizational factors in macro - interaction are expected to have a more significant effect on macro processes, under most circumstances, than the other kinds of factors and than both of them combined" (Etzioni, 1968: 103).

The essence then of social-political governance capacity lies in interventions, purposeful and directed forms of social-political interaction. The simple fact of positioning social-political capacities not exclusively at the side of government is in accordance with our basic assumption: it makes governing and governance dynamic, complex and diverse. By doing this, these capacities become more in conformity with the reality of (modern) social-political (sub)systems such as governing economies, health care, public and private transportation, education and environmental protection. Capacities in those sectors are much more complex, dynamic and diverse than much of the traditional theories assume. These characteristics make these capacities more effective and legitimate. This not only in terms of interventions as such, but also as regards their embedding and conditioning in terms of interplays and interferences. By stressing the complexity (patterns), dynamics (forces) and diversity (meanings) of interactions on different levels, governing and governance capacities are not seen as isolated and incidental top-down efforts of steering, managing, controlling or regulating, but as reflecting and representing the basic characteristics of the systems they are part of on the micro, the meso and the macro levels. This is why needs and capacities can be balanced, the subject of the next paragraph.

Governability

The complexity, dynamics and diversity of social-political systems require certain characteristics of the adjustment process between needs and capacities: this is what we call governability.

In the dynamics of the relations between needs and capacities the diversity of social-political questions should be represented. That is to say, in the way in which in the governance context images are formed about such questions the (diverse) meanings should be complex enough to understand these questions in their mutual coherence. This image formation itself should in some essential way represent the selection of composition and decomposition of parts in relation to wholes in terms of neither overcomplexification nor oversimplification. This can only be done in an interactive communication and decision-making process on the micro, meso and macro level of actors involved.

Social-political problems, as tested against the background of the 'need situation' of the involved (sub)system in its relation with other (sub)systems, requires a certain diversity of instruments: only variety can destroy variety (Ashby's law of requisite variety). From a capacity point of view the availability of solutions is a major governance responsibility. This could be called the instrumental aspect of governance. To what extent is a (governing) system able to create and preserve conditions under which a broad scala of potential solutions is manageable? Since a decade or so traditional means such as financial stimuli and laws, rules and regulations have more and more become questionable instruments of social-political intervention. This has to do with shortcomings on the governance level: always more of the same instead of trying out and experimenting with new ways of governance. The eminent importance of what Ashby has formulated as a principle on the governance level has hardly been recognized: how the creation of variety in instruments is a prerequisite for adequate governing (1957). This is a major aspect of the adjustment and balancing process between needs (problems) and capacities (solutions). Needs and capacities as defined and actualized in the governance context have their own dynamics, complexities and diversities. Because they have to do with systems characteristics, these (probably) cannot be created, tested and implemented at short notice. This requires open channels, flexibility and mutual recognition of divided and complementary responsibilities.

This adjustment process between needs and capacities has to be integrated from the 'capacities' and from the 'needs' point of view. This integration process is difficult to plan. There are many uncontrollable forces at work. For this reason the attuning process has to be constantly guarded. This can be done by the reciprocal control of governing needs and governing capacities. In other words: let them control themselves. This control is not a static concept and it does not take place in a social vacuum. But it can override the environmental and situational forces in a partly free decision moment. Without such a moment, the participants would be liable to random social-political developments. This could mean that a one-sided governing-governed relation between needs and capacities brings about one-sided communication: either from the needs (problems) or capacity (solutions) point of view. Because of the already mentioned polarized relation between state capacity on the one hand and social demands on the other, there are hardly any institutional forms of mutual and integrated adjustment of social-political needs and social-political capacities. Often the boundaries of capacities limit need formulation and vice versa. This promotes the 'hardening' of both points of view; hardly anywhere a mutuality can be found in this adjustment process.

Here the meta-quality of mutual adjustment and control, of needs and capacities, plays a major role. Meta can be seen as the ability to reflect, to learn and to adjust on a higher level. Meta is - as it were - the adjustment of needs and capacities but on one level higher. It is known that without meta-rules no genetic (r)evolution is possible. In an analogical way one could say that without meta governability rules, no (r)evolution in social-political governance is possible.

Conclusion

In this chapter I have tried to make a start with the development of some theoretical notions on governing and governance which takes into consideration complexity, dynamics and diversity as basic systems qualities. These concepts might be of help in forming an interpretative framework for new forms of interaction between government and society. These concepts are still rather abstract but in the following chapters some of these ideas are taken up in terms of more refined concepts and empirical illustrations. A final motto may be borrowed from Etzioni, indicating the kind of social-political reality we want to focus on. There can only be an 'active society', that is to say 'one that is master of itself', if governance is able to understand, to react and to use the dynamics, complexity and diversity of modern societies. For that purpose, governance should, in contrast to what we are used to, be able to cope much better with uncertainty, instability, even chaos, long-term perspectives, broader orientations and great diversity of life-styles and meanings. Exactly because of this, theoretical notions, such as they are developed in this book around these phenomena, instead of ignoring them or declaring them unwanted, put them in the centre of attention. Chaos might create order as Prigogine puts it (1984). But this order is of a different nature than most present-day governing (theoretically and empirically) points to.

INTRODUCTION TO PART II

PREDICAMENTS

In the three chapters that make up this second part of the book we want to show some of the predicaments of recent ways of governance and governing. They concern forms of incapabilities of governing systems to cope with governing needs, at least against the background of the conceptualization of social-political governance and governing.

From other points of view (such as 'muddling-through' as a strategy to cope with complex, dynamic and differentiated problems) the given examples might be evaluated differently. Although no pretension exists that the three cases give a representative overview of such incapacities, failures or other forms of ineffective governing, each highlights an important aspect of our topic.

Frédéric Royall shows how in the case of the labour market in Ireland an external 'opportunity' created by the EC membership, and its interest to develop economically weak regions of the Community, did not dynamize the governance of this sector. He gives an example of a (part of a) sector which leans so heavily on public initiatives (and probably its vested and balanced interests) that its governance is not capable of bringing needs and capacities on a higher and, for the system as a whole, more appropriate level.

Kirsti Stenvall gives an example how the public/administrative part of a governing system uses planning as an instrument not only to govern in general but also to influence the governance of a particular sector systematically, in this case education in Finland. She shows how this part of the educational governing system reduces the diversity of the 'image formation' on education in such a way as to 'restructure' the society at large in an active but not in an inter-active way.

Marijke Prins' analysis of women's liberation in the Netherlands shows the lack of capacity of a field of social-political interaction to put an important, complex, dynamic and diversified issue (or set of issues) in a proper governance perspective. This has - at least partly - to do with traditional roles of politics, public administration, and the involved women groups. Conceptualization in terms of social-political governance and governing is in her opinion a better tool than policy-analytical or government-environment approaches, not only to put the apparent failure in this case into a proper perspective, but also to give direction to possible improvements.

These three cases try to provide a view to problems in specific areas of governing and governance. With their empirical indications they emphasize the need for looking at aspects of governability and to locate some problems of modern (complex, divers and dynamic) societies.

5

LOST OPPORTUNITY: THE CASE OF LABOUR MARKET MANAGEMENT IN THE REPUBLIC OF IRELAND

FRÉDÉRIC ROYALL

Introduction

The previous chapters have set the tone for the conceptual nature of the volume. As described, social political governing and governance are premised upon two points. The first deals with an observance of the development of continuous interactions between public and non-public actors; whereas the second refers to the growing recognition by social and political actors of the complexity, diversity and variety of social and political systems. Kooiman and Dunsire (this volume) have presented arguments of these views. In essence, the governing-governance argument implies that new problems and solutions may or may not be fully brought about in the traditional central rule hierarchical government-centred approach. The question thus becomes how the challenge of complexity, diversity and variety is handled on the governance level (meta-intervention: setting standards, formulating broader, wider perspectives). A basic assumption is taken that complexity, diversity and dynamics may be problematic but may also create opportunities in terms of new needs and new capacities.

Within this framework of reference, the present circumstances of complexity, diversity and dynamics imply that social-political governance can be a 'desirable' outcome. So governance is to be found in the establishment of the conditions for emerging qualities or the development of opportunities for concrete models such as co-regulation, co-steering, co-production, or co-operative management. In other words, the principle of governance points to facilitating the conditions for the emerging patterns.

Kickert (1992-'93) shows a useful example of such emerging patterns. The author points to the case of Higher Education in the Netherlands "in which a completely new conception of government control - steering at a distance - was invented"... and "was a departure from the classical idea of top-down direct government control". Kickert argues that in the face of complexity, diversity and complexity in this Dutch policy sector, an operational way was formulated to deal with complexity, diversity and complexity, that is in terms of the relation between needs and capacities and the matching of such. Consequently, the case is made showing the benefits accrued from adapting governance principles and using them within a sector.

This chapter takes a more nuanced look at the debate on social-political governance. It attempts to illustrate the argument by reference to a policy sector in which governing does indeed take place but without much governance at all, that is governance as defined within the context of this volume, such as taking advantage of opportunities created by the emerging patterns.

At the heart of our investigation are the means by which public authorities in Ireland have been led to strike a balance between products of tensions and changes in the labour market. We look at the processes through which the system adapts itself - mainly from the point of view of the traditional central rule approach with limited and restricted inter-actions.

In this chapter the role of public authorities in labour market affairs will be described and related to the inter-organisational network of the labour market. It is not possible to understand the dynamics of the system without 'seeing' who the actors are and what are the power relationships. A brief sketch will be given of the form that governing has taken. Finally, the 'picture' will be completed by relating the form of governing with new tendencies, specifically in relation to developments towards European integration.

Role of Public Authorities

As the general economic problems deepened in Ireland in the late 1970s (represented by rapidly increasing unemployment), appropriate objectives and methods of labour market policy were very difficult to establish. For example, it was often asked where would labour market policy fit. Would it be in relation to economic policy, social policy, industrial policy, or other policy sectors? Which approach should public authorities use; which integrated? Should labour market intervention strengthen social welfare or industrial restructuring?

What was not challenged and, indeed, had come to be expected, was the state's increased involvement in and responsibility for labour market affairs. But even to this day, public authorities express great reserve and difficulty in clarifying the objectives of labour market policy. Ireland is not alone in having had to come to terms with such problems of organisation and priorities (Rose and Page, 1990). Each country has tried to resolve the issue in line with the national expectations of the state's role in managing social and economic affairs.

But measures have varied greatly. Yet, if we turn our attention to the methods of implementing the programmes, all West European countries seem to share common bonds. These are in relation to the actors that count or whose influence must be taken into consideration. This variable must not be neglected. Within such a complex policy sector there necessarily exists a plurality of interests on which public authorities depend for a degree of decision-making and effective implementation. Governing needs require that such interests be integrated into the framework by one means or another if only so that policy is not frustrated through lack of co-operation or inactivity.

Based on Metcalfe (1978), Coombes et al. (1991: 19) argue that: "the participation of social and economic interests in the management of economic development has invariably been sought in Western European states primarily as a means of managing turbulent environments for which other, more conventional instruments of public intervention have been excluded as undesirable or inefficient."

The problem has arisen as to how to accommodate varied territorial and structural labour market needs (among others) when decisions and priorities are most often established on a national basis (that is by central public authorities in the traditional central rule hierarchical government approach). Regional differences inevitably have led to wide-ranging approaches for implementing nationally based programmes.

Consequently, many countries have developed some forms of devolved managerial structures. These may range in form from local co-ordination and management of labour market affairs by local social and economic groups to regional management agencies of the central government. Such approaches do have affinities with the qualities of the various governing models (co-steering, co-managing etc.) as proposed in the social-political governance approach. In Ireland, though, administrative tasks have been reapportioned to no other structure than to regional offices of the central public authority on the basis of vaguely defined territorial units. In fact, local labour markets at times intersect the planning units established by the central public authorities. This is not the only problem. Functional duties are often undertaken in a haphazard fashion, often creating a multiplication of agencies, and in the process, leading to much confusion for both providers and users of services. For example, prior to 1 January 1988, Ireland had no less than five official labour market agencies organised at both national and regional levels and a further panoply of governmental departments and agencies (Geary, 1988). Since then there have been great efforts to co-ordinate responsible public agencies, but there still remains numerous and distinct governmental administrative agencies. The government commissioned Culliton report on industrial policy (1992) has taken a negative view of such administrative dispersal and has called for more sweeping and radical changes in the government administrative structuring for better co-ordination and service delivery.

Along this line, all European countries have a type of decentralised public administration in labour market affairs. These reflect the prevailing concepts of administration. Most of these regional agencies do have some form of functional and structural responsibilities, aside from simply distributing social welfare. In addition, they are directly involved in the procedure of governing.

Managing these central agencies and regional branches is more problematical than it might first appear, especially when local/regional interests may constrain the effectiveness of policy or even challenge the legitimacy of the central public authority to provide services. Various methods of management have been and are being devised. In their many forms and features these means inevitably require some form of participation of local/regional actors. This ranges from formalised agreements and statutory participation of government-approved interests in the workings of labour market agencies such as in the French Comités de bassin d'emploi, to ad hoc (informal) participation, as in the Irish (now defunct) Local Training Advisory Committees.

Of course, examples of private interest participation taken from the West European context must be approached with caution. In no two countries do devolved structures or greater participation of local interests in labour market agencies operate in a similar way. There is great variation not only in the functional responsibilities of decentralised agencies but also in the power relationships of the participating interests. Thus the reasons for having groups participate in formal or informal labour market boards/ agencies often have no other goal than of absorbing new elements into a structure as a means to averting threats to its stability or existence (Selznick, 1947). In Ireland this has taken the form of providing a consultative role for concerned interests rather than as a true means to grant regionally based interests an active role in the administrative responsibilities. Nevertheless, public authorities have established a network of devolved structures while exercising ultimate control over the frameworks. Coming back to Kooiman's statement (1990: 2), "the governing role of public authorities has been part of a continuous process of interactions between social groups and forces and public or semi-public institutions and authorities". In this regard, it can not truly be said that problems or needs have impinged upon public authorities to change radically the governing mechanism. Rather minor adjustments have been made to the governing procedure as the labour market situation has continued to evolve, creating new problems and challenges for public authorities (Dineen, 1989; Dineen and Wallace, 1987). Steering-at-a-distance, in Kickert's use (1991) has not been implemented as no direct threat to the stability of the system has become manifest. We now turn to reasons why this has been so.

Institutional Structures and Forms of Governing

With the increase in economic problems, specifically from the late 1970s on, successive Irish governments have sought to tackle the nature and extent of the labour market problems with what were hoped and expected to be appropriate measures. At times, the measures did succeed in resolving some issues. Many factors, such as the lack of specialised institutions or secure network relationships, combined to make the government task more formidable. Consequently, Irish institutional developments and policy measures have often resembled what Rose and Page (1990: 66) call a "part of the serial process of incremental policy-making... It has been much easier to observe problems than to know what to do about it".

From an institutional standpoint, since the initial development of an 'active' manpower policy in the early 1960s, many public agencies have been created. Their functions have varied and their goals have been at times counteractive and counterproductive (Danaher et al., 1985). Public agencies are also supplemented in labour market activity-functions by private institutions. (Teague, 1989). However, the private sector plays a relatively limited role in the management of labour market affairs. For the greater part, it is dependent upon public institutions for managerial and/or financial support. For example, it is through the public agencies that the private sector receives financial support for service provisions either directly from the Exchequer or by means of the European Community Structural Funds or Local Employment Initiatives. This leads back to the role of the agencies of the central government and to the management processes.

The conclusions to be drawn from the multitude of agencies and Departments (established in different periods, according to varying needs, and on the basis of divergent functional responsibilities) is that public agencies have been organised as the needs arose. This was done in a generally incremental fashion, that is, mainly as a short term stop gap for targeted areas of labour market difficulties, and not on the basis of any forward-looking planning process (although the situation is changing). One could hypothesis that public authorities have succeeded in fulfilling the role that was expected of them without fully resolving the initial problems. In other words, the creation of public institutions may well have been destined more to resolve the immediate political problems than the long term economic ones. As a result at present there exists a wider body of interests which must be accommodated in this policy sector, such as groups representing the unemployed, voluntary organisations, charitable organisations, business associations, etc.. Given the structures of the policy sector and the role and functions of the state, each of these interests inevitably turns to the public authorities to present solutions to the perceived problems. Complexity, diversity and dynamics clearly become problematical and emerging governance qualities could very well have been a result. But this does not appear to have been the case. Rather governing principles have been reorganised and strengthened.

So, how have these interests been catered for and the labour market governed? The answer lies in part in the approach the central public authorities take towards labour market policy and in the organisational principles for implementing such a policy. In Ireland, public authorities have taken the responsibility not only for direct labour market intervention but also for maintaining financial and administrative control. When the issue of allowing social and economic groups to participate in Irish labour market management has arisen and thus possibly of facilitating the challenge of complexity, diversity and dynamics on the governance level (meta-intervention), public authorities have attempted to control the groups in order to ensure that vital decisions remain securely vested in the domain of the central public authorities.

Many factors have contributed to the trend toward centralised control (Chubb, 1982). At present, the process continues to favour nationally based centralised sources of support and decision-making structures. This is the situation in spite of the oft expressed aspirations of some interest bodies in favour of devolved structures. The representatives of social and economic interests, likewise, have tended to converge upon the central public authorities due to the expanding economic and social responsibilities of the state. The explanation may be that, for purposes of the labour market, local public authorities have limited functional responsibilities, although they are substantial employers and providers of essential services such as support for infrastructure (housing and building, water supply, road transportation, health, etc.) (Barrington, 1980). Interests inevitably side-step the local public authorities. Unlike some mainland European countries, and France in particular, local authorities have not as yet taken it upon themselves to develop the tasks of the responsible national agencies in dealing with localised problems of unemployment. As a result, if interests or intermediary associations do try to bring about any degree of influence they have necessarily had to turn to the central public authorities (or agencies thereof).

The central public authorities have responded to the request and need for exchange by creating formal and informal institutions of consultation and management. Social and economic groups are now being included in formal structures of decision-making through their participation in tripartite bodies. Some institutions have taken the form of including 'main social partners' as members on the boards of many public agencies. But there is a problem with these institutions. Namely, it is not clear to what extent board members actually represent grass-root membership of their organisations nor even in what capacity they govern, since final responsibility for nominations to the boards and final decisions still remain with the central government.

So partnership must be approached with caution. In other words, the main social and economic groups appear to have been co-opted into the framework of management simply because their co-operation was considered as advantageous and not in order to bring about any true form of a sharing of formal power.

The institutional principle has also been extended to consultative bodies for purposes of labour market planning in such fields as training needs and social welfare. But, with no statutory or regulatory functions, these organisations again have serious shortcomings in this respect. Nothing ensures that the decisions/proposals of these bodies are not simply ignored by the accountable public agencies (Coombes et al., 1991). The effectiveness and consideration given to the 'expert advice' is understandably very much dependent upon the commitment and support of the central government. It would seem that the central public authorities were and are unlikely to welcome any form of intervention which appears to affect their own ultimate responsibility for the form and methods of public intervention.

While the selected interests appear to be involved in an aspect of management, we should not be led astray by appearance.

In another manner, Irish central public authorities have indeed devolved certain functions to decentralised non-governmental organisations. This has involved a mixture of responsibility for functions and implementations of some of the policy measures discussed above. Essentially, the trend has taken two forms: one deals with the financial support accorded to private firms in matters such as in-company training, employment maintenance, job creation, etc.; the second, which has been on the increase, deals with state support for community based groups.

We must express reservations to any view which holds that community, self-help initiatives have been a basis for new-found approaches of emerging qualities of labour market governance. Indeed, the initiatives have widened the pattern of governing and have partially made relevant such conceptions as governing-at-a-distance. But in this context, governing-at-a-distance becomes a matter of degrees.

Lost Opportunity

We have seen so far that the pattern of governing has rested upon three pillars: the extent of centralisation, the functions of the public authorities and those delegated to the state-sponsored bodies for intervention, and the moderate use of the sharing of the burden of responsibility with local/regional interests. We turn now to means by which the opportunities created by complexity, diversity and dynamics have not come to pass. It is clear that the public management of economic affairs may be curtailed by movements toward European integration. In other words, it is to be expected that the role and functions of national governments for co-ordinating public policy in economic and social affairs must adjust to the new developments in European integration. This is not to suggest that functional responsibilities will inevitably be transferred to a supra-national body with the consequent result that member-states will loose the prerogative for intervention which is for the moment theirs. Rather we stress that, within the developing framework, the role of public policy must be adjusted to the obligations which are at times beyond the control of the member-state such as in the movement toward increased European Union. In the management of the labour market this could have far reaching effects. We will endeavour to explain the reasons for this.

The European Community has already initiated steps for a progressive movement towards integration. These have taken the form of objectives for harmonious development of economic activities. Within the labour market the principal financial instrument for promoting these objectives has been the European Social Fund (ESF). The Fund, in its original form, had been intended to complement the public expenditures of member states. It was understood that intervention by this means would provide 50% of funding for projects submitted by the state. The long term intention was to meet the specific economic or social objectives of the European Community. Overall responsibility for managing the fund was accorded to the state sponsored body in charge of major labour market affairs: in Ireland AnCO (later FAS) (Laffan, 1986). Funding was to have the added function of supporting labour market projects. Increasingly, the ESF has taken the form of supplementing the Exchequer or of subsidising projects which would have gone ahead even without such funding. It did not appear to be providing added funds for projects which would not have been otherwise undertaken by the national governments (additionality). This holds true for Ireland in particular. The Irish government has striven in practice to maximise returns by submitting as many applications as possible on behalf of projects likely to qualify for the special types of financial assistance on offer by the Community. Consequently, management of the Funds had become a preserve of governmental Departments specialising in submitting projects which conformed to the prescribed enactments (Laffan, 1989). On a Europe-wide basis, these management processes for Community funding had come under increasing criticism. Main objections concerned the limited nature of the funding and also the lack of efficiency in the expenditure of funds. In Ireland, the criticism took an added form given that all projects which were submitted and the subsequent allocation of grants, were the responsibility of an agency of the central government. There was serious dissatisfaction expressed with this arrangement, particularly from social and economic interests whose projects were simply overlooked by public authorities once Community allocations had been secured.

Reform of the Structural Funds inevitably came about in the wake of renewed efforts toward integration. The February 1988 European Council agreement to double the size of the Structural Funds between 1988 and 1993 continued the general thrust of this tendency. For Ireland, both these factors and a further tendency attaching preferences in the allocation of funds to the less favoured regions of the Community have been instrumental in this regard. These regions understandably stand to gain most from the doubling of the Structural Funds (Bradley et al., 1992; Poulsen, 1992). However, conditional to increased Community funding have been a series of rigorous financial and implementation controls.

The functions and priorities of the Funds have been detailed in the EC Regulation 2052/88. Five objectives have been identified:

1) promoting the development and structural adjustment of regions whose development is lagging behind;
2) converting regions seriously affected by industrial decline;
3) combating long-term unemployment;
4) facilitating the occupational integration of young people;
5) reforming the Common Agricultural Policy.

Further to the criteria of the objectives, the Commission has placed emphasis on programmes, conditionality, additionality, and partnership.

Financial assistance has been provided on the basis of multi-annual 'integrated' regional programmes submitted by national governments and approved by the Commission within the terms of a Community Support Framework. The Commission sets the framework of support and has discretion over fixing the rates of support according to its assessment of the target area's needs. The regional plans are thus subject to monitoring by the Community to ensure that objectives are indeed met. Monitoring committees have been established in the priority regions to ensure that funds are utilised in an efficient manner and in addition to member states' financial provisions. The final aspect of the Commission's strategy, partnership, is an effort to involve regional and local actors in the planning and administrative procedures. The preparation of plans, drawing up, financing, monitoring, and assessment of programmes and other operations is to be undertaken in 'partnership' linking the Commission, member states, and the "competent authorities designated by the latter at national, regional, local or other level." (EC, 1988). European Council Regulation 4253/88 places further emphasis on Community collaboration with sectional interests and provides for financial assistance outside the framework of the multi-annual operational programmes. Financial assistance may be provided not only on the basis of operational programmes but also on that of grants for local economic development and assistance of "social and economic interests directly concerned by the implementation of the measures" (EC, 1988b), thereby circumventing the central authorities in this category.

It is a combination of all of these aspects which have presented and present opportunities for the development of governance. We suspect that in the short term the effects of the reforms and the measures reinforcing tendencies towards integration will compel the national governments to adjust governing procedures to conform to European standards. We question, though, whether the Community's approach to harmonious development of economic activities is bringing about changes in the long term form of governance of the labour market in Ireland which are closer to the Dutch model as demonstrated by Kickert.

It is enlightening to see how Irish public authorities have adapted to changes in the principle. As a category one region, Ireland has the distinction of being required to submit a national (regional) plan subject to the same criteria as other objective one sub-national regions such as Sicily, Corsica, or Andalusia. What is interesting is that in Ireland neither local nor regional authorities have ever played a significant role in managing economic affairs. Inevitably, the central government (as the objective one public authority) is responsible for the submissions of plans. This fact by itself may dampen Community assumptions founded upon local involvement and management. This means that the administrative arrangements for implementing the Community Support Frameworks is strongly dependent upon political and other factors specific to the member-state. One would suspect that such arrangements would help to check the role of public authorities in governing economic affairs. This is not so in Ireland. In this case, not only is the whole of Ireland categorised as an objective one region, but also the state has a history of central decision-making and control structures which makes the role of the central public authorities in managing economic and social affairs critical.

In the interest of analyzing the specific arrangements for labour market management and in the light of movements toward integration, we shall now turn our attention to see how the central authorities in Ireland have responded to European Community frameworks and analyze the repercussions for labour market management.

The case of Ireland is quite special as the situation of the 1988 reform of the Structural Funds has brought into focus the whole issue of central-local relationships and the effects that the tendencies or processes of decentralisation (or devolved management) would have in the Irish context. We have already alluded to the role the central public authorities holds in managing economic and social affairs. The argument against any major reform in central public administration is threefold:

1) the cost of devolving regional structures would be exorbitant for such a small country as Ireland;
2) an increase in rivalries (political brokerage) would come about on a sub-national basis (local actors both public and private would seek admission into the partnership process);
3) the issue of revenue would develop as an area of discontent (how to finance regional submissions if a national revenue programmes is in operation?).

But this 1988 argument stands in contradiction with the recent EC suggestions that regions might play a key role in relation to EC funding and monitoring. This point is brought out by Poulsen's view (1992) of how the Irish situation might evolve and the means by which newly formed regional authorities may have a role to play and be conferred a position in the preparation and implementation of the Structural Funds. At present, circumstances still do not demonstrate strong initiatives in the regard.

In labour market affairs, the case was put that local (or for that matter regional) public authorities or other authority structures do not and would not have either the expertise, financial basis, or support structures to develop and implement programmes addressing the seriousness of the labour market problems (particularly in regard to unemployment). However, it has been conceded that given the existing structures and organisation of local authorities and other local/regional actors, their participation in the administrative co-ordination and implementation of decisions taken at the national level would be necessary if only so that the implementation of final decisions would not be frustrated by objections or inactivity on the part of interest groups.

With these essentially political considerations in mind and in order to conform to the letter if not the spirit of EC Regulation 2052/88, the government established two levels of planning - national and sub-national (the latter comprising of seven newly created and geographically defined regions) (Ireland, 1988). Furthermore, and with a view to fulfilling the partnership criteria of the reformed funds structures, the government established two bodies for consultative and planning purposes in each of the newly created regions (Ireland, 1988): a 'Working Group' (representatives of the relevant government departments) and an 'Advisory Group' (comprised of the representatives of the main interest groups). These groups have since been fused to form 'Review Committees'. The new groups, under the chairmanship of a representative from the Department of Finance, and yet again assembling a wide assortment of representative of local authorities, government Departments, EC Commission, social partners, and so on, has no decision-making power. It may submit proposals and statements to the central government or convey opinions on any aspect of implementation of the programme to the operational programmes monitoring committees or to the national committee monitoring the CSF. Other than this it has no other role in the management of local economic affairs. It is also worth noting that the principal agencies of the central government for labour market affairs (FAS and CERT) have no authoritative voice in the procedures of the Review Committee. They are simply in attendance. The situation is all the more confusing for the social and economic interests which are not nominated as 'main representatives' or 'main social partners' but which are concerned in one way or another with the activities of local labour markets (such as, community groups or voluntary organisations which provide locally based labour market functions like vocational training, educational services, information, counselling). They are given access to the planning and review stages of the Review Committee by way of written submissions only and are simply not catered for in other ways in these new structures. So, this formal institution has all the appearance of regrouping social and economic interests 'that count' or whose participation is required for political reasons.

There appears to be no evidence however that the new procedures have in any significant way shifted the balance of responsibility for labour market affairs away from the central government. The new arrangements have provided a forum, albeit extremely limited, where issues affecting local affairs (and including the operation of the labour market) may be discussed. But it has provided neither for clear criteria upon which sub-national allocations of European Community funding will be distributed, (aside from politically inspired motives to satisfy sub-national clientele interests), nor for the criteria by which groups are chosen for participation. Decisions are taken and problems are ultimately resolved by central administrative arbitration.

This is quite clear in labour market affairs. There has been no shift in functions nor ultimate responsibility for labour market affairs away from the regional institutions of the central public authorities. We have seen that the Review Committees have no functional responsibilities. For example, in the Shannon Region (one of the new regional units) a proposal was tabled in 1991 to establish a Regional Advisory Committee with the objective of gathering the view of the social partners toward the relevance of its training programmes. The consultative body will have no other brief. In essence, the framework of this new body will be similar to that of the Review Committee for this region and indeed many of the same social partners will be on both.

It would not seem unfair to suggest that the principle of partnership operates within a vacuum. Community groups and other social and economic groups now find themselves even more dependent on the central public authorities. In one sense, some groups have now acquired official recognition of the fact that the functions they provide are useful in addressing labour market problems. As a result they have been elevated to the position of social partners and integrated in the formal structures of consultation. They also share the burden of responsibility for providing services or implementing an aspect of labour market policy. But in another sense, the groups are now very much more dependent on the centralised forms of financing and management. Consequently, there has not been a true shift in the pattern of governing. The ultimate outcome of the procedures has not been in any true sense a devolution of responsibility for regional or local management of economic affairs. Rather, local interest groups are now ever more impelled to turn to the central public authority, or agencies thereof, for access to the framework within which they operate and which is ultimately established by this authority.

Conclusion

If we care to reflect for a moment on Dunsire's statement of "turbulence kept within bounds" and change "steered in desired directions", then we touch upon the essence of Ireland's efforts at adjusting governing methods. Public authorities have been enmeshed in a situation of interactions and interdependencies in which changes in the labour market situation inevitably brought about tensions to which the system had to respond. We have stressed that the changes have arrived on two fronts: the first domestically, with a rapidly untenable labour market situation; and the second, internationally, with respect to efforts at European integration and the consequences this can have on collective management and organisation of economic activity. The principle of coping with the interactions has implied the directing or steering of the changes (tensions) in a desired direction. This has in fact been brought about by the continuous "process of interaction between social groups and forces and public or semi-public authorities". We do not suspect though that the new opportunities introduced by the changes have been seized as a way out of the traditional central rule approach as a means to dynamize the sector. Rather, issues and tensions in the labour market have been addressed in an incremental fashion and the public authorities have coped with the dynamics of the interactions by means of a very limited form of steering-at-a-distance: governing but not governance.

6

PUBLIC POLICY PLANNING AND THE PROBLEM OF GOVERNANCE: THE QUESTION OF EDUCATION IN FINLAND

KIRSTI STENVALL

Introduction

Governance is evident when describing politics in the modern world. However, when society is planned by politicians or the activities of public administration, the interpretations of policy objectives are brought into the realm of values, choices and actions. In such situations, governance as a form of social-political interaction is constantly recreated through the conceptualizations of society in which it is thought to manifest itself.

The aim of this chapter is to discuss the role of public policy planning and its relation to the problem of governance. The notion of governance, in the sense of interaction between government and society (see Kooiman, this volume), refers here to public policy planning in which the ways of governing are changing. These changes are linked to efforts to produce governed outcomes of societal development. Since policy planning in Western societies is faced with this type of problem, this article analyzes some of the ways in which policy tasks in public policy planning are conceptualized. Moreover, it will be suggested that public policy planning has a strong world-making role when it produces the constructions of society which are linked to policy objectives. Analyzing this type of phenomena as one aspect to the problem of governance may broaden the view of the complexity of modern societies and policy-making processes.

Governance as a form of interaction never is a matter of a single actor. From the viewpoint of policy planning, it cannot be automatically located in decision-making processes or policy-making. We may say that governance is connected to any kind of situation in which we are able to produce a reliable understanding of human interaction. Nonetheless, public policy planning is dependent on those constructions of society in which the models of interaction are supposed to work. In Western societies, the different models of welfare serve as examples of this kind of society construction. Many of the societal contexts of welfare consist of visions which are to construct the acceptability of politics in particular fields of societal problems. Translating the context of welfare in connection to government politics or policy issues, is a part of the work done in public administrations. Within this problem, the important question is how to locate the role of public policy planning in relation to the practice of its own world-making.

This chapter attempts to suggest that, despite of the relative autonomous status of public administration, public policy planning contains a great deal of world-making in the sense that it translates the contents and the contexts of the policy issues in question. By analyzing Finnish educational planning in the central state administration during the 1970s and 1980s, this chapter attempts to illustrate the ways in which new models of interaction define not only the context of education policy issue but also the content of education. Administrative policy planning is thus regarded not only as an active system which plans, steers and regulates the provision of public services but also as an agent which shapes the interpretations of the object concerned.

Administrative Policy Planning and the Problems of Governance

In Western societies, the development of the welfare state has entailed the rapid transformation of the role of the state. The changes in the economic system and the increased complexity of societal processes have altered the preconditions for understanding the present cultural changes. The division between what is said in politics and what is done in practice has produced extensive critique of institutionalized politics, state bureaucracies, ideologies and risks (Hirschman, 1991; Offe, 1989; Turner, 1986). The attempt to locate new political and economic strategies for societal development has caused a number of social scientists to focus their attention on the question of how to define the limits of growth-orientated development.

Administrative policy planning in Western societies is still understood as a wide variety of planning practices which aim at the production of the proper policies and politics for the different areas of society. Policy planning in public administration is regarded as steering, controlling and regulating the different policy areas, in which the implementation of the major issues of policies is accomplished. The everyday planning work carried out in the public administration is often thematized on the basis of the notion of controlling the future through the present actions. The more the future is understood as a factor to be controlled, the more it is believed that planning has been effective (Wildavsky, 1979). Public administration has, in this sense, a particular role in modelling future society. Additionally the planning of public services provides the visions for society management, articulation of problems and principles for development. For everyday planning work in public administration, the word 'future' does not, however, mean something above or beyond the present. The future is present in the proposals and plans concerning the tasks of policies. This kind of orientation within policy-planning creates the idea of effective and rational planning for the administration and its public. At the same time, it expresses the attempt to have a problem-solving policy and the role of active agent in formulating policy objectives. One result is that the political meaning of policy-planning has increased. Particularly after the 1960s the development of corporative systems is seen as the result of a growing interest to participate in the planning processes (Wilensky, 1976).

However, characteristic of all policy planning is the aspect of world-making, regardless of who is taking part in the planning process. Just as policy-planning produces the importance of some issues, it produces the insignificance of others. The emphasis on certain policy tells the preferences and linkages to 'the world outside' of the administration. This kind of status places policy-planning in public administration in the position of subject, supposed to behave according to the demands of the participants and the public. It could be said that many of the present administrative planning practices work on the basis of the idea that different emphases on policy issues are a central locus of world-making. Rather than approach planning as a neutral practice of public administration, it is described below as ways in which planning is involved in world-making.

The Constructive Character of Policy-Planning

In West European countries, the establishment of planning systems in public administrations has grown with the expansion of the activities of the state. The earnest attempt by governments to capture society's interests has also changed the role of planning, by making them the main tool of policy-programming. The translation of reality into policy issues and the composition of different political interests has affected the status of planning systems and emphasized their meaning in the reconstruction of values and political tasks. One consequence is that no problem is eliminated without careful consideration of planning and the better practices which are thus produced. Since planning is produced within the administration, new administrative networks are needed to maintain both valuable and problematic planning issues. This has led to criticism and slight scepticism concerning the role of policy-planning (see Crozier, 1964; Richardson and Jordan, 1983). E.g. in the case of Finland, it has been argued that the planning systems are based on the illusion of 'an automatic society', which guarantees an automatic balance and coordination based on calculated alternatives and lacks recourse to unreasonable argumentation (see Summa, 1990).

There is also extensive discussion about public policy-planning as a means of redistributing incomes within Keynesian macro economic management (see Gough, 1979; Hirschman, 1991). It has also been discussed what kind of evaluation is necessary to improve the efficiency of planning (Wyatt, 1989). In most discussions, different arguments revolve around the themes of democracy in connection with the allocation, delivering and regulating of public services. In spite of the connection of planning practices to different interest groups, politicians and research activities, policy-planning in public administration is supposed to steer societal development objectively and neutrally in the sense of taking all the aspects of public demand into consideration. Active and selective world-

making is not considered to be the framework of the idea of a public
service administration. Nevertheless, constructions of society by world-
making is one of the most important aspects of any kind of planning in
modern society.

When concentrating on the constructive aspect of policy-planning, we
are forced to conceive the role of planning as a practice in which the
meanings of policy objectives change in relation to their context and
content. Due to the nature of societal planning in general, the world-making
aspect of administrative planning can easily be found in the administrative
documents and official plans of governments. In the case of educational
planning, it has been widely argued that the different constructions of
society concerning the images of an educated person as well as his/her
position in the labour market, are dominant in official planning texts (see
Taylor, 1984). Illustrations of how to steer the social mobility of population
on the basis of educational systems can be located in the government
argumentation. Central themes to the descriptions of population are how
many people should be educated for industrial professions and how many
people for the agricultural sector. The reality-constructing nature of public
policy-planning is part of the everyday practice in public administration
and it also illuminates the process of decision-making. This kind of policy-
programming is generally regarded as one of the main tasks of administrative planning work as well. The modelling of society is not only understood
as necessary because of the existence of the formation of public policies
characteristic of modern politics. It is also important in the framework of
the whole notion of policy-planning which is, in many administrative
practices, regarded as an effective and impressive method in proceedings
of 'public issues' (see Wyatt, 1989). It is also noticeable that planning
officers who are working in public administration have to produce evidence
and legitimacy for their administrative work and find their own 'magic'
to affect the development of society (Järvelä, 1991: 33-4). When such
attitudes prevail, the conception of policy has to exist for the administrators
either as a concept or as 'ink' when they are writing the word 'policy'
(Ahonen, 1987: 76).

Analyzing the administrative policy-planning as world-making also
emphasizes the meaning of the language used in the planning. Language
in this sense can be understood as a translation mechanism or as a device
to construct the policy issues. The languages in which reality is represented
are said to play a crucial role in the translatability between the level of
political rationality and the specific programs which seek to make
government effective (Miller and Rose, 1990). The language of planning
is especially important because it reveals how reality is transformed into
policy issues and how these issues are brought into the political and
administrative discussion (Hood, 1991). Administration must represent
somebody and something in its activities (see Pekonen). Administrative
policy-planning produces its own discourse in locating the contents of the
policies and the ways in which to speak about them. We may say that
language creates a vocabulary for the modelling of policy issues in public

administration. Speaking on behalf of others is a way to gather support and resources for planning activities. In addition to administrative language, there are also other mechanisms through which administrative planning operates. One mechanism taken into consideration here is the construction of society in which the models of interaction are supposed to be achieved. One question is about the transformation of the societal interests attributed to administrative planning. As Callon and Law (1982: 618) note, collecting interests is a part of 'marketability' which is a system of persuasion involving actors. The result can be that many diverse interests are identified, attracted and transformed in such a way that other actors value them as their own interests. At the same time interests become 'provisionally enroled' in the scheme of others (op. cit.: 619).

The important difficulty facing policy-planning is the design of the context and content of policy issues in a complex society (see also Metcalfe, this volume). Transformation of societal interests may cause negative governance between different groups in education (for example, between vocational training and higher education) and between institutions (schools, universities). Constructions of society are an important aspect of governance. Therefore, it is useful to talk about world-making as problematic in the exercise of governing.

Administrative Planning and World-making: the Case of Education in Finland

Western societies have created complex administrations which include a great deal of coordination of personal and documented interaction. The different planning activities, such as the participation of interest groups, organizing governmental committees, building planning units or writing plans are part of the work of the Finnish central state administration. Within these general frameworks, one task of administration is to create problem-solving methods and to maintain political rationalities in the different sectors of welfare policies.

By concentrating on the planning of education in the Finnish education administration, the following illustration aims at describing how this kind of planning process has been put to work. This task is examined by paying special attention to the role of administrative planning in inventing, producing and exerting such kinds of policy mechanisms which are to produce new realities in society. Planning as a part of the work done in public administration is value-orientated and cannot be regarded as an objective practice. Below, Finnish educational planning is described as a practice to produce a special kind of constructions for socio-political development.

Educational Planning and the Constructions of Society

A future-based planning orientation was characteristic of all the administrative and political planning discussions during the 1960s and 1970s in Finland. New planning principles, methods and techniques were adopted as a basis for the construction of the future (Summa, 1989). Additionally, the role of the social sciences was utilized for the purposes of the new goal-oriented planning. This 'scientification' of planning became a research object among social scientists and 'intellectualization of steering' was one of the main tasks of social scientists during the 1960s and 1970s (Wittrock, 1989). A new group of planning professionals was formed in the public administration to emphasize the importance and necessity of expertise for the planning work.

The planning orientation of the 1970s was not only a response to the perceived decision-making problems of the growing public sector, but it also shaped the reality to be planned. (See Summa, 1989: 22-68). In Finnish education administration, the main question in the planning concerned the implementation reform directed at all levels of the educational system. Among the questions to be solved was the position of the educated population and the 'new' hierarchy of qualified and professionalised citizens. Due to the widespread call for an effective administrative planning of education, the strong belief in governing social development was dominant in every branch of the education administration (Sarjala, 1982: 7). Building new educational strategies, such as those based on ideas of high expertise and labour effectiveness, was a part of this planning orientation. In Finland, growth-oriented planning arguments were used to emphasize not only economic development, but also the notion of the reconstruction of knowledge concerning the steering of societal processes. Partly due to the growth of the economy, models of welfare were developed and applied to the different policy areas. The general orientation to develop the welfare state guided policy-planning and also political decision-making to a certain extent. Planning was the means by which societal problems had to be solved (Djupsund, 1984). In Finland this was accepted by an agreement to strengthen the role of the state in steering the direction of policies.

Interpreting educational policy has many variations but its central theme is simple. It is regarded as a state activity to govern society through the effective education of the population. As Lundgren (1979: 35) argues, education has usually been understood, both by the state and by individuals as a visible instrument to be utilized to attain a better economic and social position. In accordance with this basic principle, education is usually treated as something to be maintained without the need to verify the existence of the system. In Finnish society it is also widely accepted that the main function of the educational system is to ensure the transmission of cultural models of the present to the next generation. It can be said without much doubt that education has clearly become a part of the political economy in Finland (Antikainen, 1990). The usual mode of thought in the official educational policy is that the qualifications and merits produced by educational systems are natural because of man's occupational destiny in society. Despite of the practical problems of carrying out this policy, society, as the context of education, is functionally argued about in administrative planning according to the idea of 'cultural progress'. The official goal of comprehensive school instruction is "to encourage children's growth into balanced, fit, responsible, independent, creative, cooperative and peace-loving human beings and citizens" (Developments in Education, 1990: 18).

Educational planning engaged in the idea of the governability of society has often been committed to the instrumental model of society-steering to emphasize the necessity of planned development. This instrumentalism can be found in many official Finnish planning documents in which the attempt to diagnose future society is framed by calculations concerning educated citizens. The calculating with age-groups, the statistics of student numbers, the divisions of the professions and the changes in qualifications are examples of instrumentalized government as it is practised by administrative planning (see Kivinen and Rinne, 1992). There is always the problem of producing strategic principles concerning the function of the education system in changing the context of the meaning of education as, for example, along the lines of the prevailing general atmosphere in the public sector.

During the 1980s the mobility of labour has become a key-word in planning. The purpose of education administration is said to be to develop planning towards 'knowledge revolution' and 'the new organization of work' (Kehittyvä Koulutus, 1990: 84). For the educational administration, the interest of mobilization is to make the system more effective. In the plans and reports concerning the whole educational system between the 1960s and the 1980s we may find a moralistic rhetoric, which serves to demonstrate the advantages of being educated in modern society (see also Kivinen and Rinne, 1992). This kind of persuasive rhetoric is also found in the official planning documents of higher and adult education (Hovi et al., 1989) and the line of thought can be found clearly in the idea of continuing education. It has been demonstrated that the strategy of strongly relating societal and individual interests is expanding, not only because of the competition on the labour market but also because of a marketing of basic services (Panhelainen, 1992).

The structural changes of Finnish society during the 1960s and 1970s were partly possible because of the expanding educational system. The educational reforms, which were implemented during the 1970s, were connected to the demands of societal progress and economic growth. These trends of development were formed together with the concept of equality which characterized the educational optimism of the era (see e.g. Kivinen, 1988). During the 1970s and 1980s, the Finnish education system changed its character. For example, legislation pertaining to vocational institutions was revised during the 1980s. At the same time, the functions, activities and administration of educational institutions were modernized. The development of higher education was governed by the Development Act, which covered the period 1967-86. The aim was to direct the flow of students to fields which were relevant to the labour market and society at large. At the same time, new principles were adopted as guiding lines for education policy. Effectiveness, rationality and cost-accounting are the dominant themes in Finnish education policy during the 1990s.

The increase of educational planning in Finland during the 1970s not only codified the principles for the distribution of financial resources for the new educational system by allocating the services regionally and providing supplementary funds for building schools and universities, but also intended to arrange the structure of the labour market, the relations of social groups, the definitions of 'good' knowledge and the norm for interaction between educated citizens. This orientation was mainly defended on the basis of the state's ability to govern societal changes. Many of the planning ideas of the 1970s and 1980s were borrowed from international bodies such as the OECD and UNESCO, which produced the new ideology for educational policies in the industrialized countries in Western Europe. During the late 1970s and 1980s the planning of education in the central state administration also expanded and was explicitly connected to the structural changes visible in the economic development. For instance, the demand for flexibility between the educational system and the labour market led to a new administrative language which emphasized the importance of changing the professional structure of manpower according to the idea of the new 'information society'. This emphasis not only referred to the new constructions of society, but also to the changes in the conceptualizations of the principles of how society should actually work. The idea of teleological progress, which dominated the political debates of the 1960s and mid-1970s, was replaced in the beginning of the 1980s by the mentality which emphasized the quick transformation of society. The term 'flexibility' constantly emphasizes the notion of mobilizing the population from one position to another according to the needs of labour market. Administrative educational planning has also become more dependent on the development of the labour market than before. Economic development is utilized as a reason not only to fulfil the need for highly qualified labour but also to point out that the mentality of the steering of education has to be reorganized.

The new conceptualization of the status of education in Finland also modelled the image of an educated citizen during the 1970s and the 1980s. The notion of a flexible society presupposed a change of the arguments concerning the status of individuals in education. To be educated properly, students had to meet criteria set by the labour market and not those of their own. The content of education was no longer to be viewed as the opportunity for 'the right' to learn. Rather, it was understood from the perspective of different learning interests which aimed at the recognition of a profession. Efficient education was to be achieved through practical skills. Work and study could complement each other and provide students satisfaction in later occupational work. However, it is possible to say that the focus of this new orientation during the late 1980s was individual. A well-planned society was understood as one in which a concern of learning is the responsibility of each individual. The nature of 'good planning' should be in a position to improve "the educational mobility of individuals" (Kehittyvä Koulutus, 1990: 86).

It is usually argued that educational policy and the values which underlie it, interact with the 'moods and fashions' of the time. The actions of politicians, interest groups and the professions are "both the products as well as the producers of the changes in values in social needs" (Kogan, 1975: 26). The interpretation of educational policy in Western countries has many variations, but its central theme is simple. It is regarded as a state activity to govern the development of society through the effective education of the population. Also in Finland, it is widely agreed that the main function of the educational system is to ensure the transmission of the cultural models of the present to the next generation. Education as an institutionalized phenomenon is treated as something that is maintained independently without the need to verify the existence of the system. Educational policy is thus regarded as one of the well-established activities of the welfare state. The planning documents as well as the governmental committees for educational administration indicate that the main strategy of policy has been to increase the mobility of the population in the labour market and to extend the formal qualifications of vocations and professions. The emphasis on improving the economic positions of different social and professional groups has become clearer. In many governmental committee reports, these are presented as the result of the prediction or the prognosis of the future development which are known in advance (see e.g. Väestön Koulutus, 2000).

According to Latour (1987: 223), events, places and people situated at a distance and in relation to each other can be bound together by inventing means which render them mobile, keep them stable and make them combinable. This view is applicable to the idea of planning as well. In the case of Finnish administrative educational planning, it could be argued that the constructions of society are defined by inventing strategies or techniques which are binding together persons in education. Individuals to be educated, are in official planning language, characterized by the structural elements of society, their own combinability which is to improve governed development. The constructions of society concerning labour, knowledge and socio-political structure, functions as a network for 'new' interactions. It could be said that to create the constructions of society for describing policy tasks and the conceptualizing policy issues is one of the main features of this kind of world-making in public administration.

The Problem of Universal Governance

In this chapter, one area of policy-planning was illustrated as an example of how ways of governing have changed, and how governability in the sense of creating order is a part of the socio-political process in which the policy tasks are conceptualized. One may, of course, wonder why it is interesting to study this kind of world-making. Following the analysis made here, one could even become pessimistic as to whether there is a possibility for 'good governance' at all.

The point here has been to stress the importance of one aspect of policy-planning. This aspect, which concerns policy-planning that has to produce advanced planned constructions of society for society-modelling, is not always the most legitimate way to speak in the name of others. It is evident that planning a policy is the way that politicization and depolitization of things and phenomena occur (see also Pekonen, this volume). This can be called either bureaucracy or modern society in action. However, planning is expected to model political and cultural values. The result of this modelling is not always a hard bureaucracy of administration or administrative language without any 'deeper' meanings. A policy announced to govern society may face the problem of values better than the one which does not express such purposes. In areas of welfare policy-planning such as education, it is easily found that the mechanism of transforming the meanings of policy issues also creates new principles for planning. Much of the argumentation prevailing in the educational planning in Western countries could lead to the thought that arrangement of social relations has become to represent one aspect of governability. Planning education by emphasizing the meaning of governed development can lead to a situation in which there is no room for manoeuvres (see Prins, this volume).

We may also notice that there is another aspect characteristic for the tendency of strong world-making in public administration. This is one which operates through the categorization of population according to the general practice of sectorizing policy issues as 'social', 'economic' and 'political'. For administrators and planners this means the right to speak about the various combinations of elements such as the socio-economic aspect of professions. Categorization of the population has expanded its domain. Here it has been illustrated that people to be educated are viewed from the perspective of labour performance. It can also be argued that professional language in public administration is becoming an important aspect of linguistic networks cumulating knowledge in planning institutions. As a consequence, we can argue that planning directed at making programmes for public services, produces its own techniques and programs which are based more or less on the visions of future society. It also produces the notion that society could be administered better in a given programmatic form (Miller and Rose, 1990).

In sketching the implications of the educational planning commissioned to have the status of world-making, one cannot bypass the role of policy-planning from the viewpoint that it produces a special kind of 'governance'. For such an emphasis, it can be concluded that there is a feature of strategy that attributes interests according to the status of the planning in relation to other administrative units and to those of objects (i.e. the whole population). This means that the implication of the government, the ability and the mentality combined with the status of an authority, is in a position to create specific constructions of society. In the case of Finnish educational planning, this strategy of associating different interests by mobilizing the population can also be understood as a form of power in which people are expected to act in the given situations. In education-planning, this kind of society-building may foster the gap between the individual need for education and the control from outside. The special authoritative status of educational planning, to which a prior position concerning the practical arrangements of education is given, may only legitimate its own position.

Conclusions

Translating the meaning of welfare in connection with policy issues has become a part of a technology in which the design of values, beliefs and moral commitments is central thinking of the management of structural changes in modern societies. When planning public policies, for example educational policy, the issues concerning the contents of the policy are often understood on the basis of economic priorities or conceptualizations of professional preferences in the labour market.

As mentioned above, the present development of Western societies is increasingly characterized by the enlargement of the administrative apparatus with its concomitant 'planning logic'. The tendency of Finnish educational planning to use this 'logic' has not been made a policy only to function. A great deal of planning is working, but patterns of formulating society have changed. This chapter does not make any suggestions or recommendations on how to cope with these changes. The central 'message' of this chapter is that new measures and evaluation of planning are also needed in public administrations. There is no reason to stop analyzing policy-planning just because it is merely planning rather than decision-making or fighting 'real' political battles in public. The political-administrative system as a whole is one of the examples of an area which is often utilized as a strategic point to dissipate the exertion of power. This mentality can be said to contain constructions of rules that is different from practices in other parts of the political system.

It is often argued that the present 'crisis' of the welfare state has both political and economic effects on the planning of public policies. It could also be assumed that many of the present constructions of society may lead to epochal programs which often hide the natural common-sense understanding of politics and policy issues. At this point, we could hypothesize that these programs may reveal the world as a highly programmed market of impersonal pretensions which can lead to 'negative governance'. When it comes to governability in the sense of creating order, a world which remains inaccessible to human intervention, can also not be affected by its argument or logic. Since societal planning builds its world-making on strategies, the best way to govern could start about pointing out how not to argue about good governing.

7

WOMEN'S EMANCIPATION AS A QUESTION OF GOVERNANCE: ACTORS, INSTITUTIONS AND THE ROOM FOR MANOEUVRE

MARIJKE PRINS

Introduction

In recent years a public governance model has broadly been sketched as an interactive social-political governance approach. The core of this approach is the idea that the governance of society does not take place from an 'Archimedean point', a central controlling point (the central government). The tendency to regard the government as the axis around which the world turns has been characterised as control-centrism (Den Hoed et al., 1983: 43). This simplification that the state plays a central role is no longer generally accepted. Governance capacity of the state is more clearly linked to its 'environment'. Gradually, the insight grows that politics can no longer be equated with policy, nor can the 'environment' be regarded as a given fact (Scharpf, 1987). There are different environments for different actors, each with their own traditions, objectives and interests, to be considered against a background of social relationships and developments.

In contrast to the traditional rational actor model, the interactive approach allows more actors to play an active role in the decision-making process. Contrary to the rational actor model with its strong internal policy-centred view, the interactive approach takes into account the broad social context with all the actors involved. An important gain compared to the discussions in the 1980s was the insight that societal actors should be left out of consideration. This is important because public administrators have the tendency to neglect social actors and to more or less treat social-political questions as a neutral subject, which leads to the assumption that problems are technical and managerial and 'always resolvable' in the short term. Social-political governance aims at more than the mere rational discussion of objectives and means and the relations between them.

Perestroika in the Netherlands

It is understandable that the discussion about governing and governance is once again topical. After all, when problems arise in hard reality which cannot be solved by existing theories and methods, it is possible to speak of a 'crisis' of the means of government policy and a 'crisis' in the controllability of the state's instruments. At that moment a discussion becomes paradigmatic in the social sciences (Kuhn, 1962: 77-91). When there is a crisis of means and a crisis in governance, and when both lines coincide, then public administrators and their 'supporting disciplines' are faced with the question: what should we do now?

In political science and public administration in The Netherlands much has been written about 'controlling conceptions, 'control paradigms' and 'control theory' in the last few years. This discussion has so far been carried on with little system and little conceptual consistency. For example, the concepts of governing, governance, control and administration are still used interchangeably (Kooiman, 1990: 408-25). These concepts refer to a new phenomenon, a new direction in public administration. Apparently, Perestroika was also needed in Dutch public administration.

New concepts such as governing and governance are being introduced and can be regarded as an indication of paradigmatic changes in public administration. An interesting question is, in which direction public administration will develop and to what extent this process is already going on? Are there new developments within public administration that can offer a new theoretical and practically relevant alternative? In other words, have new conceptions of public administration been formed in the Netherlands, which not only shed a new light on the theoretical and practical presumptions of public administration, but can also substantiate claims that they have a certain amount of 'puzzle-solving capacity' in terms of the relationship between governing and governance (Kuhn, 1962: 77)?

I am especially interested in concepts, that are suitable for the evaluation of broad questions of governance which imply a strong societal conflict, and on the basis of which strategies for solutions can be indicated.

The use of those concepts will be illustrated with empirical evidence from women's emancipation in the Netherlands. I will mention some important guidelines or points of departure which have proved to be useful for evaluating some of the tense and complex relations between actors in the field of emancipation. This will be followed by an attempt to relate the concepts of social-political governing and governance with notions such as 'room to manoeuvre', 'institutionalization' and 'political climate'. From my empirical findings I will show that by means of these notions, the case of women's emancipation can be understood better and analyzed more precisely (Prins, 1989).

A Diagnostic Model

The interactive approach can be interpreted as an analytical and diagnostic model: a conditional model. The period of universal judgements seems to have come to an end. In fact, each problem requires its own approach. In this context the interactive approach offers certain advantages. It enables one to cover a greater area than is usual in public administration. The social-political approach clearly relates governing and governance with their environments. In this way, the question of governing and governance is in fact expanded into a question of the science of Public Administration and Political Science. Although it is still at an embryonic stage, the interactive approach is a social-political theory of action.

There is a change in perspective in which not only the rational-economic dimension is taken into account, but also social and political dimensions are considered. Not only the policy context should be taken into account in the interactive approach, it should also explicitly include the relations between State and Society. Continuing this line of reasoning, it could be said that the concepts of state and society can be regarded as reciprocal concepts, although they are not interchangeable. State and society are not interchangeable concepts, but the state in itself can be regarded as a mirror image of social actors. And society can on its turn be regarded as a series of sectors with self-governing capacity and as such as a contributor to changes. Ultimately, the state cannot enforce any changes if they are not desired and tolerated by that society. This process of reciprocity has been adequately expressed by Romein in his book "On the interface of two centuries": 'The state permeates society... and society permeates the state' (Romein, 1967: 316 et seq.). The concept of 'inter-action' comes close to this (Kooiman, 1988).

It is the difference in approach to the way a problem is defined, which can give rise to conflicts. One requirement for effective governing and governance is therefore very important, namely that all the relevant participants, should have an idea of the major problems involved, their backgrounds and also have an idea of potential solutions. The second guideline is therefore: make an adequate problem analysis of the interdependencies (cohesion) between the relevant participants, institutions and government actions. Patterns of interdependencies between actors, institutions and government actions can be found within a given framework, without stating universal things by that. In the interactive social-political model the emphasis is on interactions, forms of reciprocity in the relations between actors and between different levels (macro-meso-micro). By making these interactions visible, deeper societal conflicts such as women's emancipation will also come into the picture.

Extension of the Conceptual Framework

Following what is meant in this book by the concepts of social-political governing and governance, I would like to suggest to extend the conceptual framework with notions such as 'room for manoeuvre', 'institutionalization' and 'political climate' (Prins, 1989). It is clear from my empirical findings that emancipation can be analyzed more profoundly and precisely using these notions.

The assumption I make here is, that the impact of change by institutions and actors on social and political governing and governance, depends on the room for manoeuvre, the degree of institutionalization as well as on the existing political conjuncture or climate (Schmidt, 1987). In other words, factors such as time (political climate or conjuncture), environment (contexts like institutions), and also the way actors and factors interact with respect to the problem of governing, should explicitly be taken into account.

By the idea of 'room for manoeuvre', I mean the relation among the actors themselves as well as between actors and the institutions involved (see also: Prins, 1989). The relations between actors - the interactions which influence behaviour, that is, by extending or limiting it - and institutions determine the freedom of manoeuvre. Together these determine the room for manoeuvre, which can vary in time and is also dependent on the sort of actors and institutions which are involved in the discussion.

By the notion of 'institutionalization', I mean the mutual acceptance of certain formal and informal rules and codes of behaviour and the role, connected to this, of political, societal and policy actors (Schmidt, 1987: 10 et seq.).

Institutionalization is not only a question of 'structures' , but also of those formal and informal processes in which actors and factors interact with each other. An important requirement for an adequate process of interaction is therefore: the mutual acceptance of certain agreements and procedures by each relevant actor involved.

Without the 'willingness' to accept certain agreements and procedures, institutionalization will only be partially successful. This is also the case in the process of institutionalization in the field of emancipation.

By the term 'political climate' or 'conjuncture', I mean a change in outlook on norms, values and social behaviour under the influence of different, new, political ideas, which can partly be derived from general social developments, particularly socio-economic and socio-cultural ones (Braun and Keman, 1986). As a consequence of this, issues often acquire a new meaning and intensity and this process shows itself in changed political outlooks, political power relations, change in party behaviour and priorities for government policy.

Problem Analysis of Emancipation

If we apply the above mentioned prescription of making a problem analysis to emancipation, then we see five specific characteristics of women's emancipation (Prins, 1989).

The first important characteristic is, that women's emancipation, has to be defined as a question of social-political governing and governance, since emancipation is a matter at the intersection of state and society. The question of women's emancipation is not a simple, politically neutral subject, but a deeply contested question in society, concerning power relations between men and women. This means that it is more than just a problem of implementation of certain policies. It is understandable that this question cannot be translated easily into terms of governing and governance, let alone be 'solved'.

Secondly, there is a number of actors involved. The policy actors (the Coordinating Office for Emancipation Policy; the DCE); the social actors (the women's movement and advisory boards) and the political actors (members of parliament, State Secretaries, Ministers), exercise an influence, separately and reciprocally, on the issue of emancipation.

Not only do these actors operate centrally, they have an effect at three levels: macro, meso and micro. An assessment of the effects of fifteen years of emancipation policy is then strongly dependent on the perspective you choose. After all, results of the emancipation policy carried out by the government cannot be attributed to a single actor, the central government, but they are the outcome of processes taking place within a dynamic political and social field of influence.

Thirdly, there are difficulties in translating emancipation into terms of social-political governing. The interactive model teaches us that this translation is a process with some very specific characteristics (Kooiman, 1990). The course followed by a problem in this translation process is full of moments of choice. These choices have a great influence on the question of whether a problem is tackled, and if so, how. From the entire course in which emancipation has developed from a social question to a question of governing, it is clear that the idea of emancipation is difficult to make operative in governing terms, and also difficult to express in government actions. As a result of this, the women's movement has only formulated emancipation as an issue on a societal level. The positive result of that was that the subject has been recognised and emancipation placed on the political agenda. But in order to be included in the public governing circuit, emancipation has to be called something else. Emancipation is designated as a particular policy area. In this way it is abstracted from the societal reality and the relation between state and society becomes an even more complex one.

As a fourth characteristic we can mention the fact that, although women's emancipation has been accepted as a political goal, adequate policy-making and implementation proves to be more problematic than is often assumed. The emancipation of women, with as central element the achievement of equality and parity between men and women, is not enforceable in the short term nor can it be realized by planning in the long term. There is no short-cut towards equality and parity between men and women, neither is it simply a matter of long-term planning.

Finally, there is the fact that a deeply contested question like emancipation, is politically highly sensitive. Fifteen years of emancipation policy-making has taught us that the changes in the political-ideological views that are taking place and its ramifications for policy-making and implementation must be taken into account. Emancipation has turned out to be very dependent on time-specific events.

Looking back, we could state, that the room for manoeuvre for emancipation has been too dependent on how the political wind blows. This has had far-reaching consequences. For example, we could characterize the first period (1974-1981), as one of building up, becoming accepted and organising governing and related implementation of emancipation with respect to the Dutch political system and bureaucratic agencies. The second period (1981-1989) however, can be viewed as a 'watershed' between the more progressive political tendency of the 1970s and the 'swing' to a more liberal-conservative one during the 1980s. This has been a crucial phase for emancipation. The consequence of this change in political-ideological view was a decline in the room for manoeuvre in linking direct and concrete measures to continuing emancipation. This leads to the question: what went wrong after a potentially promising start in the seventies?

Empirical Findings

During the period of the Den Uyl cabinet (1973-1977) the political and official infrastructure for the new policy had a quick start. A governmental apparatus was developed which corresponded to the broad policy perspective. Certain material and immaterial resources were allotted to the policy area, such as: the appointment of a coordinating government minister (1974), an emancipation committee (1974), an official coordinating agency (the DCE in 1978), an interdepartmental coordinating committee (1977), a sub-committee of the Cabinet, and the ministerial committee on emancipation policy (1986). From the organizational point of view the conditions for an integrated policy were fulfilled. Emancipation had its own bureaucratic machinery. So far so good! At least, so it seemed. In the sense of the interactive approach, the institutionalization of emancipation has been only partially successful. There was an important requirement with which had not been met, namely: giving a content to the policy. The translation of the emancipation concept, in terms of policy design, took place before there was a clear definition of what the emancipation policy should contain, and what conditions had to be fulfilled if the policy was to have a chance of succeeding.

Evaluating the policy since its start in 1974, societal, political and policy actors have not made enough of a coherent connection between the contents of the policy and the organizational design of the policy. Not the contents of an integrated emancipation policy to be carried out (or rather, the governing), but emancipation reduced to an organizational and managerial problem of governing, has become central. In 1977 the choice of an integrated policy was mainly an instrumental choice and began to live a life of its own. It means that the discussion was concerned with government programmes, strengthening of the infrastructure of the policy, with the political weight and responsibility of the Secretary of State for Emancipation.

If we stick to the guidelines of the interactive model of governing then we know, that strategic decision should not be made in isolation from the womens' movement (the social environment). Where that happens, many disturbances in the action-reaction-action process between societal and policy actors may arise (Easton, 1953; Kooiman, 1988; 1991). This is exactly what happened in the case of emancipation. The tragedy of Murphy's Law in its purest form!

Government and bureaucracy have chosen to use a 'two-track' strategy to solve the problem of governing emancipation. They chose to follow a two-track strategy, which aimed at two goals at the same time. Within this strategy, not only the principal bureaucratic policy actor (the DCE), has an important responsibility, but the role of the women's movement is also important. The women's movement is expected to mobilize parts of female society in order to legitimize processes of change initiated by the state. DCE, the coordinating agency, being the principal bureaucratic policy actor, is responsible for implementation in all ministries.

The pursuit of the two-track policy, which includes following a sector and an integrated policy, refers to the coordinating and integrative role of DCE.

Sector policy refers to the granting of subsidies to support and stimulate the emancipation process in society in order to get the women's movement involved in the policy. Integrated policy refers to the goal to stimulate the departments to participate in the execution of the emancipation policy.

Both goals have to support each other. As the coordinating administrative unit, DCE has to realize this expectation and presumption. DCE has been given the task of ensuring that both tracks lead to a coherent policy. The way of dealing with this tension has been the 'dual-purpose' strategy on the one hand, in which the combined trajectory aims at cooperation and consensus among the different ministers. On the other hand, the sector-specific trajectory directs its measures at specific issues and women's interests. An important task for the DCE is also to ensure that the two-track policy is not only conducted internally but can count on enough external support and understanding. The will to realise both a sector and an integrated-policy objective has been decisive for the way in which the government has given expression to emancipation over the last fifteen years.

Looking back we can say that the two-track strategy has accomplished little. The mobilization has been misdirected, and turns out to have been more effective at the level of groups (meso-level) than the level of the relations between state and society (the macro-level). There is a rather tense relation between the societal actor and the bureaucracy, which is by and large due to the different system levels (meso and macro level) on which each actor actually operates. There is insufficient support for the policy from the movement and DCE cannot operate alone. Without the support of the women's movement however, there is not enough room for manoeuvre for DCE within the departments.

That the idea of emancipation could be institutionalised on political and official levels is an important point for the women's movement. They obtained what they wanted: 'access'. However, getting 'access' soon proved not to be the same as 'acceptance'. Integration cannot be brought about by decree. Problems in the emancipation-integrated policy would prove to mainly concern the degree of institutionalization.

A bureaucratic machinery offers a certain room for manoeuvre, but it is not the case that all the players are also immediately ready, willing or able to see it, or to accept it. Institutions create latitude but do not guarantee successful interaction.

A governing body like the DCE is limited in its operations because it has to work within existing formal institutional patterns. Existing institutions have to be conquered so to say. Integration does not occur overnight. Integrated policy implies change in attitude and continual application of resources. That's why activities and initiatives from the field are indispensable for DCE. From the government side, the subsidy instrument is deployed as a very suitable means to 'politicize' the process of emancipation or the women's movement.

Despite the good will on both sides, both sectors (women's movement and DCE) failed to explain enough about their own actions, their own room for manoeuvre and the changed political climate. It seems that these two participants have grown more or less apart, in stead of coming closer to each other in terms of mutual acceptance, support and shared intentions.

It is remarkable how often in the past solutions for emancipation problems have been sought in the establishment of new institutions. The Emancipation Council recently made a plea for the establishment of a professional public affairs bureau for the women's movement (Recommendation to the Dutch parliament, 1988). The suggestion of a lobby bureau paid for by the government was keenly investigated during the national conference in June 1990 of 'Women and Political Strategies for the 1990s', on the assumption that it would solve two problems (Goudt and Dorsman, 1990).

Firstly, such a lobby bureau was supposed to improve the inadequate interaction between women's movement and policy.

Secondly, a lobby bureau was supposed to be an excellent means for the women's movement to exert a positive influence on the integrated emancipation policy in the various departments.

The question is, however, whether a number of problems can be solved just by instutionalizing them. The establishment of institutions in the area of emancipation, with the intention of improving the relations between the women's movement and policy-makers is ,after all, not in itself a guarantee for a better and more effective emancipation policy. Over-institutionalization however does not lead to a solution of the politicization problem but to more bureaucracy and routine. Not to mention the fact that it offers no solution to the question of how we should start an integrated policy.

Two Working Hypotheses

It is obvious that, or an adequate interpretation of 15 years of emancipation policy-making, we explicitly have to consider it in the context of all the relevant societal, bureaucratic and political actors, which on their turn are related to time-specific events. I want to emphasize that emancipation, given its broad content and given its special relation with a pluriform societal actor (i.e. the women's movement), can only be sufficiently analyses if it is viewed in a broader context than that of policy analyses alone. Not only the policy-context must be taken into account, but also, and explicitly, the relation between State and Society.

We can now deduce two hypotheses from the interactive social-political governing model. These hypotheses are meant to 'test' the explanatory power and usefulness for evaluating emancipation policy-making of the above-mentioned framework.

1) Insufficient effect is not only a consequence of insufficient money (means) or political obstinacy on the part of (non-left-wing) members of the government, but mainly of an inadequate interaction between the government as a policy actor and the women's movement as a pluriform actor.

2) Above all insufficient effect is the consequence of an inadequate forming of the picture of the problem and a lack of an inadequate strategy, which operates both 'from the inside out' and 'from the inside in'.

ad 1) Within the departments the governing need of emancipation is contested. They themselves have no need for new financial commitments and interferences with the policy. In order to be able to exert pressure on other ministries, support and concentration of forces from the women's movement for DCE (as the policy coordinator) is very necessary. However, this has not occurred often enough. It is clear from my research that the strength and the action potential of the women's movement cannot be measured or expressed in terms of measures at the government level. The real action potential of the movement has mainly been oriented not towards the central level, but rather towards the individual, in the case of the meso level. The women's movement has mainly come to DCE for financial support. It needed that instrument and it was also granted to them. However, there has been no support from the movement for the DCE in the solving of policy problems, i.e. social pressure.

The consequence of this is that DCE has to concentrate relatively strongly on the internal organization in order to survive. Attempts to strengthen the policy have mainly been aimed at the carrying out of improvements of political and official coordination structures and not enough at strengthening the relation with the women's movement. Political and bureaucratic actors were (too) much occupied with questions such as; 'by which department could the interests of emancipation be promoted best' and 'whether the government member responsible should be a minister or a state secretary'.

To put it briefly, despite institutionalization there is little interaction: the room for manoeuvre for DCE seems large but remains limited. On the one hand this is caused by departmental reluctance and on the other hand by divided support from the women's movement for the government network.

The long march through the institutions is only half-over, and we have yet to find a reasonable and adequate use of them to make emancipation policy more effective with respect to the emancipation of women in the near future. Further institutionalization is necessary, leading to sufficient room for manoeuvre for an effective implementation of the emancipation policy.

However, the problems of attunement in the interaction have to be solved first. In order to create a better relationship with the women's movement, DCE should devote more attention to the so-called input side of policy. The ties with the women's movement must be made stronger and real interaction between women's movement and policy-makers set in motion, so that a clear societal counterforce can be relied upon.

ad 2) Emancipation is translated into a number of issues and transformed into manageable terms of bureaucratic policy-making. The conditions under which the two-track policy could do well, were not made explicit enough from the very beginning. The ratio of objectives and resources was not structurally laid down. No criteria were developed for this. That is, however, a condition for working on a serious solution to this 'problem'.

It was decided to follow the existing traditional model of governing. In stead of 'structure follows strategy' the more classical route was followed: 'strategy follows structure' (see Kooiman, Introduction, this volume). This choice was made however, before the necessary content of the policy had been defined. Insufficient attention was paid to what the development and execution of the policy objective meant in the practice of governing and governance.

An important consequence of this was that the relation between governing and governance was weakened and even led to an unbalanced discussion.

The governing and governance of the question of emancipation has been reduced to choices of pursuing sector and integrated policy in instrumental terms. This is an important explanation why emancipation policy has turned out to be insufficiently effective so far. It is the consequence of the lack of a strategy which operates both 'from the inside out' and 'from the outside in'. With a changed political climate in the eighties, due to among other things the influence of cuts and a receding women's movement, emancipation policy came to play a 'paper' role.

A more flexible approach of the two-track strategy is the best way to proceed. However, it is necessary that governance and governing should no longer be regarded and treated separately. Instead they should be attuned. Therefore it is essential that clear and feasible objectives are formulated by all the major actors involved. The strategy can only be useful and feasible if an operationalized criterium of evaluation exists. This criterium could and should be emancipation aiming at equality and parity amongst men and women in order to attain 'social justice'.[1] This also means that it is not a solution to do away with sector-specific actions (as is often suggested in the Dutch debate), rather they must be genuinely combined with the compounded trajectory.

Contribution of the Interactive Model

The interactive social-political model is applicable not only to 'solve' the case of 'women' emancipation from the 'public administration' point of view, but also to understand and evaluate this case from a wider perspective. This model turns out to contribute to an understanding of the tense and complex relations between actors and those within the state machinery.

My empirical findings show that by using notions such as 'interaction', 'interdependency', 'attunement of governing needs and capacities','room to manoeuvre', 'institutionalization' and 'political climate', emancipation can be analyzed more profoundly and precisely. The rudimentary interaction between the relevant actors constrain their 'room to manoeuvre'. Hence the effectiveness of political guidance and congruent implementation of politics is limited. The choice for the strategy to follow a two-track policy, requires a lot of the administrative qualities of the parties involved. Careful monitoring of the development process is necessary, not only in terms of instruments, but also in terms of legitimacy, democratic content and political will. For decision-making, effort and good will is not enough. The concept of 'willingness' or 'readiness to' is a moral-philosophical category and can be regarded as a very important meta-quality of governance (Kooiman, 1988). However, actors may desire all kinds of things, but the room for manoeuvre - the options and constraints for action - is determined by organizational structures and the political climate.

My conclusion is therefore, that the influence of institutions and actors on the governing capacity of policy depends on the room for manoeuvre, the degree of institutionalization and the prevailing political conjuncture.

---

[1]   The English philosopher, Janet Radcliffe Richards (1980), elaborates on Rawls' idea of justice in 'The Sceptical Feminist' and tries to apply this idea to the emancipation of women. A strategy for emancipation in Richards's sense, instead of an 'all or nothing' attitude, would lead to a strategy which tries to base itself on the principle of compensating inequalities. Argued from this perspective, emancipation would also be seen in a different light.

Framing at a Lower Level

Assuming that we analyze things more and more from a micro- and meso perspective, the question arises, to what extent existing concepts and approaches of planning, control, steering or governing and governance are still adequate? It seems that, the more we move away from the routine macro level, the more difficult it becomes to say something about the interplays and interdependencies between the meso and micro level. When the focus is only on the macro level, society as a whole, there is insufficient insight into the effects of policy on a meso and a micro level, or certain groups and people, let alone insight into the individual quality of governing.

By this, I do not want to say of course that governing is not necessary any more. On the contrary. Government action is a fact. For instance, every government has an obligation to use governing and governance at the same time, based on a number of criteria, like effectiveness, efficiency and social justice (Lehning, 1986). In my opinion, government action has to prevent suboptimal effects, for society as a whole. However, the reality is that there is a tendency that groups and people remain or end up more and more in the margins of society. This raises the question of social and political responsibility, or the ethical basis of welfare.

In recent decades, the moral and ethical dilemmas of policy have been shunted into the background. In this context, broadening our focus from a macro level to a meso and a micro level, means a renewed attention for normative and ethical aspects in the relation between politics and policy. Basing the interactive social political approach on humanitarian values could improve the quality of governing and governance. The moral-ethical dimension, with attention to social political problems, should be placed fairly and squarely on our agenda.

Finally, this reorientation to the meso and micro level could also lead to the forming of more open relations between the practice of government, policy-making research circles and a great number of scientific disciplines (see also: Kreukels, 1989: 137-47). In this, looking outside our own scientific sector, there is a challenge for further adaption and renewal.

INTRODUCTION TO PART III

EXPERIENCES

After these three chapters six examples follow of 'new' forms of interaction between government and society in terms of 'co' arrangements.

Charles Raab shows that within the field of data protection a combination of top-down and bottom-up (combination of regulation and deregulation) seems to be a feasible strategy. His analysis shows that regulation
cannot be effective (in an area like this) without a combination of
promulgation and routine enforcement on the one hand with mutual
learning and bargaining on the other hand.

The analysis of Martijn van Vliet of the options for and constraints of
the emergence of communicative governance in the field of environmental regulation of trade and industry, shows a number of conditions
under which a strategy directed at mutual understanding of the involved
public and private actors, might work. He mentions: recognition of
mutual interests; recognized interdependencies; learning through the
dissemination of information and increasing support of the involved
actors.

Vincent Kouwenhoven sketches the conditions under which interaction
between governments and the business community in the form of so-
called Public-Private-Partnerships can function. From case-studies he
made of this subject in The Netherlands, a checklist of such conditions
has been developed to be used by co-entrepreneurial projects between the
public and private sector.

Michèle Breuillard analyzes the effects of the building of the Channel
Tunnel in the two directly affected regions in France and the UK. An
important outcome of this study is that the challenge of such a dynamic
and complex event 'taken up' so differently in the two countries and
regions in terms of 'different degrees in capacity to adapt themselves to
the context imposed on them'.

In his study of the voluntary fire service in Belgium, Geert Bouckaert
offers a strong argumentation for the need of 'co-procuration' in areas
like this. Only in co-productivity terms an operational acceptable balance
can be reached between matters of legitimacy and effectiveness.

Herman Aquina and Hans Bekke finally show that the complex,
diverse and dynamic task of allocation in a modern social-political system
(case of The Netherlands) almost by necessity is a complementary one of
public organizations and private associations. How such a complementarity is (or should be) actually organized, remains a question in which
efficiency, political and ethical considerations play a role; the outcome
may greatly differ from system to system.

8

THE GOVERNANCE OF DATA PROTECTION[1]

CHARLES RAAB

Introduction

Data protection is a new but rapidly developing field of public policy in which governments and international. bodies have sought to enforce standards and rules upon the practices that are associated with information systems that employ personal data, and that are increasingly crucial to the workings of states, societies and economies. Sophisticated information systems have rapidly permeated all fields of economic, governmental and social activity and at levels that run from individual to very large public and private sector data users. Vast amounts of data about named, living individuals are used within organisations and transferred between them, often across the public/private divide as well as across national borders.

Formidable problems for policy and implementation are presented by the attempt to regulate systems and practices that are technologically advanced, widely dispersed, rapidly changing, and employed by powerful economic and governmental interests. It poses questions about the adequacy of central steering as a mode of control. How can public policy come to grips with these issues? What novel structures, organisational relationships and interactions are developing in the governance of data protection, whether by design or ad hoc? What part is played by mutual learning between the state and society in the co-production of better privacy protection and of the conditions for the benign development of 'informatisation' in both spheres? This chapter examines such issues in the light of approaches to the study of governance and seeks to locate data protection as a field of regulatory policy within them. It illustrates the subject by discussing the governance of data protection in Britain.

Data Protection as Policy

Since the beginning of the 1970s, many countries have enacted data protection or privacy laws, especially for data that are held on computers. Data protection has provided an arena for learning and experimentation

[1] This chapter is in part informed by research being carried out with C. Bennett, to whom I am grateful for comments on earlier versions. I also acknowledge the similar help of other contributors to this volume at meetings in Colchester and Amsterdam, and of H. Burkert.

in the arts and sciences of regulation, both nationally and internationally, and detailed accounts and comparisons of these processes have begun to be available in the academic literature (e.g. Bennett, 1992).

Data protection systems take their cue from a number of sources, including the precedents set by other countries (Bennett, 1992). Among the most important influences have been the efforts of the Organisation for Economic Cooperation and Development (OECD) and the Council of Europe, which have for many years played a powerful role in shaping such systems through the establishment of guidelines and standards (Council of Europe, 1981). The Council enunciated principles that resembled the OECD's and established a benchmark for systems of data protection ever since. These principles form a common core of data protection that each state's legislation is expected to incorporate, although the manner of implementation may vary.

In brief, the principles concern the fair and lawful obtaining and processing of personal data; the purposes for which they are stored and used; the adequacy, relevance and non-excessiveness of the data; the limitation of the period of their storage; the conditions under which especially sensitive data may be processed; and the security conditions under which data are held. They also seek to give data subjects the ability to find out what is held on them and by whom, to obtain copies of the data and to have them corrected or erased if the principles have been violated, and to obtain other remedies. The adoption of these principles through the enactment of national laws and the ratification of the Convention by states is intended to create a safe international zone for transborder data flows, and thus to reconcile the values of free interchange of data with the requirements of privacy protection.

The principles' generality, however, has occasioned further interpretation and Council of Europe recommendations on their application to particular sectors, and a sectoral approach to implementation is also an important feature of national systems as an adjunct to their general data-protection legislation. Moreover, the principles are not self-enacting. Most commentators who have studied national or provincial systems (for example, as in Germany and Canada) take the view that effective data protection owes a great deal to the institutional machinery that is put in place to implement it, and to the leadership provided by regulatory officials (Flaherty, 1989). The absence of such machinery in the United States, for instance, is lamented by proponents of more effective data protection in that country (Reidenberg, 1992; Schwartz, 1992).

Regulatory organisations for data protection possess important resources of independence and expertise. They implement policy only in part through bringing sanctions against users of personal data who violate the law. A great deal of their activity is devoted to the encouragement and dissemination of good practice, as well as to consciousness-raising efforts amongst data users, the general public and politicians. The meaning and application of the principles (for example, what does it mean to obtain data 'fairly'?) is elaborated or clarified through the practical experience of debate, contestation and learning that takes place between regulators and data users, and through judicial rulings. Regulatory institutions are therefore important in the broad implementation of data protection, and not only in their law-enforcement capacity.

Legislation varies across countries, but typically involves the establishment of a regulatory system by which the law is to be implemented, including sanctions and penalties against 'data users' who offend; rights and remedies for members of the public as 'data subjects'; and machinery such as an independent organisation or agency to control or otherwise steer the implementation. Britain passed its Data Protection Act (DPA) in 1984 (Bennett, 1992). It gives protection to personal data held on computers by requiring data users to register the fact that they hold data, and to describe their kinds, purposes, sources and potential recipients. It gives individuals access to their own data as well as remedies, and establishes a Registrar as the principle central agent for implementation.

Privacy and the safeguarding of citizens' interests are only one set of objectives of data protection. In many cases, the facilitation of the free flow of personal data for governmental or economic purposes through the establishment of safeguards has been of paramount importance, however cosmetic the latter turn out to be, and the privacy of citizens has had to be balanced against this objective in data protection laws and systems.

The idea of a 'balance' between objectives has become a paradigmatic assumption in developing and implementing data protection (Blume, 1992; Raab, 1992c), and will be discussed later on in the British context.

Sometimes this balance might be struck through settling upon a level or scope of regulation that minimises the real or incipient conflict between data protection and other purposes, and instead turns data protection to advantage in facilitating these other pursuits. Public confidence in government, for example, may well be strengthened by the knowledge that personal data are well protected, and by the transparency of the procedures in which they are employed. In turn, administrative efficiency and effectiveness are enhanced if organisations are not hampered by excessive, inaccurate, obsolete or insecurely-held information. Data protection addresses itself to these pathologies of information systems, and to private as well as public organisations. The doctrine of 'balance' puts into mechanistic and rhetorical language a process of bargaining that reflects the relative power positions of various interests, and that glosses over the political or economic conflicts that inhere in information conflicts (Burkert, 1984) It points up the way in which the outcome depends less on the wording of legislation than on the structures, contexts and interactions through which it is implemented.

The Environmental Context for Data Protection

Not only is data protection a highly complex matter of governmental or public learning and institutional experimentation, it is a policy that operates in an unfavourable environment. The latter conditions the prospects for successful governance, and consists of several interrelated factors. It includes, first, the configuration of interests in the rapidly-developing computerisation of organisations' information practices. Data users wish to use personal information for commercial gain, administrative convenience, or the delivery of public services. They favour a low level of regulation, although they may find it advantageous to be seen to subscribe to laws or rules of 'good housekeeping'. Interested groups in the public sector may be close enough to the centres of governmental decision-making to keep data protection off the agenda, or to restrict its impact. The private sector may be able to mobilise resistance to proposed schemes of data protection. Data subjects as citizens and customers have an interest in better public administration and in better commercial dealings, primarily in their own cases but also as part of a general public interest. On the other hand, they also have an interest in privacy.

Second, the environment for the system of governance is one of *complexity*, *dynamism* and *diversity* in technology, information systems and human purposes. The possibilities for sophisticated, automatic processing of large quantities of personal data have expanded enormously, and new applications of information and communications technology continue to unfold (Taylor and Williams, 1991). There has been a rapid dispersal of this technology from what was once a centralised, expensive computing capability housed in special buildings, to the desks, laps and pockets of today. Knowledge about technology and its uses is thus widely distributed to the periphery, and tailored to a vast diversity of sectoral purposes that can be served without central direction, and without central control. At the same time, however, there are growing central capabilities for gathering, collating and transmitting personal data, as for example in certain aspects of policing or of welfare systems; 1984 has passed but '1984' may still lie in the future. These developments present severe challenges to regulation, which must itself become better informed and more sophisticated.

Third, although there is public apprehension about uses of personal data that intrude on privacy or that adversely affect life chances, these problems may be of low political saliency in some countries. Many members of the public complain about the gathering and transfer of their personal details without their knowledge or consent, especially when these practices lead to annoyances such as 'junk mail'. Demands for regulation may arise when adverse decisions are taken on the basis of erroneous or irrelevant information by credit grantors, health specialists or others. Where there is public suspicion of authority, however, issues concerning personal data become more prominent. This makes it more difficult for regulators to rely upon continuous political or public 'effective demand' for regulation, and thus upon effective support for regulatory instruments.

Fourth, although the existence of an international policy community as well as transnational factors shaped national legislation from the 1970s on (Bennett, 1992), in the 1990s there are even greater pressures for harmonisation. These not only affect the making and revision of statutes, but also the process of interpretation and implementation within countries. Currently this process can be most clearly seen within the EC, where stronger measures of regulation are likely to be enjoined on each Member State, in the interests of privacy as well as of the completion of the Single Market, in which transborder data flow is a crucial element. These international developments overtake important parts of national agendas and change the domestic politics of data protection, even in non-EC countries.

Data Protection and Governance

What models of governance - emerging patterns or order - are found in these circumstances? Amongst the variety of approaches that data-protecting countries have adopted, Bennett (1992) identifies a number of discrete but overlapping and combinable regulatory strategies. These include voluntary control by data users, control by data subjects, licensing, registration and the establishment of a data commissioner. Each has its strengths and weaknesses, and does not itself represent the totality of a country's approach. From the viewpoint of governance, the strategies run the gamut from forms of central control to forms of societal self-regulation, and there are many combinations within and between these poles.

This means that the governance of data protection in a particular country (or on the international or sub-national level) may be a pattern that extends in a complex web from top to bottom; but what do these terms signify, and how might they be used in analyzing governance? Before turning to look at the British system of data protection in the light of this observation, it is important to note briefly some conceptual aspects of governance that relate to the analysis of a regulatory field like data protection under the conditions and constraints outlined above.

'Governance' bears a close relationship to other research strategies that also involve perspectives in inter-organisational dynamics in policy processes, especially when these processes bring governmental and societal organisations into intimate contact in producing order (Kooiman, this volume). In the present case, an ordered system of data protection depends upon co-production through such processes, and not solely or even mainly upon the enforcement of regulations. In part, the concept of governance reformulates such strategies in terms of cybernetic and systems-theoretic frameworks (e.g. Deutsch, 1963), in which patterns of communication and control are studied and the dynamic properties of systems are emphasised, as they move from one state to another, as is arguably the case when data protection moves from low levels to high ones.

Other chapters in this volume (for example, Dunsire and Kickert) also emphasise dynamics, but point up the way in which governance need not be predicated upon traditional ideas of central steering. Thus governance need not take place through an intensively-acting and directive governor, if there is, instead, autonomous self-regulation and 'collibration'. Much of the effort devoted to implanting data protection into information systems involves practitioners in public organisations, in businesses, or at the industry-wide level seeing the value of changing their practices and of adopting higher standards for reasons beyond that of mere compliance, and thus (quasi-)autonomously sustaining these changes. The social anthropology of acephalous societies is also relevant here, for it explains the occurrence of order and collective action in societies in which there is no exercise of political authority through hierarchical structures; the role of networks and trust is highlighted in this area of research (Raab, 1992a).

'Governance' points in the direction of a variety of inter-organisational models, but scepticism about the part played by formal authority should not lead either analysts or practitioners to abolish the concept of authority at a stroke. Kickert (1991) argues that 'steering at a distance' should not be confused with non-steering, or with the abandonment of control. It complements organisations' self-control but retains the idea of goal-oriented steering. Thus it is important not to lose sight of the fact that data protection is a statutory public policy, although the route to its execution might lie through inter-organisational networks.

Several authors in this volume retain some notion of authority, although not necessarily in its more accustomed form of imposed hierarchical control. Dunsire's 'collibration' is expounded in terms of steering and authority, intentional and purposive management, albeit exercised in a very different, low-key, non-regulatory mode of intervention by a governor whose thumb is on the scale of societal forces. Kooiman maintains that final authority is important to governance, even though it might not reside with government, whilst for Metcalfe management involves accepting responsibility for steering in order to improve results, and concerns getting things done through other organisations in a policy network. This point is directly relevant to the case of data protection systems in which an official agency is charged with such responsibility and can use authoritative sanctions to carry it out. Despite the attractions of theories of self-control and self-organisation for a theory of network management in situations of dynamics and complexity, Kickert concludes by reaffirming the continued relevance of public government and of control. Although this does not betoken rule or command, it could be construed in terms of authority in some sense, and of managers and controllers whose formal or legal authority at least counts for something, some of the time.

More strikingly, Aquina and Bekke specifically retain the premise of government as an authoritative allocator, especially where its unique function of balancing interests for society as a whole is concerned. Some notion of a controlling authority is also intrinsic to Mayntz's 'Steuerung', even though this takes place within complex patterns of interaction. She sees the intended outcome of these interventions as the purposeful changing of the autonomous dynamics of the 'object' of steering. The stipulation of a (central) steering authority is linked partly to the need for some stable point of departure in empirical analysis, and does not preclude seeing this actor as also being acted upon within the system that is steered; nor does it obviate an understanding of the steering difficulties encountered by political authority vis-à-vis social subsystems. Accordingly, the analysis of the governance of data protection might start at the top but would certainly not end there; nor would it assume the primacy of any authoritative central steering.

These views in many ways extend a well-rehearsed debate concerning the proper angle of vision for studies of interaction of the kind with which governance deals. Bogason (1991) equates control and steering, linking these concepts to a 'top-down' approach to implementation; a connection which seems to ignore wider meanings of steering, self-regulation and interaction that are usually considered as part of 'bottom-up' approaches. Likewise, Sabatier's (1986) comparison of contrasting approaches also ties steering to 'top-down' implementation and ties strategic interaction in a policy network to 'bottom-up'; so, too, does Hanf (1982) in outlining his 'implementation structure' approach. Hanf, however, makes it clear that 'bottom-up' analysis does not preclude the possibility that the determinant actors may actually be located at the 'top', although this does not necessarily mean that implementation is hierarchical and 'top-down'. For his part, Sabatier (1986) advocates a synthesis of 'top-down' and 'bottom-up' approaches, preferably through a focus on policy-oriented learning over very long periods of time by actors grouped in various interacting coalitions within a policy subsystem.

The elements of his research strategy seem to fall comfortably within the familiar range of conceptions of governance, networks and change that we have already seen. If one adopts a problem-solving strategy, as Hanf and O'Toole (1992) do, then the question is one of contriving a relationship of joint action amongst interdependent actors. Analytically, this is to focus upon the inter-organisational network itself as a unit of analysis in order to provide, as far as possible, a knowledge-base for more effective design. 'Network', they show, can thus be either an analytical construct or a vehicle of action. As an analytical or explanatory construct, and as a concept for prescriptive or design purposes, 'network' has become a key focus of attention of many studies of policy processes (Jordan and Schubert, 1992). In an applied-science mode of thought, networks conceived as vehicles for desirable action bring into full view 'steering', inter-organisational management and the prospects for concerting action towards some objective. Recommendations for improved data protection often implicitly reflect this constructive approach to the network-building. The activities of participants often exemplify deliberate attempts to create organisational relationships, whether for promoting the goals of data protection, or perhaps for cushioning the impact of implementation.

The conclusion that should perhaps be drawn is that states matter; how much, and in what ways they matter in any field of governance is a matter for empirical research, as in Hjern and Hull's (1982) 'empirical constitutionalism'. One should avoid the a priori assumption that states and governments count for little in a world of pluralistic policy-making in which networks abound. Nor should the actions of the 'top' be equated only with 'top-down' imperative command through hierarchies, rather than to an attempted, sometimes successful exercise of leadership in policy networks that include many other structures and actors. The distinction that Hood (1986) draws between 'comptrol' and 'interpolable balance' as ideal types of control over public bureaucracies is one between different modes of state (or at any rate, authoritative) action; the latter - akin to 'collibration' - involves the manipulation of self-control processes that occur elsewhere in the system, for the purpose of achieving desired goals. 'Interpolable balance' does not merely describe what happens or advocate a hands-off approach in the face of some 'natural order'; it is (or describes) a strategy of intervention in the patterning of incentives, rewards, rules, pressures and other elements, and is therefore subject to design.

Analogously, Hanf and O'Toole (1992) emphasise the importance of considering the management of implementation structures, employing the insights gained through understanding the multi-organisational network properties of governance in a world of complex problems. Governments, in this sense are not necessarily determinant actors, but are important parts of the system of co-ordinated action and control. Co-ordination of this kind is also a major theme in the work of Kaufmann and his colleagues (1986), in which the possibilities of institutional design are explored. They are concerned with lengthening the chains of action amongst a multiplicity of actors who are capable of self-regulation and learning, and whose co-ordination cannot happen solely through hierarchic control by a centre.

Steering Data Protection: The British Example

The implementation of regulatory policy for data protection exemplifies much of the variety of these approaches to governance, implementation and steering. As with Mayntz's (1978) or Hanf's (1982) work on air quality control programmes, and with Hancher and Moran's (1989) approach to the complex interdependencies that are involved in economic 'regulatory space', it is appropriate to apply perspectives on multi-organisational, negotiated action to data protection. The relationship between authoritative control, self-regulation and learning are at issue in analyzing the data protection system and in its deliberate design and reform.

In Britain, if there is an authoritative 'top' that makes policy and is responsible for its implementation, it is located in the Home Office and in the Office of the Data Protection Registrar. The former is the 'lead' department of state as far as overall policy is concerned, whether purely domestically or within the wider European or international arenas in which British interests are represented. The role and influence of other government departments, principally the Department of Trade and Industry, are very significant, at least where private-sector commercial interests are affected by data protection.

The Registrar's Office, however, is government's instrument for implementing the law within the constraints laid down in policy-making circles, although it is not without influence to shape policies and thus affect the parameters for implementation. The Registrar has mandated functions and powers, but outside his Office there is no clear-cut 'hierarchy' through which he can exercise his authority. Out there might just be 'out there', not 'down'. To be sure, in the last resort - perhaps when negotiation and persuasion break down - he can have offenders prosecuted and punished. However, the uncertain, disputed interpretation of some of the data protection principles means that his sanctions do not always rest on secure foundations, but must await rulings of the Data Protection Tribunal.

Most often, however, in order to achieve the objectives of the policy, he must operate in a multi-organisational, 'bottom-up' world of competing interests. These operations, including overt exercises of authority, depend crucially on knowledge about particular personal-information practices in specific sectors or fields of application. In at least the early phase of a data protection system, but in some senses perennially because of continual innovations in technology and in new commercial or administrative purposes to which it is put, such knowledge is more likely to be held by data users than by the official regulators. Regulators like the Registrar's Office must move up the 'learning curve' if their activities are to be effective (Raab, 1993). Perhaps a more immediately relevant area of knowledge for regulators concerns compliance. The Registrar, for example, must find answers to questions such as: who are data users?; which data users are complying with the Act?; how can their personal-data practices be monitored, controlled, or steered towards better data protection?; on a meta-level, what procedures must my Office develop in order to know about these things and to gain experience in dealing with data users and others?

Answers to these questions are conditioned by the complexity, dynamics and diversity of the fragmented world of data users in various industries and sectors, which aggravate the problem of regulating computerised personal-data systems. These environmental factors exert powerful influences over the organisational structure, strategies, and resource-deployment of the emergent system of data protection. For example, at the inception of the system in 1984, there was no accurate estimate of the numbers of data users who would have to register, and therefore only a rough idea of the dimensions of the administrative tasks lying before the Registrar's office. There were no bureaucratic routines or familiar policy networks at hand to assist with this first, crucial step in implementation. On the first page of his first annual report to Parliament, the Registrar poignantly explained that *'[s]etting out with an Act and a blank piece of paper raises a question as to how to start. Resources must be conjured up and I have begged, borrowed and bought help where I could.'* (HMSO, 1985).

Putting the legislation to work involves considerable experimentation and innovation in developing not only new forms of public bureaucracy but new patterns of relationship between the official regulators, those who are regulated, and the public at large. The formal authority that is vested in official data protectors is no guarantee that other will comply, and may only be exercisable on certain occasions. The data protection system would be largely unworkable without the formation of general and sectoral implementation structures for negotiation, bargaining, learning, and the encouragement of self-regulation. There has been a considerable but varied development of these relationships from the outset, although some of them have become strained where conflict has been at its sharpest, as with the credit-referencing industry in its justiciable disputes with the Registrar over the use of third-party information.

The contacts that are cultivated link the Registrar's office with the diverse worlds of data users and data subjects as well as with other parts of the administrative and political system whose policies help to form the milieu within data protection must make its way. In Hood's (1983a) terms, the Registrar's 'nodality' is a resource; his strategic position in information channels and networks enables him to build up a rounded picture of the world as well as to affect it with advice or persuasion. Inter-organisational relationships, whether structured and permanent or informal and fleeting, go hand in hand with the nature of data protection as a learning process that embraces not only the Registrar and those with whom he deals, but that stretches across organisations and individuals within and between sectors in ways that are amenable to 'bottom-up' investigation.

Space does not permit an extensive development of this perspective here; some aspects of the learning-system properties of British data protection are discussed in detail elsewhere (Raab, 1993). The question of learning in public systems is a central focus in a number of sources, especially in cybernetic approaches such as Deutsch's (1963) and in Schon's (1971) treatment of organisations and networks. Learning is relevant to steering and to the social organisation of implementation, perhaps especially where authoritative powers are weak or untried, where the environment is complex and changing rapidly, and - as will be discussed later - where goals are somewhat unclear; data protection fits these conditions.

In the British case, the Registrar draws connections between learning and the consultation in which he engages for the instrumental purpose of gaining compliance (HMSO, 1985). This points up the close relationship between innovations in the social organisation of implementation (second-order learning) and the cognitive prerequisites of effective data protection. Learning is seen as essential to the widespread understanding of the data protection principles that form the essential core of the regulatory system, and which are indispensable in any attempt to encourage self-regulation through the adoption of good practices by data users. The Registrar's office monitors the effects of its own activities, and also tries to learn about the resources they wield and how they might best be organised, given the constraints, opportunities and uncertainties they face.

Such learning is facilitated by extending the range of contacts within networks of similarly-placed data protectors abroad and in international organisations, a policy community of considerable significance. The Registrar's learning was also assisted through his formal consultation of a vast number of data users in Britain about the workings of the DPA and the regulatory system (HMSO, 1989). Those consulted constituted the global British network, including sectoral networks, of actors with whom the Registrar had previously dealt. As in other ways, this enabled him to tap the considerable expertise that lies at the periphery, amongst data users whose knowledge and experience of data practices as well as of the implementation process are important to governance.

A high degree of self-regulation among these users can also be seen as an essential element in data protection. Every data user who abides by the principles is, in some sense, an implementer of data protection, just as every motorist implements environmental policy by purchasing unleaded petrol. On the other hand, these discrete instances depend upon wider organised systems for recognising and dealing with problems in terms of public policy, in which incentives, penalties, norms, monitoring, or enforcement play a part. These systemic and, indeed, authoritative processes provide the context for individual, disconnected, and mundane activities; they also provide it for activities at those collective, organised levels where the 'self' of self-regulation is a sector of, say, industry or government, or some other corporate actor.

For these users, self-regulation goes beyond basic compliance to embrace the further development of good practices and their dissemination within organisations and industries on their own behalf, albeit under the urging and assistance of the Registrar. As Ziegler-Jung (1991) shows, some degree of self-regulation is a common feature of several systems in Europe, especially the Dutch, in which formal, statutory procedures surround the official certification of sectoral codes. This kind of self-regulation is heavily controlled from the 'top', and cannot be construed as spontaneous voluntarism. In any case, the relationship between sanction-based authority and self-regulation is a crucial one, for the latter only operates within the parameters of the former. Regulation and self-regulation intertwine to a considerable extent in British data protection. Self-regulation is particularly stimulated by the statutory duty placed on the Registrar to encourage the adoption of codes of practice by data users, as an adjunct to their adherence to the principles. Codes now exist or are being developed in a number of sectors, including the police, local authorities, the health service, property management, computer bureau services, direct marketing and banking. Consultation and machinery have evolved within sectors in order to concert approaches to the whole question of data protection, including the formulation of codes of practice and their monitoring and enforcement.

The Registrar's office plays an important part in the collaborative development of these codes, but he has also expressed some doubt about their possibility in some sectors. He has considered whether self-regulation should not be supported by central formal approval, so that the quasi-judicial Data Protection Tribunal can have a broader basis for its decisions about applying sanctions. Codes of practice, of course, may be seen merely in a cosmetic, public-relations vein by sectors as public evidence of their own 'good housekeeping', and thus may have commercial or other value if clients, customers or citizens are sufficiently reassured. On the other hand, codes may actually help to rationalise organisations' information practices, and increase their effectiveness and efficiency for the benefit of the data user and the data subject as well. Data users may perhaps prefer self-regulation to engaging in adversarial relations with regulators, especially if the terms on which they regulate themselves are bargained rather than imposed.

It is important to note that the changes that are sought by data protection are not merely institutional and functional, but cultural as well. This is because the prospects for the protection of personal data are enhanced to the extent that data protection is not merely bolted on, but instead, built in, when information systems are designed and operated. This presupposes a widespread permeation of certain understandings, amounting to a cultural change, into organisational practices and technical specialisms, and also amongst the general public whose role as data subjects pursuing claims based upon rights are an integral part of the system and its potential success. The Registrar told Parliament that he was *'involved in a massive educational exercise which is trying to change the attitudes as practices of the whole nation'* (House of Commons, 1990).

Accordingly, from the outset the Registrar has emphasised the importance of publicity, information and education in a planned campaign backed by considerable resources. The educational exercise has been targeted particularly upon data users and data subjects, and has involved the production of vast numbers of guidance publications, public meetings, advertisements, press releases and the like. The channels of dissemination have occasionally included representative organisations in the sectoral policy networks themselves, through which co-production may thus be tinged with an element of neo-corporatism. These bodies themselves independently engage in educative activities amongst sectoral data users, even if the main purpose is sometimes only to heighten their awareness of the threat that data protection poses and to mould them into a constituency for exerting pressure upon policy; politics and learning thus reinforce each other. One of the Registrar's declared aims is to co-operate with these bodies and to provide them with support and material for their own activities (HMSO, 1990). His reliance upon 'peak' organisations suggests that there are advantages to this strategy beyond their simple convenience in the face of scarce central resources.

Although recent budget cuts have curtailed much of the Registrar's publicity, the educational campaign's place in the broader system of compliance has been a notable feature. The Registrar has monitored and researched its effects upon the level of public knowledge and awareness of data protection issues, and related questions, in an attempt, through feedback, to guide his achievement of objectives. His office's learning, however, depends in part on its learning capacity (Deutsch, 1963), which is a function of its internal organisation and resources. Staffing restrictions, and the considerable proportion of organisational resources that have had to be committed to maintaining the register of data users, place severe limits upon the extent to which the Registrar's office can extend its supervisory and investigatory roles. These tasks are not only important in terms of enforcement, but in terms of inter-organisational networking and the mutual learning that occurs through these channels. Perhaps more crucially for the future, however, limitations on resources impeded or delayed for several years the office's ability to devote attention to some of the major emergent issues in information practices that appear on the policy agenda, such as ID cards, data matching, DNA profile databases, police information systems, and many others. These innovations involve new technology as well as new administrative applications of it. They open up new issues for regulation, but may present a formidable challenge to the learning and networking capabilities of the official regulators as well as of data users and subjects who play a part in the system of control.

The Registrar has said that his research endeavour *'assists the Office to monitor its progress towards achieving its main aims and objectives'* (HMSO, 1990), and has observed that the Registrar's office had a key role *'in making the ways clear for those who journey'* (HMSO, 1985). This implies a conception of steering, of moving from one state to the next, and of achieving goals. However, it is in regard to decisions about how to devise the system of data protection, including its principles, structures, relationships, legal prescriptions and learning, that the configuration of goals poses a difficult question: towards what objective should the system be steered?

If there is a principal goal, it is to enhance the protection of personal data, and hence of privacy, through regulations that limit the possibilities afforded by modern computer technology (Blume, 1992). Putting privacy first may lead to strong measures of data protection. However, as mentioned earlier, this may conflict with another goal, that of safeguarding commerce or administration, which may therefore lead to the adoption of only the minimum of privacy protection that is necessary for this purpose. This duality of goals makes compromises likely, albeit compromises that are not necessarily unsatisfactory in practice: 'the free flow of protected data' is conceptually sound, although rather hollow because it does not indicate the extent of privacy that is afforded. Nevertheless, the duality of goals reduces the ability of regulators to act too zealously as advocates pursuing privacy as a paramount objective, lest the threat that was posed to the interests of data users caused issues to be resolved in political arenas in which data protection claims were weakly supported.

Moreover, governmental policies and organisational activities in other fields may take precedence over the protection of personal data. Some of these are encapsulated in the various exemptions to sections of the DPA, in which national security, public safety, the monetary interests of the state and crime control prevail against data-protection considerations. These values are among those that are advanced in the rationales for the increasing computerisation of public bureaucracies, such as improved service-delivery, administrative convenience, and public order; these objectives attract more political and public support and enjoy greater legitimacy despite the potential dangers they pose to individual privacy (Raab, 1992b).

In these circumstances, it would be less sustainable for an official regulatory agency to construe its role single-mindedly as an advocate for data protection as an absolute, and indeed the British Registrar has argued for a 'balancing' approach in the judgements he makes (HMSO, 1988). The concept of 'balance' was touched on earlier. In Britain, balance is built into the process and structures of implementation themselves more than it is the product of a countervailance of the data- protection system and other public policies. This colours the negotiations that take place within the inter-organisational networks, although the Registrar has also endeavoured to project himself as a privacy advocate in the first instance, as indeed have his regulatory counterparts in other countries; the explicit privacy goal enunciated in the proposed European Community data protection regime (Commission of the European Communities, 1990) has been appreciatively received in British regulatory circles.

'Balancing' in the sense of 'interpolable balance' might be a conceivable strategy for 'steering at a distance', where, say, the Registrar assists knowledgeable data subjects to challenge data users who violate the law, or encourages sectoral data users to challenge each other to raise the level of data protection in their industry. On the other hand, the meaning of 'balance' as a trade-off between goals is quite different. If it is taken seriously, and not just as a rough-and-ready slogan, it poses questions of value concerning these objectives: how much efficiency is an ounce of protection worth? should the balance-point differ across different sectors, and if so, why? It also complicates the evaluation of data protection, especially if performance measures that are applied to the system are predicated upon privacy as the goal, but also if incommensurable multiple goals are taken into account (Raab, 1991).

This is further complicated by the very nature of data protection as a co-production steered by officials and others in inter-organisational networks. The object of evaluation may not be only to measure the performance of an agency like the Registrar's, but to judge whether the data protection system as a whole is achieving its goals. The 'value added' by the Registrar might only be realised indirectly, through the efforts of data users whom he has encouraged and with whom he has collaborated, and therefore may not be easily separated for the purpose of analysis or for public accountability. This problem is endemic in measuring the effectiveness of public systems generally, whether in Britain or in other countries.

Conclusion

Evaluative questions need to be addressed by new approaches to social-political governance that are predicated upon the empirical reality or the prescriptive desirability of inter-relationships through which steering take place and order is produced. If the network as a whole is argued to be not only the proper unit of analysis but also the unit for design and improvement, then evaluations of performance are already presupposed. These are political questions, not merely of interest to policy analysts and management technocrats, insofar as they relate to the accountability of public and other organisations for their performance in processes of policy implementation.

In a similar vein, some might argue that one difficulty surrounding the question of 'balance' between objectives is that it may not obviate politically-laden disputes about the existence and/or the value of a particular state of affairs that is claimed to be 'in (or out of) balance'. On the other hand, the more that such issues are matters of political disputation, in the sense of reasoned arguments and evidence deployed in public arenas, and not left as matters that are best argued out within technical and bureaucratic networks, the higher the status that data protection, privacy, and the uses of information technology will enjoy as serious issues on the political agenda in Britain.

These may be provocative notes on which to conclude an exploration of governance models as they apply to a regulatory field such as data protection. However, it is worth noting that the Registrar's Deputy, perhaps only half-seriously, has envisaged the proper implementation of data protection as a situation in which his office had worked itself out of a job through the full compliance of data users with the principles of data protection. This goes beyond 'nodality' to a very bureaucracy-sparing (Hood, 1983b) mode, and is one political vision amongst others. It would imply a successful, self-steering and mutually-adjusting network of well-schooled practitioners. It is not easy to envisage this except as a long-term institutional ideal that is only achievable if data protection has been steered to its change-of-state goal. But this would be to accord no importance to the plural interests and values that inhere in implementation, and that operate not necessarily as obstacles to be overcome but as part of a process in which their proponents are managed and self-managed.

Such values and interests do not disappear just because a new state has been reached. Their disappearance would imply that the future environment of the regulatory system for data protection will resemble the present one, generating no qualitatively new problems. This is an unlikely prospect; what may be required are not only new rules grounded in new understandings of problems, but new learning to be facilitated or imparted, and new 'macro-management' (Metcalfe, this volume). More important, they may require debate and decision in political and judicial arenas, which must not be omitted in any account of governance.

9

ENVIRONMENTAL REGULATION OF BUSINESS: OPTIONS AND CONSTRAINTS FOR COMMUNICATIVE GOVERNANCE

MARTIJN VAN VLIET

Introduction

The problem of environmental degradation is often been highlighted by Hardin's (1968) *Tragedy of the Commons*. The dark image of the collective problem-resolving capacity of interacting human beings - social systems - with regard to environmental problems is considered as an enormous challenge for contemporary political and social systems (O'Riordan, 1983; Ostrom, 1990).

Environmental degradation is seen as a collective-action-problem in which separate actions of autonomous but interdependent social actors lead to a negative and often catastrophic outcome. Usually, public intervention is considered to be the normal way of acting when collective-action-problems arise. As a result, public intervention and public regulation in the field of environmental protection began to rise in the period when the polluting impact of industrial activities became a subject of public and political concern.

However, research in the field of political science and public administration has shown the low effectiveness, the enforcement problems and the sometimes negative effects of a lot of public regulation: besides *market failure*, there also exists *bureaucratic failure* (Majone, 1986). Also and maybe, just in a relatively new area of public intervention as protection of the environment, the outcomes of public intervention lags behind the original political and social expectations. The (articulated) need for the regulation of activities leading to environmental degradation is not satisfactorily met by government with 'traditional', bureaucratic and strictly legal means (Mayntz, 1978; Downing and Hanf, eds, 1983). A problem of governability exists.

The main theme of this chapter is the question whether and how the gap between market failure and bureaucratic failure, and the resulting gap between the governing needs and governing capabilities (Kooiman, this volume) can be closed in the field of environmental regulation of industrial activity.

In this chapter, a solution, which I will call *communicative governance* is presented and discussed.

In the second section, the concept of communicative governance is discussed. Its theoretical background is highlighted and the main expectations and bottle-necks of communicative governance are formulated. In the third section the role of this concept within the Dutch system of environmental regulation of business is described and practical experience with government-business cooperation is analyzed. In the fourth section, the confrontation between the concept and the practice of communicative governance results in some remarks about the perspectives for communicative governance in the field of environmental regulation of business.

Communicative Governance in Theory

The development of the concept of communicative governance must be seen in the light of the shift in focus within the science of public administration from 'monocentric' to 'polycentric' approaches, in which processes of governing and governance are not considered as a relation or a process between a governing actor (the state) on the one hand and a to-be-governed object (society) on the other, but as a relation or interaction between two or more 'acting' subjects: 'Political governance in modern societies can no longer be conceived in terms of external government control of society but emerges from a plurality of governing agents.' (Marin and Mayntz, eds, 1991: backflap). This shift in focus can be observed in analytically oriented literature as well as in the design-oriented literature.

The starting point of alternative forms of governance is the observation and acknowledgement of the existence of *networks* of organisations that are centred around societal problems or public programs (Rainey and Milward, 1983; Wright, 1988; Raab, 1992; Hanf and O'Toole, 1992). These networks, in which different public and private actors play a role and in which processes of problem-solving, planning and policy-making take place, are characterized by:

- the complexity of the problems, which have to be dealt with;
- the interdependence of the actors involved;
- the negotiational or 'game-like' character of the developments within the network;
- the learning processes which can take place within and between the involved actors.

I will link these characteristics to the problem of environmental degradation.

Complexity is a term that is often used and misused. Misused, in the sense that references to the complexity of (social or political) problems or solutions are often made to cover administrative and political unwillingness to tackle a problem or to resist powerful actors. A situation that often occurs in environmental politics. This improper use of the word does not mean, however, that it is possible to ignore the word but that one must be careful in using it. Complexity refers to the multitude and diversity of the parts and the interactions between these parts, which are present in (social) systems, problems, solutions, etc. (Dunsire, this volume; Kooiman, this volume).

The complexity of modern society is said to be growing, and so are the problems within modern society. Environmental degradation can be seen as an example of these modern and complex social problems. With regard to environmental degradation, the relation between causes and consequences is not always clear and, more often than not, the reaction chain covers a long time-span and the 'right' solutions are not always evident. Besides to the Entropy Law environmental solutions often seem to be subjected to the 'Law of Preservation of Misery'. In addition to the ecological system dynamics, the diversity of human activities involved in environmental degradation and, therefore the diversity of social interests involved, make environmental problems complex ones. This complexity on the one hand limits the practical range of formal laws and rules and as a result the capacity of unilateral governmental intervention and on the other hand it suggests that a part of governing capacity has to be found within the target groups of public intervention.

Interdependence between public and private actors is seen as the result of the growing complexity of modern society. Social problem-solving involves many different actors and interests and effective problem solving is dependent on the coordination between the actors involved. Governing and problem-solving capacities are spread over many actors, and no one is capable of enforcing coordination against the will of other actors. With regard to environmental problems, this interdependence can be analyzed as the capacity of each actor to obstruct the achievement of the objectives, set by other actors. Generally speaking, the achievements of environmental objectives is on the one hand dependent on the knowledge of the production process by trade and industry themselves and on the other hand on the making of binding rules for all by the government. The need for the effective regulation of environmental problems necessitates forms of cooperation, but the 'obstruction power' of each actor means that there is a risk that adversary, non-cooperative behaviour will lead to the obstruction of environmental as well as economic objectives.

Negotiation is seen as the normal way of governance. The broad range of implementation literature has taught us that even in the most legalistic approaches, negotiation is the normal practice with regard to rule-making, permit-procedures and rule-enforcement ('negotiation under the shadow of law'). The need for some kind of cooperation increases the interest of integrative negotiations directed at joint problem solving. The possibilities for integrative negotiation are dependent on the extent in which positive-sum elements can play a role and are dependent on a certain degree of equality in the power relations between each of the interested actors (Bacharach and Lawler, 1983).

Being confronted with complex problems in difficult circumstances, governance is more and more seen as a process of *learning*. The new doctrine seems to be that instead of making the 'best' decision in advance, governing activities should be directed at the creation of learning processes within the interested actors or society in general (see f.e. Kaufmann, 1986; Reich, 1985). The attraction power of learning-theories can be found in the link between the idea of an ambitious public policy with a complex, often contradictory and unpredictable reality (Koppenjan and Hufen, 1991). Negotiations enable the exchange of information, building a relation of credibility and even trust, and a process of mutual learning can take place. However, learning does certainly not necessarily lead to cooperation. It is possible to consider the adversary relations between government and trade and industry in the USA with regard to environmental regulation as a learning process, but one in which the interested actors have learned to distrust each other and in which the targets of government intervention have learned how to avoid and obstruct public rules and regulations.

As a result, new governance patterns are addressed to stimulate learning processes that will lead to cooperative behaviour and mutual adjustment, so that responsibility for managing structural changes is shared by all or most actors involved (Metcalfe, this volume). One such an alternative form of governance which is based on the image of complex problems in which problem-resolving capacities are spread over autonomous but interdependent actors, is described as communicative governance.

As the starting point, I take a description given by Vermeulen (1989: 172, my own translation): 'In this model the transmission of information, knowledge and valuations, is central. Persons are supposed to act as conscious and rational beings, whose changes in their insights will be followed by changes in their behaviour.'

In this description, a form of rationality is presented in which social actors are considered to be 'reasonable citizens'. It is clear that by rationality, described as 'reasonableness', another kind of rationality is meant than the selfish, opportunistic profit- or benefit maximizing kind of rationality with is used in economic or public choice theory. In a market economy, business organizations are expected to act rationally in a economic sense and their rights and conditions of existence are evaluated on this basis. However, communicative governance is based on a different form of rationality, namely one which is based on reasonableness and public interest.

The call upon the 'reasonable citizen' corresponds with the way Dryzek (1987) connects the concept of *communicative rationality* with social problem-solving and conflict-resolution. In his opinion, situations which are characterized by complex problem-solving are suitable situations for forms of communicative rationality which can replace instrumental and functional forms of rationality.

Communicative governance can be considered as an attempt to approach the ideal of communicative rationality as closely as possible in the decision-making process on complex collective-action problems, or as, Dryzek calls it: 'communicative rationality in practice' (p. 437).

The concept of communicative rationality was developed by Jürgen Habermas. In his view communicative rationality is based on the interaction of human beings; truth and knowledge are based on a (temporary) intersubjective understanding. In this view communicative rationality flourishes and prospers in a process of intersubjective interaction, clear of domination, strategic behaviour and deception, in which the actors are equally communicatively competent and there are no restrictions on the possibilities of participation in the debate or dialogue. In the 'ideal dialogue situation', the only remaining authority, is that of 'the good argument', which can be related to empirical as well as normative judgements. Habermas confronts 'communicative action' which is based on mutual understanding ('Einverständnis') with 'strategic action' which is based on (instrumental) mutual manipulation by power or money (Habermas, 1989).

The main question that must be asked is whether it is possible to put this form of communicative rationality into practice in the tough reality of politics, social problem-solving, policy-making and planning. As a rule, within collective decision-making, the place the use of power, strategic and opportunistic behaviour and deception has is considerable, certainly when the interests at stake are great.

On the basis of an analysis of different mediation- and negotiation processes in various policy areas including environmental dispute resolution, Dryzek concludes that there are options for putting communicative rationality into practice. Mediation procedures often succeed in forming a consensus between the interested actors with different interests at the start, but low public participation makes this kind of procedures vulnerable for critics which state that there is more attention for reaching an agreement between well-organised special interest groups than for serving the public interest (Dryzek, 1987: 439, 440). Dryzek concludes that actors decide to participate in negotiations if they see good reasons for it, such as: a stalemate in other procedures such as legal ones, a real desire for improved communication, and naked self-interest (ibid.: 440).

Dryzek admits that some kinds of self-interest influence the vitality of decision procedures based upon communicative rationality. However, he does not see this conclusion as the end, but as the start of a flourishing future. In his opinion, 'increasing social complexity raises the chances of a calculus rooted in self-interest leading actors into communicative rationality' (Dryzek, 1987: 440). In his view increasing social complexity means increasing interdependencies and increasing possibilities of positive-sum solutions that are not visible at first sight but can be negotiated on.

A 'strong' version of communicative rationality, in which communicative action is strongly separated from strategic action does not hold long in practice. However, *if Dryzek is right*, elements of communicative rationality can penetrate in the 'real' world of economics and public decision-making if the interests involved are not ignored but taken into account. The possibility of this penetration depends on:

- interdependence: each of the actors involved has to have an (some) interest in taking part in a dialogue-situation;

- positive-sum solution: there has to be a possibility or a prospect of an outcome of the dialogue/negotiations which is acceptable for all interested actors.

Communicative governance is on the edge of naivety. Naivety, in the sense of denying power-relations and not recognising 'strategic' or opportunistic action, risks that the opposite of what is intended, will be achieved. Namely, in stead of joint problem-solving, the development of symbolic decision-making and the avoidance of responsibility resulting in the subordination of environmental interests to political and economic interests.

That is why it has to be stressed that communicative governance is more than an 'interest- and power-free' dialogue. The nucleus of communicative governance is that in the real world and confronted with complex, long-term and ambiguous political and social problems, forms of joint decision-making are more adequate than traditional forms of coordination as bureaucracy and markets. Majone (1986) suggests 'mutual adjustment by debate and persuasion'. In his view, a dialogue advances a process of social learning through which solutions can be found which cannot be found through market or bureaucratic processes. He emphasizes the necessity of public participation and the public nature of the dialogue / debate as a counterbalance to professional misuse (Majone, 1986: 455).

The 'translation' of communicative rationality into practice takes place especially by public participation and guarding the public nature of the process. Communicative rationality in practice is pursued, not by way of making the 'dialogue' 'free from power' but by way of broadening the process of governance.

It is claimed that communicative governance fits in well with complex and dynamic social problems, like environmental degradation. These 'contemporary' problems can be solved because communicative governance enables the creation of sufficient cooperation and coordination between interested actors, even when it is confronted with the complexity of problems and the multitude of actors and interests involved.

It is expected that the results of communicative governance are defensible from a 'public' interest point of view and does not only satisfy the needs and interests of the most powerful actors. It is also expected that the involvement of interested actors leads to support for and commitment to the mutually agreed objectives so that the willingness for cooperation increases and communicative rationality dominates political and economic rationality. Furthermore, it is expected that as a result of improved coordination mechanisms, the capabilities of shifting actual decisions and actions in a socially (environmentally) responsible direction are enlarged.

However, this section has also made us aware of some important bottlenecks of communicative governance. Actual and observable interdependencies between the actors involved should create a situation in which all actors feel enough incentives to be prepared to reach an agreement. Apparently, a paradox is that situations in which actors have mutual 'obstruction powers' seems to promote this preparedness. The actors must be 'condemned to cooperation' (see Wassenberg, 1987). Effective communicative governance strongly depends on the availability of positive-sum solutions for the problem-situation. Last but not least, the legitimacy of communicative governance has to be taken into account. Alternative decision and conflict-resolution procedures have to be embedded in normal procedures within parliamentary-democratic systems, and interested 'third parties' such as environmental organisations and citizen groups have to have access to the alternative procedures, acting at least as a counter-balance against business interest.

Communicative Governance in Practice

In the 1980s, the structure of environmental policy-making in The Netherlands has reoriented in the direction of responsibility of trade and industry themselves for the ecological consequences of their activities. The reorientation is partly related to the internalization strategy as it was promoted by the former Minister for the Environment, Pieter Winsemius (1982-1986) (Winsemius, 1986). The internalization strategy was a way to develop an environmental policy which corresponded to the 'no nonsense', 'withdrawing government' (quasi-Thatcherite) ideology of the centre-right-wing cabinet coalitions from 1982 till 1989, being the political-administrative expression of the 'spirit of the times' (see Jørgensen, this volume) of the eighties. Although 'internalization' is a rather vague concept, it was the starting-point for the development of, what is called the *target group policy* today. The target group strategy is the overall strategy by which the National Environmental Policy Plan (NEPP - published in 1989) is implemented. The strategy has developed into a general negotiation and consultation strategy with organized sectors of trade and industry in which the partial responsibility of the 'target groups' for environmental measures should be expressed. The core of the concept is the view that an environmental strategy directed at sustainable development (Brundtland, 1987) is dependent on a preventive and source-oriented approach of environmental problems, which is not enforceable by a unilateral rule-making government but which depends on the cooperation and the (partial) responsibility of the main relevant social and economic sectors. The target group approach, then, is directed at the joint consultation of relevant public authorities and sectors of trade and industry. In this strategy the targets of environmental policy have to be made operational with the help of a coordinated and structured approach of the economic sector or branch of industry concerned, reckoning with the specific character and dynamics within the branch or industry. It is hoped that the support for environmental measures within industry will increase. This as a result of the involvement of representatives of the business community in the development of the specific branch- or sector-oriented strategies and of the translation of the nation-wide targets for different forms of pollution into integrated branch- or sector-specific targets.

Of course, this reorientation has not been without criticism. The non-committal nature of the agreements between governments and trade and industry and the influence of business representatives on public decision-making are questioned. The capture of governmental agencies and cooperative bodies by business representatives is feared. One of the leading Dutch environmentalists and environmental scientists, Lucas Reijnders, has even spoken about the threat of the development of a 'fifth column' within the environmental directorate.

Because of the early stages of the implementation of the NEPP and the limited experiences with the target group approach, it is too early to give a definitive evaluation of it. However, it is possible to give results of an evaluation of a consensus-oriented project which started when the target group strategy was still in its founding phase but which is seen today as an early example of the target group approach and can be regarded as a first testcase for this approach.

This project is named KWS 2000 or, in English, HC 2000. The project is directed at the reduction of emissions of hydro-carbons (HC) or volatile organic compounds (VOC's). VOC's react with nitrogen oxides into ozone. In contrast with the situation in the stratosphere, there is too much ozone in the lower two to three kilometres of the atmosphere. Ozone formation contributes to the ecological damage that is generally attributed to acidification.

Because of a lack of confidence in unilateral rule-making (due to the plurality of emission sources and the lack of knowledge about abatement strategies) and the penetration of concepts as internalization and target group approach, the environmental directorate decided to develop a VOC reduction strategy in cooperation with trade and industry. Between 1985 en 1988 a project group with representatives of business organisations and different central and local public authorities developed a reduction strategy which should be implemented between 1988 en 2000.

The reduction strategy is directed to a reduction of VOC emissions from industry, small companies and households from 225 kiloton yearly to 100 kiloton yearly in 2000. The measures focus on prevention of pollution instead of end-of-pipe treatment (e.g. using water-borne paint instead of gathering and burning of organic solvents afterwards). Within this reduction strategy the consensus between public authorities and business organisations is laid down. The basis for this consensus is formed by an exchange in which trade and industry gets ample time for implementing environmental measures and the government can expect an active efforts of companies to use their knowledge and capacities to abate VOC-emissions. This willingness to cooperate has its price. Trade and industry receive in return:

- influence on the kind of measures which are to be taken;
- influence on the conditions that have to be met before environmental measures are taken; measures are dependent on technical and international developments;

- a generous time-path because of which a large part of the pursued reductions only have to take place in the last years of the implementation period;
- reasonable certainty that governmental policy with regard to VOC-emissions will not change in the coming decade and protection of VOC policy against intensification of governmental objectives.

The conditions which are set on the implementation of measures, lower the probability and certainty that the objectives will be achieved but these conditions increase the flexibility in the implementation period. This flexibility creates room for making use of learning effects, particularly the further development of not yet practical applicable techniques and products. However, this flexibility can be misused by non-cooperative corporations to delay or cancel implementation of pollution-abatement measures.

The main problems regarding the implementation of the created consensus between representatives of authorities and trade and industry, is the 'translation' of the HC 2000 programme into 'real' activities within individual corporations and public authorities. That is why the strategic interactive discussion which has led to the programme is followed by the creation of a project organisation that is entrusted with the implementation of the programme. Within the environmental directorate this coupling of the 'strategic-choice' or 'strategic-discussion' approach with the establishment of a project organisation is considered as an important innovational experiment.

It is hoped that as a result of the involvement of business representatives in the strategy development and the implementation process, the practical implementation on company level will take place on a voluntary basis but a 'certain measure' can also be obligatory in a juridical sense if local or regional authorities embody these measures into licenses or if the measures are made obligatory in nation-wide regulations. In practice, the HC 2000 strategy is playing a more and more important role in license procedures, in the sense that companies and local authorities both use the HC 2000 strategy document as a basis for their negotiations concerning issuing of licenses. There is evidence that there are some regional authorities which have been slowed down by the HC 2000 programme as well as evidence that public authorities have been stimulated by the programme. The latter seems to be dominant.

The national environmental directorate as well as organized sectors of trade and industry are aware that HC 2000 is an important testcase for the viability of 'environmental policy in partnership' as the target group approach is often called. This awareness leads on the one hand to commitment to the objectives which are partially adopted by individual companies as well, but on the other hand it leads to the view that the strategy has to be assessed positively by the directorate and trade and industry, whatever the real results are.

Two main targets of the HC 2000 project are described as the *paint network* and the *petroleum network*.

The *paint network* results from the interdependencies between the various actors that are involved in the production and application of paint and varnish. With regard to the paint network, HC 2000 is focused on product innovation, in which organic solvents based paints are substituted by water-borne paints. A change in the composition of a product will inevitably lead to some change in the properties of a product. The major and minor problems related to these changes can only be solved by a cooperation between the various actors within the paint network: starting from the producers of basic products, which have to develop different basic products, to the applicators and consumers which have to accept changes in ways of application, duration, maintenance, appearance, etc. This environmentally based product innovation is dependent on the realization of a connection between the technological developments and market acceptation.

In recent years, the global paint production industry has increasingly concentrated. It is believed that the world-wide top ten's market share in paint production, will rise from 20% in 1980, and 30% in 1987 to 50% in 1995 (European Coatings Journal, 1989: 340; European Chemical News, 13/11/89: 22). The decreasing numbers of independent paint producers and the concentration of production of basic chemicals and paint in large chemical multinationals, is partly the result of what is sometimes called the environment-technology spiral: 'Capital will have to be found to upgrade paint factories, develop new paints, improve production processes and change application methods among industrial customers.' (ECJ, 1989: 337). This tendency can also be seen in The Netherlands, where two paint producers are increasingly dominating the market. They are both daughters of, Dutch- and Belgian-based chemical multinationals respectively. In fact, there is an international trend to production of low-solvent paints and varnishes.

It is not believed that The Netherlands is on the vanguard line regarding the introduction of low-solvent paints. The HC 2000 project has the possibility of making use of this international trend in product change. The HC 2000 activities directed at the introduction of low-solvent paints does not mean a fundamental reorientation within the paint-producing industry but, chiefly, an effort directed at speeding up a process that fits in close with the developments within the sector itself. The question is not whether it is possible to use low-solvent paint, but under which circumstances, at what rate and in which specific applications these alternative paints can be introduced.

An important part of the introduction of alternative paint is conditioned by (technical) quality requirements and market (consumer) acceptation, and a gradual implementation is allowed. 'Quality is sufficient if so agreed between producers and users' (HC 2000 report (English version): 53). As a result of afore-mentioned conditions, the pressure on the paint network as a result of the HC 2000 project does not seem to be unacceptably high.

The paint producers and applicators can change their behaviour (and public image!) into a more environmentally friendly one without being confronted with high financial costs. Especially the metal industry has got the opportunity to prevent the construction of expensive end-of-pipe facilities, by participating in the HC 2000 project. So, one should not to be amazed that the HC 2000 strategy is not only supported by the paint-producing industry, but is also approved by the two main branches of paint and varnish application, painting enterprises in the housing sector and the metal industry.

In addition to the paint network, the *petroleum network* constitutes an important target for the KWS 2000 project. This network refers to the gasoline production and distribution process from the refining stage to the distribution to the individual automobile. The HC 2000 project is focused on recovery of vapours (which mainly consists of VOC's) that escape in various stages during the production and distribution process. Recovery instead of destruction of those vapours is the best approximation of the prevention objective. However, the product (gasoline) is not changed and the environmental facilities are generally seen as additional. As a result, within this network, financial considerations are important. In some stages of the production and distribution process, the rewards of the recovered vapours makes an additional investment profitable (sometimes with the help of an adjusted excise charge). However, in most cases, there are no advantages from an economic point of view in the construction of these facilities. It is not possible to create so called 'win-win' situations and it is difficult or impossible to achieve consensus.

An interesting and illuminating issue within the petroleum network is formed by the decision-making process about the way in which VOC-emissions have to be reduced when gasoline is distributed from the gasoline station to the automobile. There are two solutions for vapour emission in this stage. Firstly, it is possible to install within the automobiles carbon canisters that absorb the vapours, the costs are born by the car producers. Secondly, it is possible to install vapour balance systems at the gasoline pumps' filling hoses (this solution is called Stage II), the costs are borne by the oil companies. The carbon canister versus Stage II controversy is an international one. The oil companies hold the view that the car producers must make room within their cars for the carbon canisters, whereas the car producers are of the opinion that a stage II facility is the best and cheapest solution. Both actors recognize the fact that it is essentially a financial discussion: no one wants to bear the investment costs.

In the HC 2000 strategy report, a decision on this issue has been consciously shifted to future and it is laid down that this decision will depend on international decision-making, although the environmental directorate is in favour of Stage II facilities. A report made in order of the HC 2000 organisation is in favour of Stage II but the conclusions are heavily disputed by the Oil Contact Committee. The differences concerning the financial costs of both solutions are striking. It is not possible to achieve consensus and the environmental directorate does not seem capable of forcing a decision against the opinion of the oil companies without outside help. This outside help came from the German government when it finally cut the knot and decided in favour of stage II in August 1991. As a result of this decision the inclusion of an implementation scheme for Stage II in the Dutch directive concerning environmental measures in gasoline stages became possible. This directive, however, is scheduled for 1993. Therefore, it is concluded that the time-table of the original HC 2000 report will not be met within the petroleum-network. The search for consensus is a time consuming-affair and, furthermore, when consensus fails to emerge, it leads to delay of decision-making.

The approach as has been followed in the HC 2000 strategy is successful with respect to sources of emission, if there is a consensus about the kind of solution or about the direction in which a solution has to be searched. In these cases, the discussions are especially directed at the conditions which have to be met before a measure can be taken or a new technique is applicable and at the question which time-path for implementation is possible. Under these circumstances a 'reasonable' discussion, directed at joint problem-solving, is possible. It is possible to find solutions which are mutually beneficial, and it can be expected that involvement in decision-making will lead to a commitment to the agreed objectives. However, when fundamental and especially financial differences of opinion exist, and strategic action is dominant, the consensus-oriented approach is much less successful. The structure of consultation within the HC 2000 project leaves enough room for the discussion of fundamental differences of opinion; the pro's and con's of different alternatives are presented, but the orientation on consensus prohibits an energetic cutting of knots when a consensus is not achieved. Furthermore, it cannot be expected that, even if the knots are cut, the actors which will lose, will be committed to the decision that is made.

Discussion

The analysis of the HC 2000 project so far has taught us that it is possible to formulate a strategy, based on cooperation between government and business, which is - at least in principle - in accordance with the 'public interest' as it is formulated by the environmental directorate. However, because of the formulated conditions and uncertainties, at this moment it cannot be determined whether the outcome of the strategy will not differ much from the targeted 50% reduction. The HC 2000 project supports the expectation that involvement of interested actors leads to a certain amount of commitment to the mutually agreed objectives that goes further than when decisions are made unilaterally. In the stage of the strategy formulation it was possible to create a situation in which joint problem-solving was dominant. Furthermore, the analysis suggests that the connection between mutual strategic discussions and an implementary project organisation forms an important instrument in the conversion of environmental responsibility into environmentally sound behaviour.

However, it should be clear that the created consensus is based on the formulated conditions and uncertainties. In the paint network, this formulation creates a basis for further consultation and action directed at the removal of these constraints. The interdependencies within the paint network seem to be better exploitable than in the petroleum network. In any case, the available technological possibilities are the most important deciding factor for the options for positive-sum solutions and the room for agreement and consensus. The HC 2000 project chiefly a business-central government affair. Local and regional public authorities have played a minor part and environmental organisations and were only consulted after an agreement within the original project group between government officials and business representatives had been reached. Apart from the societal acceptability and legitimacy which are questionable, the double role of the environmental directorate, both as the defender of the environmental interests and as the process controller limits environmental directorate's space of manoeuvre. An important condition on communicative governance has not been met. It is also for this reason that it is not possible to give a final evaluation of the options and constraints for this mode of governance. However, the analysis of the HC 2000 experiences suggests that communicative governance in-practice has to take into account:

1) *The importance of private interests*
    a) Negotiation as joint problem-solving is strongly dependent on the opportunities for finding solutions which can take into account the interests of the involved actors. There is no room for naive opinions about communicative governance. Companies' bottom-lines are at the least defined as the continuation of their existences. Therefore, it is necessary that the involved interests (both of industry and the environment) and the perceptions of these interests are adequately represented.
    b) The effectiveness of communicative governance will be increased if it is taken into account that economic and financial arguments necessarily play a dominant role when environmental measures are implemented in individual companies. That is why mutually agreed objectives on a macro or sectoral level have to be translatable into clearly formulated requirements for individual companies that are supported by incentives or the targeted companies.
    c) Furthermore, it is concluded that it is obvious that communicative governance is not suitable for environmental problem-solving when environmental and business interests are sharply contradictory: in these cases the search for consensus will only lead to delay of decision-making.
2) *The importance of interdependencies* between the interested actors is expressed in the mutual possibility of harming each other and

obstructing the objectives of others. This is most clear in situations in which interdependence is lacking. Paint producers and applicators are risking loss of markets or obligatory end-of-pipe measures when should they ignore the developments regarding low-solvent paints. Car producers and oil companies which do not give in, do not risk much. When the rewards for obstructing the decision-making process are substantial, the search for consensus will be time-consuming and will lead to delay of decision-making.

However, communicative governance can reckon with:

3) The phenomenon that exchange of information is leads to learning effects in terms of increasing knowledge about problems and solutions and about one's own and others interests, also when consensus is not achieved. Within the HC 2000 project, learning effects are clearly recognizable. The knowledge about the nature, the scale, and the seriousness of discussed environmental problems is growing and is spreading to more actors. The insights regarding solutions or environmental problems and with respect to involved interests is growing. This growing knowledge and insight can support the purposiveness and as a result the effectiveness of specific interventions.

4) Involvement in the decision-making process increases the support for the formulated strategy. Although the consent of trade and industry of the HC 2000 strategy is for mainly based on the formulated constraints, the preparedness for environmental action is increasing. However, because societal 'interested third parties' such as environmental organisations, only play a minimal part in the project analyzed, the prospects for a broader social support of HC 2000 have been ignored.

10

THE RISE OF THE PUBLIC PRIVATE PARTNERSHIP: A MODEL FOR THE MANAGEMENT OF PUBLIC-PRIVATE COOPERATION

VINCENT KOUWENHOVEN

Introduction

Public private partnership is a specific form of social-political governance, which has been at the centre of interest for some years. It has been the subject of many publications, both in European and American specialist literature, and symposiums on this subject draw large audiences. At the same time, this new form of cooperation is being examined and put into practice by actors within the public and the private sector.

The growing interest in cooperation between public and private actors is not a solitary case. For some years, there has been a re-appreciation of the roles played by the public sector (particularly public administration) and by the private sector (particularly the business community), partly under the influence of economic, social, political and cultural changes. In relation to this, there has been a change in the views on the relationship between public and private actors. Whereas in the seventies the relationship between public administration and the business community was characterized by a great degree of alienation and estrangement, there has been a reverse movement in the eighties. There seems to be a mutual re-appreciation of the roles played by public administration and by the business community, no longer dominated by emotions, but in which transactions are paramount. As a result, the question is raised more and more whether certain problems could not be dealt with more effectively and efficiently by public and private parties together rather than separately. Such forms of cooperation are often referred to by the term public private partnership (PPP).

The expression PPP gained popularity from the beginning of the eighties, initially within the context of a number of spectacular examples of new forms of cooperation in the field of urban renewal. Meanwhile, this type of cooperation is being applied in a multitude of different markets and areas of policy, including infrastructural projects (financing of roads and bridges); environmental projects (implementation of environmental policy plans, exploitation of waste-processing plants) and employment and education projects (jointly setting up and managing business centres).

As such, cooperation between public and private actors is not new. In many fields, different forms of cooperation between miscellaneous public and private actors emerged in the past, some of which still exist. However, public private partnership distinguishes itself from prior, more institutional forms of cooperation, by its more dynamic/ project nature and by the more businesslike distribution of inputs, risks and returns between the cooperating public and private parties, both directed towards synergy.

PPP distinguishes itself in a number of ways from other forms of sociopolitical governance, such as those discussed in this volume. Striking aspects are the businesslike, pragmatic line of approach and the apparent lack of ideological foundation of PPP, as compared to the communicative governance conception, for example, which is directed towards generating 'shared comprehension'.

Positioning PPP as a businesslike, pragmatic form of cooperation, I will focus in this chapter on the development of a model which can serve both as a descriptive frame and as a prescriptive model.

Defining PPP

In this study, the phenomenon of PPP is examined in terms of organizations as well as in terms of organizing. Attention is being paid to both structural and dynamic process aspects of PPP. The governance-and-network theory in particular offers several starting points. As a result of this approach, PPP as a research object is regarded as a form of joint governance by public-private networks.

However, a more detailed definition of the research object is necessary. There are several definitions of PPP, which are often linked to a specific theme or to a specific organizational connection. The latter condition, however, does not do justice to the process character of PPP. This leads to the distinction between PPP in a narrow sense and PPP in a broad sense. In the narrow sense, PPP refers to legally formalized forms of cooperation between public and private parties (joint-ventures), whereas the broad definition also includes less formalized consultative platforms.

Another distinction is the one between so-called 'policy PPP', which refers to policy development and planning, and 'administrative PPP', which is directed towards implementation and the potential financing of policies. Thus, PPP can be applied at several points in the policy cycle, with the objectives and results varying greatly for each phase.

In this study the term PPP is used if: *there is interaction between government and business, the focus in achieving convergent objectives is on synergy the objectives have both social and commercial characteristics, and the respective identities and responsibilities of the parties involved remain intact.*

In the definition used, the dichotomy between government and business does not do justice to the variety of potential actors. The essential point, however, is the synergetic effect they expect from their interaction: more effectiveness and/or efficiency than would be the case if they acted independently. A prerequisite to the convergence of objectives is that they should not be incompatible. Only if they are compatible, is it possible for private means to contribute to the solution of public problems, or for public means to be used to respond to commercial opportunities or threats. PPP also distinguishes itself from comparable organizations by the preservation of the respective identities of the parties involved.

On the basis of the above definition of PPP and the research approach explained, one can conclude that PPP is considered to be a specific governance interaction (cf. Kooiman, this volume). Governance interactions can be studied from various viewpoints, taking either an internal, an external or a mixed perspective. In this study, the latter has been chosen, in other words, the focus is on the whole of relations between organizations. This also demonstrates the importance of examining the interorganization theory, which will offer important starting points with respect to the issues in this study.

Motives for PPP

Within studies based on interorganizational theory, the common denominator is the interdependence motive, which constitutes the basis for cooperation (e.g. Levine and White, 1961; Pfeffer and Salancik, 1978). This interdependence is related to the turbulence and complexity of the environment in which organizations operate. An important addition is offered by Ackoff (1981), who holds that organizational effectiveness is to a large extent determined by the way in which organizations deal with interdependencies.

Although it is difficult to establish unambiguously whether organizational interdependence has increased in the 1980's, it is possible to establish that there has been an increasing recognition of the necessity to 'channel' or even to 'exploit' interdependence by means of cooperation (e.g. Miles and Snow, 1984; Jarillo, 1986).

It could be hypothesized that the rise of PPP in the mid eighties can be explained by the recent trend of growing recognition, by both government and the business community, of the need to channel or even to exploit mutual interdependencies by means of cooperation.

The analysis of scores of actual applications of PPP, such as those which came into being since the mid eighties, has identified two main motives for PPP.

First of all there are *financial-economic motives* for applying PPP. These concern the limited financial capacity of governments for investments, which is mainly related to setting standards for budgets at governmental and municipal level. In this light the prospects of private (co-)financing are of importance. Where the government faces a budget deficit, the private sector shows a financial surplus, especially in the case of the institutional investors. The private sector parties have different motives for meeting this need. They benefit themselves from removing social bottlenecks, or, in the case of institutional investors, there is a need for participation in remunerative investments. The desirability of participation in PPP applications seems to be determined in particular by the expected returns and the prospects of diversifying risks. Various publications also refer to motives of the private sector which result from the expectation of leverage and spin-off effects.

From the analysis of the financial-economic motives involved in PPP projects involving rather substantial investments, we may conclude that a certain degree of mutual interdependency is present.

Especially at the macro level, to which this analysis applies, the recognition by both government and the private sector of the necessity to channel or even to exploit interdependencies is evident.

Against the background of the government's budget deficit, PPP has often been dismissed as a fashionable phenomenon. After all, if government policy were successful in eliminating the budget deficit, the need to apply PPP would also disappear. There are indications, however, of more fundamental - and therefore possibly less fashionable - motives for applying PPP. This concerns the second type of motives identified.

An important indication of *managerial-strategic motives* on the side of the government is connected with the reorientation within government during the eighties. This reorientation is dominated by the drive to bring about a more efficient and effective (i.e. more businesslike) functioning of government.

By applying PPP, government can often use specific market know-how which is present in the private sector. The efficiency of certain projects can be influenced positively by greater cost awareness in the private sector, and by making agreements with private parties in the context of PPP, the effectiveness of policies can be enhanced. This implies arriving at acceptable and implementable policies by establishing them in direct interaction with the parties involved.

As far as managerial-strategic motives in the private sector are concerned, we can refer to the increasing importance which this sector attaches to maintaining adequate 'government relations'. This expresses the strategy of reacting less passively to the influence which the intervening and regulating role of government has on the functioning of businesses.

In some situations, businesses motivate participation in PPP by the differential advantages they expect in comparison with competition. These can be of a direct or indirect commercial nature. For example, the motivation to participate in PPP in order to create a better understanding and to gain improved insights in the way public administration operates, and hence to be able to anticipate policy decisions, seems to be of a less direct commercial importance.

On the basis of the above, the previously formulated hypothesis concerning the recent rise of PPP seems a plausible one. From the beginning of the eighties, a mutual re-appreciation of the roles played by government and business has coincided with economic recovery. Compelled by an external necessity (interdependencies), parties start to realize that their actions are increasingly intertwined and they start to grow towards each other (convergence in ordering principles).

The rise of PPP during the middle of the eighties is therefore explained by the perceived recent increase of the recognition by government and the private sector of the necessity to channel, or even exploit, mutual inter-dependencies by means of cooperation.

Towards a Model for the Management of PPP

Sometimes, public and private parties have diverging characteristics, qualities and interests. As a general rule, governments will pay special attention to the social pay-off of activities, whereas market parties will be interested primarily in the commercial return. Governments are generally committed to specific rules, such as the general principles of proper administration, whereas market parties follow the rules of the market. As a result, governments and businesses show partially diverging interests. By and large, governments have a less flexible, more hierarchical organization than market parties, although governments generally have more control mechanisms at their disposal.

Such contradictions highlight the relevance of identifying the conditions which are of importance to the emergence, existence and successful functioning of PPP. Specific models, indicating which conditions are of importance to the emergence of such networks and their effective administration, have not readily presented themselves and the contribution of existing interorganizational theory to the understanding of the actual functioning of networks is outright disappointing. Even when it comes to interorganizational studies focusing on the emergence and functioning of networks, they generally show important limitations. For instance, many of these studies refer to specific sectors, often non-profit ones, and to health care in particular. Also, the theory is generally based on one or a few case studies at the most, which limits the possibilities of generalization.

Consequently, in the study on which this contribution is based, an alternative, explorative research approach was opted for. Partial researches into specific aspects of PPP take a central position. During the past few years, a number of research reports have been published which pay attention to organizational, financial and political-administrative aspects of PPP.

By means of a secondary analysis of these aspects of PPP, a preliminary model was established, in which the so-called start and process conditions have been incorporated. Before this model is presented, several of these aspects will be discussed in brief.

The manifestations of PPP differ as much as their applications. They vary from very loose connections between government and businesses, as is the case with more or less non-committal consultation, to stronger connections, in which relations are laid down contractually, or in which even a joint corporate body is created. These different manifestations can even be encountered in one single application of PPP, which underlines the dynamic process character of PPP.

As far as the legal aspects are concerned, parties can choose from several forms of cooperation from public and private law. The public and private parties involved can also jointly decide the form of cooperation.

In respect of the *financial aspects* of PPP, the question of the distribution of costs, risks and returns is of particular importance. The literature studied shows that this distribution may be very unequal. It is of paramount importance that it is clear to the parties involved, both before and during the process, what each contributes individually, how risks will be diversified and in what way the expected returns will be distributed.

Where the *political-administrative aspects* of PPP are concerned, attention is paid to the issue of public legal responsibilities involved in governmental participation in a PPP. The most important considerations will be discussed first.

On the face of it, there seems to be a certain tension between government involvement in PPP and the responsibility concerning public interest. During the past few years, several publications have been devoted to indicating limiting conditions within which the government should operate when participating in PPP in order to guarantee that the democratic duties be observed. Special attention has been paid to the legality of government action with regard to PPP, as well as to the careful protection of the rights and interests of 'third parties'. The involvement of third parties may incur or prevent appeal procedures, which is an aspect to which the business community should pay attention.

Marginalia to the Model

On the basis of these aspect studies, complemented by more general literature dealing with cooperation processes, we have developed a preliminary model, which will be explained below. In line with the specific governance character of PPP, which was described in the second section and which is the central topic of this study, only those conditions have been identified which are of importance from the perspective of the joint governance by public-private parties.

The selection of the conditions to be included in the preliminary model is based on their relevance to all occurring applications of PPP within the context of the definition used in this study. These conditions must be considered as 'minimum-conditions' for the emergence, existence and successful functioning of PPP.

The model thus developed may be used as a framework for describing actual cases of PPP. It can perhaps also be used prescriptively. The application of the preliminary model to the analysis of actual cases (see next paragraph) intends primarily to test the descriptive value of the model. It is possible that, on the basis of this 'testing', the model will be adapted or expanded. The finalization of the model's status will only take place after analysis in the context of the case studies.

In itself, the determination of the prescriptive value of the model demands a different research approach, for which the two case studies analyzed are not adequate. The confrontation between model and practice, however, can be a stimulus for using the model in an explanatory and predictive way, albeit with the necessary guarantees.

The following conditions apply to the emergence of PPP, and are considered to be primary start conditions:

- Interdependence
- Convergence of objectives.

The increasing recognition of interdependence between governments and businesses has already been advanced as an explanation for the rise of PPP at the macro level and can also be considered to be an essential condition for the emergence of actual applications. Meeting this condition is essential, but not sufficient.

It has already been observed that the objectives of the different parties in a PPP need not be identical. The condition of convergence of objectives means that, in order to bring about cooperation, the partners' objectives should at least not be incompatible.

Recognizing interdependence and identifying convergence of objectives is facilitated if at least one of the following, so-called secondary start conditions (also referred to as 'linking mechanisms' (Waddock, 1986: 279) is met:

- Presence of a network
- Presence of a broker.

A network in which individuals of the various parties meet one another informally creates the opportunity for open communication channels and consultations situations. Sometimes the existence of this network will be impossible or inadequate. In such cases a broker, preferably an independent one, can act as an intermediary or 'facilitator'.

Process Conditions for PPP

For the successful functioning of PPP, the conditions mentioned below, which are considered to be process conditions, have to be met:

- Mutual trust;
- Unambiguity - and recording - of objectives and strategy;
- Unambiguity - and recording - of the division of costs, risks and returns;
- Unambiguity - and recording - of the division of responsibilities and authorities;

- Phasing of the project;
- Conflict regulation laid down beforehand;
- Legality;
- Protection of third parties' interests and rights;
- Adequate support and control facilities;
- Business and market oriented thinking and acting;
- 'Internal' coordination;
- Adequate project organization.

Trust is of importance for the entering into and functioning of cooperation relations. It brings about mutual respect and adaptation and constitutes the lubricating oil in complex cooperation relations such as PPP.

In view of the principally diverging interests of the respective parties, there may be ambiguity or disagreement as to the objectives - or as to the way they should be achieved. It is therefore strongly recommended to lay down such matters unambiguously. This also goes for the division of inputs, risks and returns, and for the division of responsibilities and authorities, both between and within the partners. A good coordination between the various levels of public administration involved in PPP is of particular importance.

As PPP is a process, it is subject to dynamics, for example with respect to participants, power structures and the rules of the game. The process condition of phasing aims to do justice to the required flexibility and continuity and creates good administrative possibilities.

In view of the diverging interests of the parties involved, continuity will be threatened by conflicts. It is therefore recommended to include a dispute regulation in a PPP-agreement and to define conditions for changing and, if necessary, terminating the relationship.

A PPP cannot be called successful if it is beyond the pale of the law, certainly from the government's perspective. This does not only refer to applying the law in the formal sense. Government, being the 'guardian of common interest', must also weigh the interests which it wants to serve by PPP against the interests of all people and organizations directly or indirectly influenced by PPP. Their means of defense should be guaranteed by, among other things, controllability.

From the private sector's point of view, government must take into account the conditions for commercial orientation. The government needs business know-how, in particular if the participation in a PPP is a risk-bearing one. The businesslike functioning of government requires a comparatively quick completion of procedures.

In a PPP, the involvement of government will cover the many relevant organizations and administrative levels. If these are not coordinated by internal coordination, successful functioning of a PPP will be hindered. The same goes, mutatis mutandis, for the private sector. A project organization forms the ideal linking mechanism which guards and controls the effectiveness and the efficiency of a PPP's functioning, regardless of its exact structure. It is desirable to appoint a project leader who is accepted and respected by both parties, preferably an independent one, and who has far-reaching authorities with regard to coordinating activities of importance to PPP.

This way, the process conditions, directed to a successful functioning of PPP, have been identified beforehand. Contrary to the start conditions, they are not sine qua nons, but they are often success factors which are critical to effective and efficient governance by means of PPP.

Application of the Model to Two Cases

CASE 'THE ENVIRONMENTAL ACTION PLAN RIJNMOND'[1]

In this section, the model outlined above will be applied in the analysis of the implementation of a so-called 'policy PPP', in this case the Environmental Action Plan Rijnmond (EAP-R). The Rijnmond area is one of the major industrial areas of the Netherlands, situated near the port of Rotterdam. In the seventies, the district was given the status of redevelopment area, because of its deplorable environmental quality, which was mainly the result of the high concentration of chemical plants. The EAP-R concerns the joint development of environmental action plans by government and the private sector, on the basis of objectives laid down in advance by the government. On the one hand it concerns the improvement of the air quality in the Rijnmond area (social objective), and - related to this - on the other it concerns the lifting of the status of redevelopment area (commercial objective). This status had very disadvantageous consequences for the businesses established, in terms of attracting investors, personnel, etc.. After a difficult start and with considerable delay in respect of the objectives, the parties agreed on a joint action plan which offered possibilities both for substantial improvement of the environmental quality in the district and for considerable improvement of the commercial settlement climate, with regard to the lifting of the status of redevelopment area.

Within the framework of the collective responsibility for the creation of the EAP-R, a contact group was formed with representatives from the authorities involved and from the private sector. The objectives of this contact committee were defined by the government and could be guarded by governmental committee members. The private sector, which could negotiate the objectives and the action plan based on it within the contact committee, was expected to initiate the formulation of adaptation measures. Synergetic effects were expected from the know-how of the businesses concerning the sources of pollution and the possibilities for adaptation within standards acceptable to industry.

---

[1] This concerns a limited summary of an extensive case study as explained in Kouwenhoven (1991).

The presence of the primary start conditions is evident. With regard to the secondary start conditions there was a network in which local government and businesses established in the district met. Rivalry between the two parties, however, was such that the existing network had a negative rather than a positive influence on the implementation of the PPP. Therefore, the presence of a broker, in this case the then Dutch minister of environmental affairs, a former McKinsey-man, was of even greater importance. The parties involved did not exactly show a 'natural inclination towards cooperation'. Only after the explicit recognition of interdependence and the important role played by the broker, was it possible to set the first step towards this 'policy PPP'.

Of the process conditions identified, the existing distrust, the ambiguity of objectives and responsibilities, and the initial lack of an adequate project organization in particular caused a considerable delay in the implementation of the project. In the course of the cooperation, however, all conditions included in the model were more or less met.

The observed effects on the degree of success of this PPP caused by the absence of various process conditions or their not being met completely offer an initial perspective on the possible prescriptive value of the model focused on in this contribution.

CASE 'DE N.V. ECONOMISCH HERSTEL ZEEDIJK'

This section centres around a so-called administrative PPP, the N.V. Economisch Herstel Zeedijk (NVEHZ), in the light of the start and process conditions identified in section four.

The NVEHZ is a public-private corporation, founded in 1985 with the aim to deal with the criminality which threatened to ruin the Zeedijk, one of Amsterdam's most famous streets. It concerns an application of PPP in the field of urban renewal, which can be described as a small-scale revitalization project.

At and around the Zeedijk there was a downward spiral, resulting from the interaction between increasing criminality (drugs trade!) and decreasing economic activity (retail shops). A public-private corporation was founded to break the vicious circle by a combination of efforts directed towards, on the one hand, economic revitalization and, on the other, an increase of the efforts directed towards maintaining civil order. The start condition of interdependence has evidently been met.

A number of private financiers, most of them banks, and the city of Amsterdam participated in the NVEHZ on a 50/50 basis. The private partners were primarily responsible for the economic revitalization, which also served to realize their commercial objectives. The primary task of the authorities was to restore civil order, which expresses their social task. By dealing with both objectives at the same time it was possible to create a broader basis and to diversify the substantial risks. This shows the presence of the second start condition, convergence of objectives.

A necessary but unforeseen increase in the pace with which parts of the projects had to be completed created the need for additional funds soon after the start of the process.

The private parties involved, however, refused to share the resulting greater risk, which subsequently had to be borne by the city government alone. Against the background of a less adequate realization of relevant process conditions, the adapted and unbalanced distribution of risks caused the existence of the NVEHZ to be the subject of much debate. A large number of the activities planned, however, have been completed. The maintenance of public order has been greatly improved and the economic revitalization is - slowly but surely - making progress. The return prospects are certainly positive.

The analysis of the process conditions with regard to the NVEHZ shows that an important factor for success or failure is clear agreements concerning objectives, inputs, risks etc. Inadequate agreements beforehand threatened the very existence of this PPP for a short while. We have observed, however, that all remaining conditions have been met and that new process conditions which might be of importance to the successful functioning of this form of public-private governance, have not emerged.

Conclusion: Determination of the Model for the Emergence and Functioning of PPP

The analysis of the cases, a brief summary of which has been included in the previous section, does not show a need for adaptation or expansion of the preliminary model.

Because the descriptive value of the preliminary model has been tested against two quite diverging variants of PPP, the plausibility of the model's usefulness with regard to a broad range of applications of PPP conceivable has grown.

It is clear that the weight of the various conditions may vary. Depending on the context within which actual applications of PPP take shape, some conditions may be called points for attention, whereas others are considered to be critical conditions for success.

The importance of the start and process conditions identified has been established, but the analysis of two cases provides insufficient evidence to conclude that the model can be used prescriptively. With regard to a prescriptive use of the model, it should also be stressed that selection of the conditions has taken place within the limited context of the governance-and-network approach.

This implies that the start conditions can be considered as sine qua nons with regard to the emergence of PPP, but that certain content-related conditions may stand in the way of a PPP coming into being. The same is true, mutatis mutandis, to an even greater extent for the process conditions. In the model, however, these content-related conditions are considered 'ceteris paribus' conditions.

Therefore, with regard to the prescriptive use of the model, the conditions included in the model should be considered as 'minimum conditions'.

Evaluation

This contribution aimed to demonstrate that there is a rise of new, specific forms of social-political governance, which are actually being applied to an increasing extent in a number of policy areas and markets.

It has been argued that fundamental dynamics lie at the basis of the rise of these forms of cooperation. It is related to the recent, fundamental shift in thinking about organizations in terms of networks of a private-private, a public-public, and a public-private nature, which coincides with the recognition of the need to channel, or even to exploit, the underlying interdependencies.

Against the background of the comparative unfamiliarity with such forms of cooperation, in particular those of a public-private nature, the explicit need for models of management of such processes comes forward. The start and process conditions identified in this contribution constitute a first step to that end.

Further research on more specific models of PPP is underway. With regard to the specific nature of studying public private networks, further research is desirable, as the model developed in this study does not only offer points for attention, but also raises various questions. Detailed case descriptions, in which among other things the underlying processes of PPP are described, can generate more insight into the emergence and successful functioning of future applications of public private partnership.

11

DYNAMICS AND ROOM FOR MANOEUVRE IN GOVERNANCE: THE CHANNEL TUNNEL DECISION IN FRANCE AND BRITAIN

MICHÈLE BREUILLARD

Introduction

As noted in many chapters of this book, the political and social crisis of the Welfare State became thoroughly evident in the last two decades and opened a new era for government studies: political research on the State and on public policies has enjoyed increasing interest and has been developed in comparative works. Indeed many more academics have widened their scopes beyond their home countries to trace similar phenomena with varying impacts and consequences, given the different political, cultural, social and economic contexts. Indeed comparative analysis has been imposed as one of the tools to be used for assessing the capacity of governing bodies and actors to respond to the citizens' needs and expectations.

Studying a decision-making process in terms of 'capacity' and 'responses' implies that we move from the static description of political and governmental functions or responsibilities, as laws and statutes enact them, to the dynamic analysis of mechanisms and processes at work which determine actions but also re-actions within socio-political systems. This capacity could be a mere synonym for 'governance' if only the Welfare State's crisis of the seventies had not entailed a crisis in the State and in politics too. In the late seventies, Bourricaud (1977) explained that governance depends on the adequacy between, on the one hand demands and expectations which are spread among competing groups and, on the other hand, rules for allocating resources and putting them into practice efficiently. Nowadays the very idea of any adequacy tends to be doubted and the previous question 'how are democracies governed?' has been rephrased as 'can democracies still be governed?'. Crozier (1975) contends that the modern state is becoming all the less powerful as the number of decisions it has to take increases: 'Decision-making does not only generate power but also vulnerability'. As a matter of fact, these thoughts raised new questions among politicians and decisions-makers following the new trends in political research: comparing different public policies does not only mean assessing the outcomes but mainly - and preferably - trying to understand and master the ways important decisions are to be addressed and tackled. Then it may be the political scientist's task to explain how and why some states which are so close to one another in geographic and historic terms, can produce so different solutions in response to problems they experienced in similar ways.

The Channel Tunnel project provides for such a comparative analysis in offering the opportunity for experiencing and assessing the progress of a bi-national scheme. The Eurotunnel scheme is the twenty-seventh and probably the final attempt to link Great Britain to continental Europe physically. As such it creates a new field for political research because it represents an unusual case-study as it is an international and private joint-venture with financial, technical and economic implications to be agreed on by two states with opposed ideologies, a sort of mythical symbol becoming a sophisticated piece of infrastructure to be operated in common.

It is common wisdom to say that one could not imagine a wider contrast between two neighbouring regions than that existing between Kent, 'the Garden of England' and Nord-Pas-de-Calais, 'le Plat pays'. Beyond socio-economic and political features, the contrasting images of the French and the English hinterlands of the tunnel are the results of several different divides: present ideologies at central and local government levels, traditional views on local government functions and responsibilities especially in the field of economic development planning, competition between rail and road traffics.Whatever the people's expectations and fears are, the Channel Tunnel could not be bored elsewhere; it could not be constructed between Calais and Newcastle for example, as a cartoon in a newspaper once designed it to symbolise the North-South divide on the subject in Britain. The fact is that the tunnel will not only shorten the travel-time between two regions and two countries; in the new context of the Common Market it generates new expectations in the existing relationships between the United Kingdom and 'Europe' as the British usually call the mainland as if they were not at all sure to be Europeans themselves!

When it is fully operational the tunnel will offer two types of services that make it impossible to consider it as just a new route across a gap in the continent. As it is designed for through-rail services from the main lines and also a shuttle-service for cars, coaches and lorries, it will operate a new means of land-transport with specific tasks. Its impacts then have far-reaching economic effects which are not limited to the tunnel-affected areas around the portals at Sangatte and Cheriton, or to their hinterlands, the city of Calais and the district of Shepway around the town of Folkestone. Both Kent and Nord-Pas-de-Calais are affected, not to mention Northern France and South England at large. The tunnel will not just connect existing road and rail networks from both sides. A whole range of new or improved roads, a High Speed Rail Link and up-graded railways lines, new railways stations, new industrial estates and business parks are under construction at the same time, or purposively planned... Local and regional economic development strategies are under way on both sides, which are not mere collections of factual, day-to-day decisions and can account for an example of a dynamic process of decision-making based on interactions between several types of different forces.

Dynamics as an Aspect of Governance

What the title of this chapter seeks to express is this multifold interaction-system between needs, or what are said to be needs, and responses, in the example of the tunnel between central and local governments in each country, between the public authorities and the private contractors. More-over, because of the bi-national dimension of the project we must take note of the relationships each central government and local authority has established with its counter-parts, across the border, on top of the usual model of top-down or bottom-up forces and regulations within each poli-tical system. Changing attitudes and thinking, as they are observed in the political and business worlds, cannot be ignored and neither can the innovations which are brought to the institutional and legal frameworks. To that extent, the concept of governance is understood here as a possible linkage between governing and governability as referring to the key-question mentioned at the beginning: 'can democracies be governed?' Hence governance can be assessed through an analysis of decision-making processes which takes into account every kind of interaction from inside and outside a given system. Relations between the different actors can be observed as parts of a complex machinery at work: from the interactions which have been first established within a process, new and unexpected interactions can take place in a kind of chain-reaction.

Then governance is more than the mere capacity to respond to ques-tions or needs. While both governance and capacity imply a real or alleged legitimacy to be thrust upon governing bodies, capacity only seeks for coherence in pre-determined fields and for intelligence of information-gathering. So capacity rather suggests a one-way process in a stable system where the 'enabled' actor rules - or governs - through adjusting his outcomes to what he understands the responses are from the various signals he is sent back. As Dunsire and Metcalfe explain (this volume), such traditional forms of governing regulations and central control are no longer adequate. More and more complex decisions have to be taken and citizens or their representatives claim more participation, especially in modern western democracies.

So governance refers to an inter-active system as opposed to the more fixed pattern of capacity. It suggests power to enforce an outcome but also to resist confrontation and conflicts aiming at enforcing feed-backs, between what can roughly be summed-up as two spheres: the sphere of the initiators who take actions and the sphere of those who are targeted by these actions or affected by their direct or indirect consequences, of who approve or disapprove, accept, refuse or modify the initiators' actions. Here the dynamic and complex aspect of governance with different interlocked, inter-dependent loops of interactions can be seen. In this paper we will show two main loops of interactions which show complexity and inter-dependence between the two central governments and the concessionaire Eurotunnel plus the constructors Trans Manche Link (T.M.L.) on the one hand and central government and local authorities on the other hand. The two loops are interlocked on the spot in the area of the working-sites, where the four types of actor meet 'physically'.

The aim of this chapter is to analyze how the construction and the operation of the tunnel contribute to dynamize both political and institutional mechanisms in Britain and France, as it can be analyzed from the Franco-British negotiations. Here the questions to ask are: why and how could the Channel Tunnel have been agreed upon and built in two areas where at first so many people were not really in favour of it? The symbolic aspect of any fixed link is stronger in Britain than in France. So the legitimacy of the project comes first under scrutiny: once they virtually agreed on the concept of a fixed link, both central governments wanted this project to be implemented quickly, efficiently and at lower costs in order to attract the private sector's finances. They could either impose their solution on the local authorities or embark on a kind of bargaining process to reach an acceptable and feasible solution. In fact, imposing one centrally-decided scheme would have surely proved the worst at a time when citizens and sub-national governments claim more participation and local democracy.

The Politics of the Channel Tunnel: a Franco-British Compromise

As mentioned in the previous section, the decision to build a tunnel across the Dover Straits may be controversial because the cost-benefit analysis does not demonstrate an unquestionable balance to its opponents' eyes. The ferry companies contended that they could have coped with the whole of the increasing Channel traffic at much lower costs, financially, economically and socially speaking. On the question of environmental damages, it must be stressed that in both countries the construction and operation sites are situated within conservation areas. The damaging effects of the Channel Tunnel may still increase to the size of what is seen by TGV opponents as an unbearable disaster when the Rail Link spreads 'destruction and nuisances' throughout Kent and Northern France along a five hundred kilometres-long corridor.

So finally the two Governments' decision could only be based on a political will asserted on financial and technical feasibility much more than on purely socio-economic benefits. This feasibility had already been lengthily assessed at French, British and European levels, before and after the 1975 cancellation of the previous scheme. It was kept alive even after 1975 by British Rail (BR) and Société Nationale des Chemins de fer Français (SNCF) who published a much smaller scheme in 1979, a one-single track train-tunnel nicknamed the 'mouse-hole' to be used alternately from France and Britain. This was not considered with much interest by the two governments or by businessmen. The French were disillusioned and suspicious of any British initiative to reach any achievement, because they had been disappointed so many times and on the last time at their own costs. As for the newly elected Tory Government, it was not ready to let the public sector have such an expensive go.

After the London summit in September 1981 mutual consultation was resumed with the establishment of a Franco-British Inter-Governmental Commission co-chaired by a senior civil servant of the British Department of Transport, and a Conseiller d'Etat, as special adviser to the French Minister. Being involved in the Falklands war in 1982-83, the British Government only made it clear that the project should be left to the private-sector for the financing, construction and operation, or nothing could be agreed on. The economic 'positive' or 'negative disasters', as Hall (1980) classifies them, which were all public-sector initiated and conducted, reinforced the Thatcherite Tories' belief in the private industry's efficiency and effectiveness.

These ultra-liberal stands were not to meet the view of the socialist and communist coalition Government in France. But what only mattered there was the British acceptance of a fixed-link and more of a train-tunnel. BR and SNCF were not invited to participate in the delineating of the Invitation to Promoters which officially opened the competition between projects from 2 April till 31 October 1985. However, they both managed to ponder on the final choice to make it meet their own interests. For once the mother-land of railways, Britain, had given up expanding and modern-izing its network from the moment Parliament had imposed a 7% to 8% annual return on each railway investment to be approved. These restrictive conditions are opposed to SNCF's three decades of subsidized plans for faster trains, able to compete with motorways and domestic air-lines.

Here we reach an important point of systemic differences between the French and the English views on transport in general and on the tunnel in particular. For the English, BR only offers a transport service and a train-tunnel is just one of the many ways to cross the Channel. In France, transportation is not an isolated service to run. It is part of the overall policy of 'aménagement du territoire' which dates back to the post-war Reconstruction period and cannot be satisfyingly translated into 'country-planning' because it also encompasses national and regional economic development planning as well as transport policy. Hence SNCF, a nationalised enterprise, is closely associated with it both at national and regional levels. Railways, motorways, airports or harbours are developed not just to meet transportation needs but also to help communications and exchanges within France and between the country and its foreign partners, in order to boost national, regional and local economies.

This conception also explains why the TGV is of such great importance to regional and local authorities in Nord-Pas-de-Calais: the Regional Council, the Communauté Urbaine de Lille and the city itself will pay for the 830 million francs extra-works that SNCF needs to make TGV-Nord trains stop at a new station in the centre of the city instead of outside, as first decided. This also explains why some inhabitants and politicians from Picardie battled to have the same trains running through their region while in many Kent districts their counter-parts demonstrated forcefully that they did not want to have it!

The liaison between the Channel Tunnel and rail transport, especially in the case of TGV scheme, is obvious to the French point of view: the tunnel is the missing link in the European network, especially between the main cities in the North-West. The TGV-route to England has been on the French government's mind ever since the seventies and accounted for one of the reasons for the Wilson Government to withdraw in 1975. In England the Channel Tunnel Act (schedule 42) only mentions 'any' international rail link in order to refuse any public funding for its construction as well as for that of the Tunnel.

In such a context of political and ideological division, the tunnel appears a mutual compromise. The analysis of the tunnel policy will show that in Britain the plan does not depart from the general transport policy which is based on the consumer's choice and on free market through competition and innovation. If the Channel Tunnel is asserted not simply to compete with the ferries and the airplanes but also to have an important impact on the national economy, it may well be because of its far-reaching consequences, even at the expense of the affected areas. Paradoxically this Government's ideological view is not to be met by Kent local authorities in the long run whatever the identical political majority they may have. We will then show a limited coherence in central-local relations.

In France, the Socialist majority which existed at both central and local government levels until the local elections of 1992, is not the only reason for the coherent economic strategy between the centre and the periphery. The swing to the Right after the 1986 general election did not make the Chirac government modify its predecessor's decision. The same swing in the two March 1992 local elections swept out the forty-five year old Socialist majority at Département du Nord council (Conseil général) and made the Regional Council hung for the first time in twenty years. It remains to be seen how the new alliance between Socialist and Green regional councillors is to modify the project.

But before the chapter moves to this aspect of central-local relationships in both countries, we must analyze the institutional and ideological environment of the Channel Tunnel.

The Channel Tunnel's Political Environment: Institutional Traditions and Ideological Dynamics

In order to clarify the analysis of the strategies which are developed in both countries we separate the different stages in the construction of the Tunnel from the different territorial impacts of the Tunnel-related developments.

The three stages in construction are:

1) decision-making on building a fixed-link and choosing the Eurotunnel scheme for the concession;
2) discussion on local integration of the construction site;
3) discussion on local, regional and national integration of the tunnel as a new means of transportation.

In France, negotiations and consultations on stage 3 can be said to be parts of those on stage 1 and took place before those on stage 2.

In Britain the decision-making process chronologically followed the three stages as listed because transport and economic development policies are treated separately. Furthermore, far-reaching regional and national impacts were considered more important than impacts in Kent because the Government's first idea was that if the Tunnel was to benefit the national economy its impacts should reach the London metropolitan area and beyond, the Northern regions, rather than the affluent South-East. So the county of Kent just had to 'suffer' locally. Since that time the Kent County Council's position has been 'to minimize the inconveniences and to maximize the benefits'.

The two different territorial scopes of the Tunnel related developments are:

1) the area around the portals which surrounds the building-sites, that is the city of Calais and its outskirts; the districts of Dover and Shepway (Folkestone) and that of Ashford where the International Passenger Station is to be located;
2) the area affected by the implications of the Channel Tunnel for the economy, land-use, transport infrastructures and the environment: Région Nord-Pas-de-Calais and Kent County as front-liners, the whole Northern France down to Paris; central and northern Britain to a much bigger extent than the South-East region.

The functional divisions between central and local governments' responsibilities are more clearly delineated in Britain than in France, though it is obvious that in both countries the decision to build a tunnel had to be taken at the highest level of state because it resulted in an international agreement. Since the 1975 cancellation, the institutional context of the Channel Tunnel has radically changed in both countries.

In England the 1972 reform of local government only came into force in April 1974. So no time was allowed for the new local government system to work in the seventies' venture which was to be public sector-led. The main points of the reform which affect the tunnel are that more homogeneous local authorities have been facing the 1986 private concessionaires with more clearly allocated responsibilities: the county council deals with road improvement and construction, country planning with its economic development strategic aspect, as developed by Kent County Council to respond to economic decline in traditional heavy industries areas and then to the challenge of 1993; the districts are responsible for local and urban planning and community services. However, the 1987 Channel Tunnel Act allocates a special 'Scheme of Operation' to the tunnel project which deprives the local authorities of their control over planning permission. Influenced by the example of the County's activity, most of the affected districts have set up an economic department within their own services. However, the scope for economic development in terms of liaised land planning with urban and social economic policy is neither specified nor really allocated to either council.

The old parishes have lost much of their legal importance in the present system but in Kent they show an extreme vigour on the social and political scene maybe because of the rural and traditionalist nature of the area. Kent Association of Parish Councils was one of the most active petitioners in the Parliament Select Committee hearings during the passage of the Channel Tunnel bill. It was quite successful in its part as a conservationist lobby for the protection of the tunnel-mouth area. It is still in the lead as the instigator of Kent Action Group, a very active campaigner opposed to the Channel Rail Link. So in England the leading part has been played by central government for the initial decision then Kent County Council decided to take the lead in the response to the economic and social challenge of the Tunnel, entailing positive action from some affected district councils. However, under the pressure of local officers and Kent Members of Parliament, Whitehall Departments finally had to show a stronger interest in the local development policy than expected.

Coincidentally in France the birth of the Regional Council took place in 1972 too and in operation in 1973. But it was not given a general responsibility but only some limited functions in financing social and economic investments. It was in the situation of a corporation board ('établissement public') and not of a local authority ('collectivité territoriale') like communes and 'départements'. These two reasons explain why it had a rather little say in the 1975 project. It remains noticeable that in both Nord-Pas-de-Calais and Kent the similarity between the two projects as much as the stability of staff, among the most active councillors and officers at the most important periods of negotiations, surely helped the involved authorities to respond quickly and efficiently when asked by central government or by the concessionaire. Since the decentralising 'revolution' of 1982 the new 'collectivités territoriales', the now fully responsible Regions together with 'Départements' and 'Communes', have gained executive powers and have been freed from the State's 'tutelle'.

So besides central government in its multiple forms of departments, inter-departmental committees and field agencies at local, regional, and intermediate levels, three levels of local authorities are concerned: the Nord-Pas-de-Calais regional council for training, secondary school building and maintenance, transport and economic development; the 'Conseil général' at the 'département' level of Pas-de-Calais for community and social services, primary schools, communes for urban planning. Some of these have several tens of thousands of inhabitants like Calais and

Boulogne. Some closer to the portal are very small with a population of a few hundreds. All these communes are in charge of the same responsibilities. One must not forget the intercommunal level, the special feature of French local life which is not compulsory but very active in the area.

The Channel Tunnel Policy: Political Coherence in Britain and Economic Coherence in France

The difference between the two central governments' commitment to local participation at the early stage of the Franco-British negotiations can be drawn from their consultation with the affected local authorities.

In France, the political coherence between Matignon and the Left-wing regional majority is obvious in 1981 after the presidential and general elections. The leader of the Regional Council, Pierre Mauroy, became Prime Minister, and then the minister for Harbours and Fisheries ('Affaires maritimes') was elected as mayor of Boulogne, in the local elections of 1983. Some other members of the Government were local M.P. and/ or councillors. Calais City Council had turned 'red' with a Communist mayor since the seventies. Though this is not sufficient to ensure a similar view on the question of a fixed link from the beginning of the revival of the project. If the Government's idea was that Channel Tunnel is good for France it was because it reinforced the French central position inside the growing network of exchanges and communications within the European Community and because it also helped to sell TGV technology abroad, in Belgium and in The Netherlands, in Spain and hopefully in Britain. The project had been postponed in 1975.

But by the time the Government started to negotiate with its British counter-part, the prospect seemed much gloomier to Regional and local councillors. The tunnel scheme was relaunched at a time when the economic crisis was quickly deepening: traditional industrial activities, iron, steel, textile and coal-mining were collapsing. A fixed link was to add a final blow to the breakdown if only because it would result in thousands of direct and indirect redundancies if the ferry-companies can not stand the competition. After consultancy and discussion the Nord-Pas-de-Calais regional council decided it could be, on the contrary, a boost to local and regional development, but on two conditions:

- it was to be a train-tunnel, as this would be the least damaging to the Ferry companies,
- central government agreed on implementing a long-awaited list of public investments in road, harbour and rail improvement.

Ironically but logically too, this list duplicates the list of investments that were designed and proposed by central government in the aftermath of the 1973 tunnel project. For the Region and especially the coastal area, which is one of the most economically depressed areas, the benefit could come from the construction itself thanks to thousands of direct and indirect jobs to be created, and secondly from the operation of the Tunnel because of the related facilities in road and railways to be implemented. Here we can argue that when local politicians as well as the Chambers of Commerce in Calais and Boulogne first made such an out-cry and then so easily calmed down, although the 1986 project is quite similar to the 1973 one, we can imagine the protest was essentially tactical in order to get the highest compensation possible for a fixed-link that was bound to happen anyway. Maybe in this stance the political coherence worked effectively between the Communist Transport Minister and the Communist Mayor of Calais.

At this stage it is more correct to use the phrase 'fixed link' because the consultation started in 1982 with the local actors, that is at the very beginning of the process. The French minister's special advisor was sent to collect the local actors' points of view 'on the spot' under the official mandate of the Mission Transmanche. In parallel, an 'Association Transmanche' was set up to gather all kinds of economic and political elites to lobby for the construction of a fixed link. It is difficult to say whether it was a bottom-up or top-down initiative as it was an idea of the then Prime Minister, Pierre Mauroy, mayor and M.P. for Lille, the regional capital-city. After he left the Government in 1984 Mauroy had the same kind of initiative to voice the local will to have the TGV trains stop in the centre of the city and to create a new business and trade centre, 'Euralille' around a new T.G.V. station.

These proposals from the Nord-Pas-de-Calais Regional Council have been gathered since 1982 by the Transport Committee Chairman within the Regional Council, Alain Percheron who is also the first Deputy-Leader of the Pas-de-Calais (sub-regional) council; he is also a senator and a very influential member of the Socialist party. Like Mauroy and many French front-benchers, he is a good example of the French system of 'cumul des mandats' resulting in some complexity in local-central government relationships. The Percheron report was unanimously approved by the councillors and later on it largely inspired the regional strategic plan 'Plan Transmanche' which was officially submitted by the leader of the Region to President Mitterrand in Lille on the 20th of January 1986. The regional plan was turned into a four-year (1986-89) contract (Contrat de Plan) signed by central government and the local authorities. A second 'Contrat de Plan' was agreed for the following period 1990-93.

Why is it that, like the free express highway running from the Belgium boarder to Boulogne and called 'la Rocade littorale', the up-grading and expansion of Calais, Boulogne and Dunkerque harbours, the new 'Rocade Est' expressway connecting Calais harbour to the Rocade Littorale, all these new facilities were not built earlier, in the seventies, though the growing Channel traffic has demanded good connections to and from the hinterland for two decades? The answer only refers to political will at the highest level of the state. The British case is no exception to that, as we will see now.

In Britain, opposition to the construction of any kind of a fixed link was more serious and the Government decided to overcome it in a completely different way. Since a fixed link could be constructed to the benefit of the whole nation and with the efficient management of a private-sector project, the only way to ensure the completion was to act swiftly and at central level as much as possible. Initially most discussion passed through, or was supported by the Department of Transport. As opposed to the French planning process which mainly rested in the hands of central government and S.N.C.F., in England the decision had to be debated in Parliament because only an unopposed bill can gain authority for the construction and the operation of a bridge, an airport or a railway line. Many MP's, including Labour MP's, insisted it should be submitted to public inquiry under the ordinary rules of town and country planning as it should be the case for the Channel Rail Link (Private member) bill which has awaited deposition since 1989. It could not have been so because this procedure would have given the opponents too many opportunities to delay the construction if not to impede it completely and the link would lose its attraction for the private sector. This is exactly what happened to the Rail Link so far: Eurorail Ltd, a consortium which had been appointed as B.R.'s private sector partner on november 3rd 1989, finally gave up in May 1990 when the cost began to peak under Kent demonstrators' pressure for environmental protection.

The Hybrid bill procedure that was used instead allows consultation in Parliament to be opened for affected authorities and for people or groups having a personal interest in the subject, under the limitation of the 'locus standi' condition.

So, very different forms of elite negotiations were conducted in both countries and they accounted for a victory of corporatism rather than of democracy. In Britain the focus of the debate was on planning consent and control; the mechanism of elite negotiation was lengthy and often very public. In France the focus of the debate was on economic benefit; the mechanism of elite negotiation was an essentially very 'private' - that is limited - public inquiry procedure (Holliday et al., 1991). In both cases of the tunnel and the TGV, the prefect, in the name of central government, opened the public inquiry with the restrictive 'procédure d'urgence' within the usual 'Déclaration d'Utilité Publique' procedure which is very unpopular among conservationists in particular. To them, the procedure still needs to be more widely opened to detailed negotiation though it has been improved in the aftermath of the decentralisation 'revolution' by the Act of 1983.

The Channel Tunnel Dynamics: the Future of Governance in Nord-Pas de Calais and in Kent

In France, negotiations between local and central governments lasted four years from the moment the project was relaunched. They are still going on in Britain because the International Passenger Station in Asford, where all the international trains to and from the continent will stop, is not yet designed. The completion of regional and local development responses will have lasted as long as that of the tunnel at the very least. As far as political science is concerned, the tunnel is already in action by feeding the general debate on decentralisation and local or self-government. Being squeezed between the State and market forces the local authorities who are legally responsible for country planning do not play the same part any more. Moreover in France, the decentralized responsibilities in regional development and urban planning are not fully exercised by either the communes or the regions and the decentralisation-process still seems to be unfinished.

According to Ashford (1989), centralisation and decentralisation are not definite states of being but only tendencies in political systems which can vary in time and subjects. The Channel Tunnel really speaks for this view: France began with a decentralised way of thinking long before the passing of the 1982 Act. England can be said to experience centralism, although the Government does need its message to be enforced through local policies. However, the room for manoeuvring which is left with local actors is as wide - or as narrow - as Central government wants it to be. Local authorities still need to meet central government's view in order to get what they think is right for them. Their room for manoeuvring is even more restricted in terms of economic development planning since this is considered as 'high policy' with national consequences too important to be left in the hands of the 'locals'. So a kind of spontaneous and unchallenged distribution of the parts has been tacitly approved by all the actors of the Channel Tunnel drama. In short we can say that the main feature of the decentralised context of the 1986 project is not so much the legal allocation of responsibilities in policy-making as the boost to local councillors', officers' and economic actors' will and energy. The local authorities were allowed to have a greater say and could be more active in offering proposals and criticisms in response to the state's policy making. In France, common knowledge as well as political commentators insist on the fact that decentralisation is rather an attitude, a state of mind than a share of functions and powers between a still overwhelming centre and still weak and scattered peripheries.

This is consistent with the legal principles of individual liberties, inherited from the Revolution and the Declaration of Human Rights which underlie every aspect of the French law, whether it applies to the public or to the private sector: what is not forbidden by the law is allowed to be done. This is totally contradictory to the British rule of 'ultra vires' which restrains or at least does not encourage public bodies to take initiatives.

The point is all the more important in the case of the local authorities whose responsibilities in both countries are only devolved from the Parliament's sovereignty.

On top of the local authorities' institutional weaknesses, which are obvious in the light of the tunnel experience, we can account for their different degrees of capacity to adapt themselves to the context imposed on them. The incoherence in national and local development policies is a supplementary obstacle for the Kent County Council whatever its dynamism is. Surprisingly enough, the political coherence with Downing Street ideology did not prevent the Kent County Council from playing a much more important - close to interventionist? - part on the economic scene than was expected (Breuillard, 1991). In France the economic coherence in terms of a strategic policy implemented similarly and simultaneously at all levels has been achieved at the local authorities' costs through the contracted agreements ('Contrats de Plan') which make these latter contribute to what were previously central government's exclusive expenses (Breuillard, 1992). The main difference between France and United Kingdom is that the French periphery has guaranteed access to the centre of state power, legally and politically, through the system of 'cumul des mandats'. In Britain the periphery is deemed to remain around it, not in it, and usually likes it that way. Only on very rare occasions, when common difficulties which cannot be agreed upon need to be tackled by different local authorities, the partisan link between local councillors and M.P, or between local M.P. and Whitehall can be used to that purpose by unconventional politicians for unexpected actions (Pickvance, 1990).

In France and later in Britain the two main levels that are responsible for economic development, the Region and the County, decided to create new forums for discussions and co-ordinations which set up a new dynamics within local services from both sides: promote and develop tourism in both areas, co-operate in regional policy (transport, training, protection of the environment, economic development and tourism) and promote the Transmanche Region before the Community Regional Policy programme. This kind of dynamics was speeded up in view of the coming physical link between the North-Western European regions. The prospect of a Euroregion bringing together Kent, Flanders, Wallonnia, Brussels-city region and Nord-Pas-de Calais, has cleared up since a European Charter was signed in Lille on the 21 June 1991. It can account for the ultimate manifesto of converging wishes to gather local and regional forces and to feel stronger as a European region rather than to feel as a region in the position of a sub-national level. This applies very much to the case of the French frustrated 'collectivités territoriales' in their relationships with central government, as it does to the isolated British local authorities vis-à-vis the European Commission.

12

GOVERNANCE BETWEEN LEGITIMACY AND EFFICIENCY: CITIZEN PARTICIPATION IN THE BELGIAN FIRE SERVICES

GEERT BOUCKAERT

Introduction

Public services at different levels and in several countries have important problems in common. Mayntz (this volume) refers to problems of ungovernability, crises of welfare, and failures in controlling developments of society. These problems become visible in the fields of management (decreasing efficiency and effectiveness), finance (budget deficits), and democracy (legitimacy deficit).

There is the myth, or the conviction, or the intuition that government is doing a bad job from an efficiency point of view. Some people find the proof in the presence of deficits. Since the problem is perceived as structural, the solution should be structural too. This pattern of thinking continues saying that there are problems of public sector efficiency and financial gaps because the public sector (locus) is public and not private (focus) (Metcalfe, this volume). There is a public-private distinction on the system level and on the actor level (Eliassen and Kooiman, 1987). Market mechanisms are not applicable and budget allocation mechanisms have serious inconveniences.

In such a case there are two major traditional solutions. First, public management has to improve and private management techniques should be applied to the public sector. Second, significant activities should be shifted towards the private sector. Positions in between combine these with, e.g. contracting out. Privatisation and improved management should then cause less deficits and more efficiency because these are supposed to be features of the private sector.

Another problem of some governments and administrations is the widening gap between 'governors' and 'governed', between 'administrators' and 'administrated'. Following the law of increasing entropy, governmental and administrative systems become more and more complex (Dunsire, this volume). Their structures and procedures create red tape, but also cause a distance between the rulers and the ruled. This is a problem of legitimacy in the public sector.

This was partly solved by a traditional answer: decreasing the level of complexity of society in general and of the public sector in particular. Deregulation not only had a positive potential for flexibility and thus for efficiency. It also intended to narrow some disparities of excess bureaucracy. This may have caused an improved legitimacy of services and agencies.

A major question is to what extent these governing problems of efficiency, effectiveness, deficits and legitimacy are solved by shifting to the private sector and its management philosophy.

This traditional point of view, looking at the balance between government and society, appears not to fully match a dynamic, complex and varied reality. Therefore a shift in focus towards sharing responsibilities, rather than 'doing it alone', is necessary. A focus on governing and its interactional aspects of 'co-'arrangements between public and private sector, rather than a one dimensional analysis of the *sui generis* sectors, might be beneficial (Kooiman, this volume). Paying attention to a better match between governing needs and governing capabilities might be necessary. But what does it mean to move to a better system of governance. Kooiman defines this in terms of efficient, effective and legitimate adjustments of governing needs to capacities and governing capabilities to needs.

Efficiency is the relationship of input and output. Effectiveness is the relationship of output and effects (Bouckaert, 1990; Bouckaert, 1992). Legitimacy is the degree of acceptance of an authority by those who have to accept this authority.

Governance would be at best in society when there is an effective production and delivery of goods and services in an efficient way and in legitimate conditions taking into account the degree of dynamics, complexity, diversity and risk.

This chapter is about the participation of citizens and the new resulting interactions in the fire service in order to cope with increasing levels of variety, complexity, dynamics and risk. This beneficial interaction between different actors in society may result in a solution for certain problems of governance.

Government, Private Sector and Citizens in the Fire Service

Prometheus, the Titan who was chained and tortured by Zeus for having stolen fire from heaven which he gave to man probably didn't realize the consequences of this act of hubris for mankind.

In a first stage, mankind could not control fire and was governed by hazard. In a second stage fire was under control and could be used as part of civilisation. Changes in environment caused adapted patterns of behaviour to cope with fire. The more varied, complex, dynamic, and riskful a society is, the more sophisticated the governance system of fire has to be. In recent years, the needs and necessities to cope with this change required adapted and improved levels of capacity and governance for the fire function in society.

Different languages use different words to indicate whether a fire is wanted or not wanted. Apparently, this is not really the case in the English language.

The word 'Fire' as the phenomenon of combustion manifested in light, flame and heat existed before the 12th century (dates refer to the earliest recorded use in English according to Webster's Dictionary). The closest word referring to a wanted and controlled fire probably is 'furnace' (13th century) as an enclosed structure in which heat is produced as for heating a house or for reducing ore. If society is characterised by a situation where no fire control is possible, governance is an undifferentiated nature controlled macro equilibrium. From the moment fire control is available, the situation becomes more varied. There are four possibilities in society: wanted fire, unwanted fire, and a wanted or unwanted fireless situation. The societal complexity, dynamics, variety and risk increases. Control mechanisms have to be developed to adapt capacities to needs: prevention and fighting. The control of the fire became extremely important. The 'fireman' (14th c.) originally was a stoker, someone who tends or feeds fire. Only afterwards he became a fire fighter.

Language	Unwanted	Wanted
Dutch	brand	vuur
French	incendie	feu
German	Brand, Feuer	Feuer
English	fire	fire

Table 1   The concept of fire in some European languages

The second stage, where man fully controls fire, resulted in 'fire works' (1575) as a device for producing a striking display by the combustion of explosive or flammable compositions, sometimes handled with music. Controlling fire changed into mastering fire. The purpose then becomes to prevent fire caused disorder. But a fireless society, with a risk equal to zero, is impossible. The governing exercise consists of realising a fire reduced and controlled society where the risk, as the damage to people and goods is kept on a minimal and acceptable level. The growth of cities in Western Europe increased the level of interaction and therefore of society's diversity, dynamics, complexity and risks. Serious city fires occurred. In 1326, 2.000 houses were destroyed in Brussels. In 1405 another fire destroyed 2.400 houses, a church, and 1.400 weaving looms resulting in 15.000 homeless. 'Conflagration' as a large disastrous fire emerged and was recorded in 1656 in the English language. Even the New World was not free of destructive fire. In 1679, 155 houses burnt in Boston. This was the immediate cause for the founding of its fire 'service' in 1715. Prevention became important too. These fire departments slowly shifted from armed to unarmed. Their goals changed from external security to internal security in peace time mostly related to the protection of civilians in war time. Predominant actors were the (para)military and organised city-volunteers.

In a third stage, the increase of the importance of cities, the changes in the structure of the buildings (skyscrapers), the existence of chemical and other industries resulted in a further increase of diversity, complexity, dynamics and risk of fire in society. This affected the governing problem. New mechanisms had to be developed to create a capacity which allowed to cope with this.

An interaction of public sector, private sector and citizens emerged.

There is a traditional collaboration or partnership model between the public and the private sector. To facilitate production and delivery of goods and services by the public sector, and to solve certain problems of efficiency and budget deficits, there is a well developed relationship between the public and the private sector. A two-dimensional interaction is created between a private and public sector.

Next to private/private and private/public partnerships the private sector also developed private/consumer or private/citizen partnerships. There is a trend to get the consumer involved in the production or the distribution process of the private sector. The best example in the distribution process are the 'self-services'. There is a shift towards the consumer as an active participant in the distribution process by serving him/herself in the bank, the restaurant, the gas station, etc. A subtle combination of consumer motivation and automation caused an immediate involvement of one party in the distribution process. This may go beyond distribution and include some parts of the production. This applies to the private profit sector. This applies even more to the private not-for-profit sector. Private not-for-profit organizations sometimes rely heavily on volunteers. This is the case for churches, health institutions, cultural organizations, and environmental and civil rights movements.

The private sector, profit as well as not-for-profit, considers the interaction as beneficial. Another two-dimensional interaction is created between the private sector and the citizen/consumers.

If the private sector, profit as well as not-for-profit, develops the idea of collaboration or partnership between their organizations and their present or potential clients, why shouldn't government also take this position and develop it as a policy of governing?

The position taken in this chapter and formulated as a general hypothesis in this section is that interaction as a participation of citizens in public services is beneficial to government and to the citizens. More explicitly: the interaction and participation of citizens in public services improves the efficiency, the effectiveness and the legitimacy of the public services.

A general picture of the different actors interacting in the governing model is represented in graph 1:

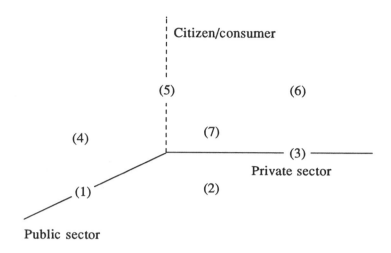

Graph 1   Public/Private/Citizen partnership

A three-dimensional space is created with three interacting axes: the private sector, the public sector and the citizen/consumers.

Seven major different positions are possible in this three dimensional space of potential interaction and partnership. These positions will be illustrated with the fire-service example.

1) A one hundred percent public service is performing the guidance, the control and the evaluation completely autonomous and independent from private sector and citizens. A fully professional fire service is an example of this.
2) There is an interaction between public and private sector. This interaction may have different degrees of intensity varying from 99% public and 1% private to 1% public and 99% private. There may be elements of contracting out (e.g. cleaning, car maintenance) and division of tasks (public prevention and private extinguishing). There may be a limited position of government just controlling contract execution and setting fire regulations and leaving the execution to a private organization.
3) There may be a one hundred percent private sector involvement with no interaction with citizens or public sector. This would mean that the fire service is an entire private matter with no government involvement in regulations, prevention or extinguishment.
4) There is an interaction between government and citizens. There may be a mix of professional civil servants and citizens. The fire service may consist of professional fire men and volunteers.

5) The service is a one hundred percent citizen matter. There are no government nor private sector organizations involved in development, production and distribution of the service. In the field of fire protection there may be just an independent neighbourhood watch that acts when fire alert is given.
6) This is a combination of a private profit or not-for-profit organization with volunteers. Fire services may be private mixed services where professionals and citizens are active.
7) The last possibility combines all three dimensions: public, private and citizens. It may be the same as the public/private interaction but with the addition of volunteers.

The challenge of governing will be to find an optimal mix between these three interacting dimensions and to make this work. This optimality may change in time and according to the situation. For each activity some positions may be more desirable than others. For some activities different combinations may be desirable and present at the same time. Interactions have to match a dynamic, complex, diverse and riskful fire reality.

Fire services probably can be organized according to all these possibilities. But the choice will be determined by contingency. Combinations are possible. In most European countries there are professional, mixed and volunteer public fire services. There are private fire services too, for private industrial purposes or for public purposes like in Denmark.

But even this interaction becomes traditional and is not fully matching present needs and capacities. Diversity, complexity, dynamics, and risk increase exponentially. High risk industrial plants have a considerable chance to damage society. The chance that something occurs multiplied with the seriousness of the event results in high risk sites. Time (speed), professionalism (know-how, attitude), complementarity of reactions , and differentiated levels of interaction (first level, second level intervention) become important for damage reduction. This results in new patterns of governing.

The three dimensional graph therefore has to be expanded and improved. More differentiated designs of fire services may match more variety, and fulfil more objectives. New types of volunteers appear: important buildings have their own responsibles with sometimes their own drills. New types of private sector involvement emerge. Industries have their own corporate fire service for a first level intervention and with a know-how which corresponds to the specific requirements of the industry. This results in new types of co-production. Traditional vectors (public sector, private sector, citizens) become more varied. Their interaction becomes more complex. This is necessary to cope with the increase in diversity, complexity, dynamics and risk of fire in society.

Models of Volunteers

The participation of citizens in public services can be classified along a variety of criteria (e.g. Brudney, 1990a). This section, however, concentrates on the volunteer as a positive, active and influencing person, who co-produces to the benefit of all citizens within the public service.

Studying the phenomenon of volunteering has two dimensions. There is a demand side analysis looking at the reasons to ask for volunteers. There is the other side of the volunteer coin, the supply side, focusing on the reasons why citizens volunteer. The two perceptions are complementary of course.

The demand side is the perception of the organization. Volunteers are wanted because it is perceived that the positive aspects are more important than possible negative repercussions. In a fiscal climate of cut back management, restricted tax potential and pressure to reduce deficits, alternative ways of service delivery are especially welcomed. Volunteers may provide a solution to these problems. They are cheap labour providing services or at least guaranteeing a minimum provision of it at a reduced cost. This may have an impact on the efficiency since the same output can be provided without a significant additional cost. It also may increase legitimacy, but this will depend on the relationship of the organization to the population.

There is also a supply side which is the position of the citizens that are willing to volunteer and participate actively in providing services. According to Brudney volunteers may have a double motivation (Brudney, 1990a). Most volunteers have a mixture of altruistic and instrumental motivations. The percentages of a survey among volunteers showed the following motivations: the desire to do something useful to help others (56%); enjoy doing the work (35%); interest in the activity (30%); religious concerns (22%); learn and gain experience (9%). Brudney concludes: 'Volunteers can - and most likely do - pursue both types of rewards simultaneously' (Brudney, 1990a). Volunteers are thus not necessarily naive citizens: 'Often, individuals will volunteer their time because they expect to benefit from the contacts they make or the feeling of being needed' (Ferris, 1984). The desire to influence policy and decision making also is a major element. According to Fitzgerald and Durant 'the primary determinant of citizen desire for additional influence in service delivery proved to be level of service satisfaction' (Fitzgerald and Durant, 1980). The conviction that one is able to influence the process of production or distribution may be a strong stimulus to volunteering.

Selecting volunteers whose motivation is in conjunction with the organizational objectives will be one of the major challenges.

Models of Coproduction

Analytically, service production, service distribution and service consumption are all very close and overlapping. Depending on whether the focus is on production or consumption, or whether the position of the consumer or the producer is more important, Arvidsson distinguishes between production oriented and consumer oriented models (Arvidsson, 1986). The focus here will be on production oriented models.

According to Mattson coproduction models have two dimensions: a political and an economic dimension. The political dimension 'stresses the active involvement of citizen-taxpayers, especially those who stand to derive direct benefits, in the execution of services' (Mattson, 1986). This is also the level of legitimacy of service policy, production and distribution (Levine, 1984). The economic dimension stresses the effects for (technical) efficiency, effectiveness (or allocative efficiency), and equity (Ferris, 1984).

Efficiency relates input and output. For a given amount of input, output has to be maximized. For a given amount of output, input has to be minimized. Depending on the skills adding volunteer time may be adding time of identical skills or complementary skills. Adding identical skills would mean an increase in the same input kind. Adding complementary skills would cause a shift in the division of labour. This may result in higher marginal yields for professionals and volunteers if these complementarities are fully exploited. In both cases additional organizational costs should be taken into account. This is the organizational perception of efficiency.

Ferris also points to the societal perspective. 'In order for coproduction to be technically efficient from society's viewpoint, it is necessary to utilize volunteers in accordance with their skill level. If a volunteer's capabilities are not fully utilized (...) then the output is not being produced at the least cost to society. The key to achieving technical efficiency, in both a public sector (financial) and societal (economic) sense, is to be able to manage coproduction arrangements so as to match the capabilities of time donors with their coproduction roles' (Ferris, 1984).

Effectiveness is about the relationship of output to effect. More effect should mean that a person or a group is better off. If volunteers can influence the service positively, if this guarantees improvement in answering true demands, then volunteering may result in improved effectiveness.

Equity may be part of effectiveness. It is also part of the legitimacy of the service. It is difficult to relate the presence of volunteers and the level of equity. According to Ferris 'there is no reason to believe that coproduction is inherently unfair. On the other hand, there is no strong evidence that it is fair' (Ferris, 1984).

The empirical research on these coproduction models is not very well developed. Data and cases are limited and are mostly situated in the fields of police (Siegel and Sundeen, 1986; Percy, 1987; Barbour, 1980), fire services and refuse collection (ICMA). Other examples are on e.g. management assistance (Brudney, 1986; Brudney, 1990a), health and rehabilitation (Mushkin and Sandifer, 1980), and a municipal zoo (Whelan and Dupont, 1986).

The Case of the Belgian Fire Service

The case of some Belgian fire services will be taken to illustrate and partly to corroborate the hypothesis that the interaction and participation of citizens in public services improves the efficiency, the effectiveness and the legitimacy of the public services.

The Belgian fire services have about 5,000 professional fire men and about 11,500 volunteers. The volunteer index (the number of volunteers per full time equivalent of professional) is fluctuating slightly over the years. For the period 1982-1987 the volunteer index varies around 2.22 volunteers per professional.

But the focus of the case study will be on the middle-sized Flemish fire services, the so-called Y-centres[1]. Y-centres may be fully professional or mixed.

These fire-services were analyzed from an efficiency and effectiveness point of view (Bouckaert, 1992). This was done by describing and relating input, output and effects. Inputs of fire services were measured in deflated financial expenses. There are different types of outputs of fire services. Two major groups may be distinguished. A first one is related to fire. It consists of prevention and fire fighting. A second group is not related to fire but consists of all other emergency interventions. These outputs may be weighted according to their input importance. It results finally in one output volume. The output volume of thirteen Y-centres from 1982 till 1987 is confronted with their inputs. This is shown in graph 2.

This graph shows two lines. Although no parametric production functions were calculated, two production functions are suggested. One function represents the mixed services, the other represents the professional services. The graph supports the hypothesis that mixed services, working with volunteers, need less deflated financial resources as input to provide the same level of output compared to professional services. Thus mixed services have a higher level of efficiency, as was proven on other places (Bouckaert, 1990).

---

[1]   Fire services belong to the categories X (e.g. Brussels, Antwerp, Liège), Y (e.g. Bruges, Ostend, Leuven), or Z and C, which are smaller fire services.

BELGIAN FIRE SERVICES
Y-CENTRES (1982-1987)

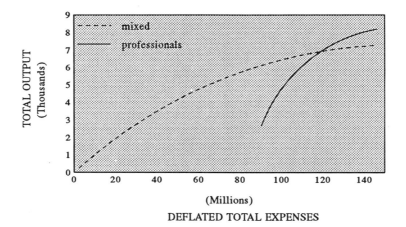

(Millions)

DEFLATED TOTAL EXPENSES

Graph 2   Deflated total expenses and total output in 13 Y-centres from 1982 till 1987

This is also shown in the relationship of the volunteer index and the productivity. Professional services with a volunteer index equal to zero have a lower productivity than mixed services with a volunteer index of approximately 2.4.

If productivity is defined as output divided by input (Output/Input) and if productivity is an acceptable indicator for efficiency, then mixed services are more efficient than professional services. The reason is quite obvious. Mixed services have a limited number of full time professionals. In cases of emergencies volunteers are called to intervene. Sudden increases in workload due to emergencies are matched with a temporal labour force that should not be paid in other circumstances. This is not the case for professional services. Full time professional fire men are full time available and have to be paid full time whether there are emergencies or not.

The next question is whether the mixed services have to pay a 'price' to be more efficient by using volunteers. The answer is probably positive.

First, the inputs of the mixed services have a different quality. Since the quality of the inputs may influence the output quantity and quality, this has to be taken into account. Mixed services have less trained and educated fire men. They have slightly older cars and machines. On the other hand, mixed services have a higher percentage of fire men beneath 35 years old (mostly volunteers), less fire men between 35 and 50, and more fire men (mostly professional officers) above 50 years than their professional equivalents. This demographic difference might give an advantage to the mixed services.

Second, since professional services have a lot of 'empty' time, they pay more attention to prevention than mixed services that reduced this 'empty' time in hiring volunteers. This reduction causes an efficiency increase but results in spending less time to prevention. Activity profiles of average mixed and average professional services show this difference very clearly. The following question should then be: is prevention effective thus causing less fires or less intensive fires. The answer is probably positive.

Mixed services are probably less effective than professional services. Input difference may be a reason: mixed services are younger, but less trained and have slightly older hardware. Activities are probably a better explanation. The lower focus on prevention may cause a lower effectiveness. Effectiveness is the relationship of output to effects. Effects can be expressed in a positive way: number of citizens protected, surface protected, and total value of goods protected. Effects can be expressed in a negative way as number of people killed or injured and total damage of goods.

1987	Prevention index	Prevention effectiveness
Belgium	1.03	0.27
Y-centre-mixed	2.25	0.43
Y-centre-prof.	4.44	0.56

Table 3   Relationship of prevention index and prevention effectiveness

A distinction is made between prevention effectiveness and extinction[2]. Apparently there is a positive relationship between the prevention index, i.e. the number of preventions per fire, and the prevention effectiveness, i.e. the inversion of the number of fires per thousand inhabitants (Table 3). This means that the less/more prevention you have per fire, the more/less fires you have per inhabitant. The relationship with the number of victims per fire was less clear.

Differences in organisation and prevention policy between mixed services and professional services probably are responsible for a lower degree of effectiveness of mixed services which is the price these mixed services have to pay for a higher level of efficiency.

---

[2] (Prevention effectiveness) times (extinction effectiveness) is (total effectiveness) or:

$$\left(\frac{\text{Number of fires}}{\text{Number of inhabitants}}\right)^{-1} \times \left(\frac{\text{Number of victims}}{\text{Number of fires}}\right)^{-1} = \left(\frac{\text{Number of victims}}{\text{Number of inhabitants}}\right)^{-1}$$

The fire service case shows that volunteers in a mixed service create a higher level of efficiency but a lower level of effectiveness. Under certain conditions they probably also should be able to realize a level of effectiveness that is at least as high as the one of the professional services. Legitimacy has not been tested in this case. Mixed or professional services probably will have no influence on matters of equity. But support of the population might be higher for a mixed service. Therefore, volunteers result in a higher level of efficiency, a conditional equal effectiveness, and probably a higher legitimacy.

This results in some governing questions. Problems of contracting out to the private sector should be joined by questions on the desirability of a shift from a professional service to a mixed one or from a mixed service to a mixed one with a higher volunteer index. The problem remains of what the optimal volunteer index is.

Changes in the behaviour of the actors (established fire services of private companies, know-how on the fire function in private businesses, training practice of the population) all increases involvement and commitment possibly strengthening the governing of the situation.

Conclusions

Citizen involvement has always been present in society. But the welfare state has nationalized (transferred to government) a lot of functions. Pressure on governments forced these to search for new and for old solutions, e.g. privatisation and stress on management. Hiving of functions to citizens has been reconsidered. A selective and conditional 'privatization' of some of these functions to citizens appears to be fruitful from a governance point of view for several reasons.

This selective and conditional transfer and increased interaction between government and citizens fits with the values of efficiency, flexibility, quality, and closeness to users and citizens. A second reason is that citizen involvement goes beyond the stress on management and the pure withdrawal from activities.

An updated interaction of three types of actors (government, private sector and citizens) creates a renewed pattern of governance which legitimizes citizen involvement. This three dimensional interactive governance pattern allows a better cope with a complex, diverse, dynamic, and riskful reality because there is a stronger potential of effectively combining means, know-how, motivation, and authority to detect needs and to solve problems.

This has been illustrated with the Belgian fire service case. This allows us to partly corroborate the hypothesis: *as a strategy of governance the interaction and co-production of citizens in public services improves the efficiency, the effectiveness and the legitimacy of the public services.*

Volunteering probably will gain momentum in the future. Increasing interference of production and consumption in services will automatically involve more citizens. Combined with a labour concept that becomes less rigid participation in production and distribution will become more accepted. Citizens get a new profile in the perspective of public/citizen partnerships. Citizen-taxpayers cannot be considered as 'passive recipients of municipal services' any more (Mattson, 1984). Not only are they taxpayers and consumers of public services, but they will increasingly participate in public production and distribution, to the benefit of the citizens, the organization and society.

Going beyond management and withdrawal, flexible interactions between government, private sector and citizens become possible and allow to cope with the increasing complexity of the situation, the variety of the responses, the dynamics in matching the situation and responses, and the increasing degree of fire related risks. This renewed form of co-'arrangement' (Kooiman, this volume) between government and society allows e.g. to combine the professional know-how and the volunteer motivation in a dynamic way.

The integration of citizens in the production and distribution of goods and services makes them part of the governance process. The participation of citizens in the fire service may not only improve efficiency and in certain conditions effectiveness. There also may be an improved level of legitimacy since the insertion of volunteers creates a new pattern of interaction, a new type of contract between society and government.

This increased legitimacy is a consequence of a (re)new(ed) form of governing and governance where governors and governed have overlapping positions and activities of guiding, steering, managing and controlling society. Therefore a conditional shift from professional to mixed fire services, or from mixed to volunteer fire services, or a general shift toward a higher volunteer involvement should be beneficial to society as a whole since it may result in a public service which is more efficient, more effective and more legitimate to cope with increasing levels of complexity, diversity, dynamics, and risk in society.

13

GOVERNANCE IN INTERACTION: PUBLIC TASKS AND PRIVATE ORGANISATIONS

HERMAN AQUINA AND HANS BEKKE

Introduction

In some countries, convicted criminals are sent to a private jail. Or privately owned hospitals are committed to a strict budget by governments, although these hospitals are actually financed by insurance companies and health services. There is more than just a public and a private sector. There is a whole sector in between that is neither purely public nor purely private. The supply and distribution of many goods and services in a society, in other words: the allocation of values, takes place by means of a network of all kinds of organisations. In this chapter we will discuss the dynamics of differentiation and cooperation in regard to types of allocating mechanisms: public, private and an increasing number of intermediate organisations. Our main problem is the proper place of government in this complex system of governance. Can other organisations be seen as instruments in government policy? Why and how is government policy involved in the actual allocation of goods and services?

A Typology of Allocating Organisations

For a long time, state and society have been discussed as if the state was something separate from society and as if the concept of society did not deserve any differentiation. The state, or political system, was in charge of the authoritative allocation of values, i.e. goods and services, for society as a whole (Easton, 1953). Any other form of allocation presumably was left to society which was equivalent to the free market for most of us. This was true for political scientists and economists alike (e.g. Haveman and Margolis, 1970). The state could be seen as an arena or as an organic chooser, it was in any case something separate from the rest of society. Things have changed dramatically. We have grown accustomed to the state as just an organisation among other organisations in society, such as associations, communities and private business enterprises (Streeck and Schmitter, 1985). Although these four categories may be interconnected in a very complex network, they can be distinguished from each other. Each of these categories can be defined by, among other characteristics, the kind of values they allocate and the kind of control mechanisms they deploy. This results in a typology of allocation mechanisms.

Communities can be seen as primary groups, for example the classical family, but also fraternities and modern phenomena like self-help groups. Their basis is spontaneous solidarity. You are a member by ascription. Communities allocate respect, mutual affection, trust and all kinds of immaterial values that can be labelled 'solidaristic'. Decision-making is rather loose and in most cases based on unanimity. Persuasion plays a major role as a control mechanism.

Associations are functionally defined groups, based on cooperation. They have a well-defined legal status, such as foundations, churches and trade unions. They allocate so-called categoric values: collective goods and services that are important to a group and its members. In many cases associations have been created deliberately to perform such a task. Members cooperate and you become a member because of the kinds of values you can obtain by membership. Usually members are well-informed about the values they can obtain as is the management about its clientele.

The *market* is defined by the competitive allocation of private goods and services. Both consumers and producers are free to do what they want to do, more so than in the case of associations and very much more so than in communities. The most important mechanism of control is exchange. The most important goal is profit.

Finally, the *state* is not defined by solidarity, as is the case with a community, or by cooperation, as is the case with associations, or by competition, as is the case in a market system. It is defined by hierarchy. The state supplies collective goods and services for a society as a whole, not just for a family or some other social group. In a modern democratic government responsibilities and tasks are clearly defined, in most cases by law. This may result in a system that is less flexible, less responsive to the needs of its clientele and more expensive than other systems. It has certain advantages as well, which we will discuss extensively. One advantage is that the state has the authoritative power to enforce the implementation of public decisions. In principle it has the monopoly of force in society, a very unique control mechanism.

These ideal types of allocation mechanisms are not found in reality. In daily practice, force is used in communities and governments may elicit feelings of solidarity. Allocation systems may use a whole range of control mechanisms, but the typology may be of analytical use anyway. The most important complicating factor is the classification in solidaristic, categoric, private and public goods for the very simple reason that only very few goods and services fit completely in one of these categories. Most values have more than just one aspect or element. For example, education may be a public good in many respects, in some other respects it is a categoric, solidaristic or even a private good. There are state schools, but some religious associations have schools of their own. Some education, even formal education, takes place in communities, or is a commodity that is for sale, as driving lessons are in most countries. Nevertheless, government may be concerned with non-state schools because of the public aspects of education. Private schools have to meet certain standards set by law in order to qualify as an educational institute. On the other hand, even in state schools many elements may be left to parent-teacher associations because they have the necessary information that a government agency has not. In conclusion then, just because there is a mixture of private, public, solidaristic and categoric elements and aspects in any value, we may expect that there will be an endless debate on who should do what. The problem becomes even more complicated because it is not always clear which elements and aspects should be regarded as private, public, solidaristic and categoric. Groups may not be allowed to have schools of their own because it is not considered to be in the general interest if they do. These kinds of decisions are in many cases political decisions, not necessarily based on the logic of any typology, but on the logic of power configurations or on ethical ideas about the good society.

Another difficulty in our typology is that the nature of goods and services is not static. It is very dynamic and it varies over time. So we may expect that corresponding allocating mechanisms change too. Broadcasting for example used to be a collective good in the technical sense, but technological developments have changed broadcasting technically into a private good. That is not to say that the organisation of broadcasting has changed from public to private. Other aspects play a role as well, but in most European countries technological developments actually did change the system. Service imperatives count. Political preferences change over time as well, which may result in changes in allocation mechanisms. This can be illustrated most dramatically by the waves of nationalisations and privatisations in the United Kingdom, depending on the party in power.

Finally, our ideas about a good society may change over time, which is also important for the organisation of the allocation of values. Widespread support for a more or less public system of social security in most European countries is a matter of ethics. It is based on the belief that anyone deserves a decent standard of living. Such a belief is not universal. Some 150 years ago, poor relief was mainly a matter of the church and the rich bourgeois, partly because poverty was interpreted in theological terms and as a matter of philanthropy and not in terms of human rights and as an economic problem.

In the following sections we will subsequently discuss problems of economic efficiency, political opportunities and ethical belief systems and we will discuss the possibility that each may influence the system of governance and the modes of governing. Although our discussion is systematic, we will not offer a general story of the genesis of the prevailing system of allocation in modern western societies. We believe that such a story cannot be written unless some very interesting developments are left out because they do not fit in the general picture. One commentator discovered at least six ways to describe the rise of the welfare state, each rich in insights, but one-sided (Schuyt, 1989). Instead, we will show that there is a variety of developments. The result may not be very coherent and consistent, but it can be understood as a more or less accidental conjunction of circumstances. This process can be analyzed in a very systematic way. However, if we turn from description to prescription and advise about the best system of allocation, we cannot do more than sum up the factors that may be relevant regarding the circumstances. This concludes to no more than a checklist that policy-makers may use.

Economic Efficiency

Classical wisdom among welfare economists holds that the market system offers an optimal solution for allocation problems. Other forms of allocation should be admitted only if they can do better than the market, which has to be clearly demonstrated. Unfortunately, there is no consensus among these political economists which values should be allocated by the market and which ones should not. Nevertheless, elements of their models play some role in political debates and may be of analytical value anyway. Let us discuss this model and see if actual allocation mechanisms can be explained in terms of their lines of reasoning.

The market may become problematic because of 1) market imperfections such as lack of information, the rise of monopolies or immobility of labour, 2) the quality of goods and services rather than the nature of the allocation mechanism, and 3) intrinsic characteristics of goods and services that result in externalities that are not effectively marketed (cf. Steiner, 1971). Consequently, the market may supply values nobody has asked for like environmental pollution. The market may also fail to supply us with what most of us would like to have such as fundamental research or social health care. We may expect to see some forms of collective action to compensate for market failure. Since both government and associations can be seen as alternative allocation mechanisms if the market fails, the problem becomes what government should do and what can be left to associations. We believe there are at least two reasons why government will be involved.

To begin with, a recent study (Weisbrod, 1988) concludes that government is the best allocation mechanism if demand is homogeneous. If demand is heterogeneous, there may be some place for associations. If groups have different opinions about collective goods and services and some variation in the supply of goods and services is possible, then each group can be given what it wants. Education is partly a collective good, but that does not mean that it should be the same for everyone, not even for every group. There is no logical need for a public educational system. Consequently, if the demand for education is heterogeneous and some variety in education is possible, it is better to let groups take care of themselves. That is the reason why in heterogeneous countries like The Netherlands the educational system is very fragmented. Certainly it is a common interest of all the Dutch that quality standards are set and that there is some unanimity about the contents of these standards, which can easily be set by government, since demand is homogeneous in this respect.

Problems arise when values are homogeneous but demands heterogeneous anyhow. Such problems are among the toughest problems in society and can be solved only in the political arena; we will continue this discussion in the next section.

The second reason why government may become involved in the supply of goods and services has to do with coercion. Market failure can be compensated by alternative supply or by regulation. But legislation to fight monopolies in a free market system, for example, makes sense only if observance can be enforced and only government has the capacity to do so. Moreover, the actual supply of goods and services may require some form of coercion. Some services cannot be supplied if funding is not secured, something that constantly worries most associations. Since only government has the power to levy taxes or make payments compulsory, the financing of much of the activities of associations is left to government.

An efficient allocation of some services eventually requires cooperation between government and associations. The implementation is very often done by associations but payments are compulsory and may have the form of taxations. Implementation is left to associations because they know their clientele best and are more familiar with their specific needs. It is almost impossible for a government to collect the necessary knowledge without creating a huge and clumsy bureaucracy, whereas associations can remain relatively small and flexible. Another example is foreign aid which is often given by foundations that are financially supported by government. These foundations are experts in their fields, they are more flexible and less dependent on the cooperation of national governments that may have other ideas about the distribution of aid than the donor government has.

Political Opportunities

The relationship between government and other allocation mechanisms is not just a question of economic efficiency. The proper place of government in a society is subject to a struggle of social forces, which may differ from one policy field to the other. It is not easy to discover some common patterns, not even in a single country.

In The Netherlands, for example, there has always been a struggle between etatists and corporatists as well as between those who preferred a strong central government and those who advocated a strong local government instead. A third complicating factor is the cleavage between social political groups such as Roman Catholics, protestants, social democrats and liberal conservatives. Over the years, ever-changing coalitions of a great variety have been formed which has resulted in an extremely complex and kaleidoscopic pattern of allocation mechanisms. To mention just two examples: the policy fields of education and poor relief, by far the two most important political problems in the 19th century and the early decades of the 20th century.

In the 19th century education was for a long time a matter of local government. Nowadays it is the responsibility of the central government on the one hand, and confessional associations that run about half of the schools on the other hand. This is the result of a long and very complex struggle that would take too much space to unravel here. Here it is sufficient to say that in the 19th century political power was in the hands of local, mostly conservative, elites. In the second half the liberals seized power on the level of the central government and they tried to improve the system by local planning. They could not do this in another way because in most local communities the conservatives remained in power. At the same time protestants, and later on catholics as well, became increasingly emancipated and began to demand education in accordance with their belief system, something that liberals were strongly opposed to. In liberal eyes, such an education system had nothing to do with enlightenment, and everything with a backward form of indoctrination. Moreover, they feared that education would become an instrument in the hands confessional political leaders to hold their rank-and-file together. Since none of the political groups could win a majority, some compromise had to be reached in order to provide education anyhow. The so-called pacification included public financing of confessional schools, which had to meet quality standards set by the central government. For the rest, confessionals were free to have their own educational program and to give the school their specific culture and character. Supervision by the central government, however, is very intense.

It is often thought that the so-called pillarization is characteristic of Dutch society but this is a very rough generalisation and it may even lead to a wrong picture. In the first place, the classical model of pillarization includes groups with interests, that are advocated by their leaders who make compromises on a central level. However, it can be demonstrated that it may have been the other way around as well. (Van Schendelen, 1984). In the second place, there are many policy fields to which pillarization in the common usage of the term does not apply. For example, most housing associations have nothing to do with any confessional group whatsoever. The same is true for most agencies that implement social security policies. Even in cultural affairs most associations have no ties at all with whatever denomination.

Poor relief offers quite a different story. Just like education, poor relief used to be a matter mainly of local associations. Local governments provided supplementary help. Nowadays local associations have virtually disappeared. Poor relief is a task of the central government with local governments as implementing agencies. The model of financial guarantees of the central government was not adopted in this policy field. One of the reasons for this development may have been the rise of all kinds of social security systems that made poor relief in its strict sense a marginal and not very interesting matter. Indeed, in the social security system we can see a pattern that is in some respects similar to the educational system. Here as well, liberals advocated a strong central government with compulsory insurance for most categories of the population, whereas confessional parties preferred action by employers' organisations. The end result was again a compromise, in which central government gives rules that are implemented by agencies that are controlled by trade unions and employers' organisations. Since we all know how important implementation is in the policy process, we could say that both government and associations control social security, especially because the government is obliged to consult associations in formulating its policy because they know the implementation problems best.

However, there is an interesting difference between education on the one hand and social security on the other. There was a heterogeneous demand for education. The liberals did not want to honour this demand and tried to supply homogeneity, thus eliciting severe political conflict that could only be solved by making the supply of education heterogeneous. In social security however, demand was homogeneous. The conflict concerned the organisation of the supply that could not be heterogeneous. The conflict was solved by committing all parties to an arrangement. Cooperation between government and associations can ensure social support for government which could not be obtained otherwise. The involvement of organisations, especially of so-called dome organisations in public policy-making and implementation, means legitimation and makes allocation of goods and services actually authoritative. In both our cases of education and social security, at least some part of the legitimation of regulatory interference is left to group representatives. Differentiation of legitimation relieves government of the need to develop a generally acceptable formula to defend decisions, a formula that cannot be found anyhow (Streeck and Schmitter, 1985).

Many observers share the opinion that associations have become the prisoners of government, especially if they depend on government subsidies. This not entirely true and even the reverse line of reasoning may be true. In the first place government is not free in giving subsidies. There are rules and regulations and in many cases there is a right to subsidies. If you qualify, it has to be given to you. In the second place, these rules and regulations, like many other rules and regulations, have very often been made by government under the pressure of associations that were trying to secure their interests. The government apparatus has simply been used by all kinds of interest groups to promote not the general interest, but only their own. Government has become the prisoner of associations (V.d. Berg and Molleman, 1975). It has been colonized. Interest groups needed government, because it can do what government can do, the authoritative allocation of values for a society as a whole.

Government has become so large, only because interest groups could take care of their own business under the aegis of government. In many western countries things have changed in the last ten years or so. Economies do not grow so fast that all kinds of new and not even well-established interests can be honoured. The turn of the economic tide in itself does not provide a sufficient explanation of the dramatic changes we have seen since then. We believe it just provided the opportunity, it was the ultimate element that caused the chain of reactions. The whole concept of the welfare state, its organisation and its methods have become subject to discussion. We will not elaborate on this, we will only mention some developments that are important from the point of view of governance of allocation.

In the first place, groups have changed and secondly, preferences have changed. Many of the old associations that built the welfare state in cooperation with government have lost their rank and file (Schmitter, 1982; Offe, 1984). Consequently, legitimation of welfare state arrangements have become ever more problematic. Parts of the electorate do not have any specific ties with whatever association and are critical about their role in public policy-making. Sensitive politicians and government bureaucrats understood what was going on. They realised that government was very often used by all kinds of interest groups which was not a bad thing, as long as interests were equally represented. Since this is no longer the case, one should not wonder that government has changed its role quite fundamentally. It is no longer the arena for some kind of corporatist policy-making because society itself has become more and more pluralistic. Consequently, government involvement in a great variety of policy fields is decreasing, whereas government control is increasing. Government is no longer an instrument in the hands of associations. Instead associations have become an instrument in government policy. Government itself is doing less, the volume of the public sector is decreasing. Interests are no longer promoted by government without answering the question of weight.

More and more often government defines priorities even in fields where it has no direct financial interests, for example in the case of health care in The Netherlands. It does so because associations do not, while social and political support for associations is becoming less and less. Most members of parliament used to have strong ties with associations but this has changed quite rapidly. Some years ago a government could hardly dismiss advisory reports to the government that are written in almost any policy field by advisory committees in which associations as well as private enterprises and government officials take part. Nowadays it happens that a government does not even ask for advice although the law reads that it should. Unmistakably, there has been a power shift, which admittedly does not mean that, all in all social developments are controlled to a greater extent or better. The contrary may be true.

Ethical Considerations

Politics is not just about power. It is about ideas as well, ideas that are part of ethical systems that include a doctrine of the relationship between government on the one hand and other organisations in society on the other hand. Most political parties are built on such a system. Catholic and calvinist parties share ideas about the doctrine of subsidiarity, that is the state should provide a social order which has to be in accordance with divine order and that is about all it should do. All other things should be left to society according to this view. The state should ensure that social groups can actually mind their own business. In the dutch version of social democracy, associations and private enterprises play a more important role than in other socialist doctrines, partly because the Dutch had to accommodate their views to the Dutch situation. In this particular version, the state cannot control everything so that must should be some form of functional decentralisation.

Quite another body of ethical considerations is a matter of what Bernard Crick (1962) calls the 'ethics of politics'. Indeed, politics is an ethical activity because it reconciles what is basically irreconcilable in a way that is satisfactory for most of those concerned. A specific arrangement of allocation mechanisms may be part of a pragmatic solution in those cases in which ethical systems themselves are not consistent. So is democracy. In any pluralistic democracy we are confronted with some dilemmas that cannot be logically solved (cf. Dahl, 1982): inalienable rights versus efficiency, equality of individuals or equality of groups, centralisation and decentralisation, and finally concentration against deconcentration. We will subsequently discuss those dilemmas and the solution that a special relationship between government and associations as allocation and control mechanisms may offer.

Sometimes, inalienable rights can be guaranteed only by a heterogeneous allocation of goods and services by associations for their members under the protection of government. In The Netherlands the right of freedom of education is fundamental; it actually is an article in the constitution. This can be honoured only by the creation of a system in which government is financially responsible for schools that are managed by associations for their members. However, it would be inefficient to allow any group to have its own school. Therefore groups have to qualify. Or, every group in The Netherlands has access to the public broadcasting system if it qualifies. The number of members is also important in this case, otherwise the system of broad casting would become very inefficient.

The efficient spending of public money poses some serious questions about public accountability of associations that have not yet been solved. Since many associations depend at least partly on government money, that is taxpayers' money, spending should be efficient under some public control. This is certainly not always the case. Accountability of associations however, even if it would be restricted to the spending of government subsidies only, is a very delicate problem. Associations are flexible organisations without a huge bureaucracy like most government agencies necessarily have. By bringing them completely under public control, one would quickly lose all the advantages that associations have. On the other hand, accountability is now often diffuse, as is the accountability of subsidized private enterprises. New budgeting systems have been tried out, for example output-budgeting instead of the traditional input-budgeting. We cannot go into all the details of these systems, they all have their pros and cons.

Government may not only be needed to secure the financing of associations' activities. It may also be needed in securing the rights of those individuals who are not serviced by any association. Associations may be very parochialistic and paternalistic. Since they have been created by members to supply goods and services that would not be supplied otherwise it is no wonder that they are parochialistic. They serve their members only. That is the reason that there are not only confessional schools but also state school, for those people who are not willing to become a member of any special group to receive education and certainly not the kind of education that is supplied by that group. Every group may have its own schools; there is an equal right to education as well. In The Netherlands the government will build a state school if a qualified number of citizens in a community ask for such a school.

Government may also be complementary to associations if they become too paternalistic. In the 19th century poor relief, for example, was a matter of philanthropy. It was the duty of all christians to support their fellow citizens. However, it was the duty of all the poor to observe the rules of good citizenship. There was no right to relief, the poor could receive it, if they behaved well according to the standards of those supporting them. Among other things it was for this reason that government intervention was advocated, because only government could guarantee equal treatment. However, it should be admitted that even state poor relief can become paternalistic, especially when means tests are introduced in the social security system.

The second dilemma in any pluralistic democracy is the group-individual dilemma. Individuals certainly have their rights, but so have groups. The problem is how groups should be defined and what should be their influence in government affairs and vice versa. Some countries, for example Austria, have some constitutional arrangements. Most western countries do not have such arrangements, but in all those countries we do see that associations are members of advisory committees to the government, often by law. On the other hand government representatives are often members of the committee of associations.

Decentralisation is one of the structural elements of democracy, but it is too easy to say that pluriformity is safeguarded just by decentralisation. The configuration of associations is not by definition a mirror of the social kaleidoscope. Sometimes government intervention is necessary to guarantee pluriformity and to support interests that are not represented by established associations or by private enterprises. In The Netherlands, the law on public broadcasting reads that the broadcasting system should reflect the pluriformity that is supposed to be characteristic of Dutch society. Programs are made by independent associations, each servicing its social or cultural segment of the population. If nevertheless some parts of the population are not serviced or if some aspects of Dutch civilization are not paid the attention to that they deserve, a special autonomous foundation will provide this. This law lists formal qualifications. Some years ago, a foundation started broadcasting islamic programs, since the islam has substantially grown in The Netherlands and has become part of Dutch society. Since it not yet represented by an association its rights are secured by a central organisation.

Finally, deconcentration is also one of the structural hall marks of modern democratic systems but for some reason we fail to apply this principle to other organisations than the core political system. If control of more or less collective goods and services is in the hands of both government and associations, or even private enterprises, why should we not apply the principle of checks and balances to associations as well. Associations often operate without any checks and even dominate government. From the point of view of deconcentration of power, the internal structure of associations and the power relationship between associations on the one hand and government on the other hand, deserve attention. In the first place, the internal structure of associations could be designed in a way that is in accordance with the principle of checks and balances. In some policy fields in The Netherlands and in many other countries, laws have been made to regulate the internal functioning of associations to make them more democratic. In the second place, associations may be seen as countervailing powers against government and government in turn as a countervailing power against associations, which would become too powerful otherwise.

Conclusions

Public tasks are not necessarily government tasks. Neither can it be said that the allocation of more or less collective goods should be under government control. Since most collective tasks, goods and services not only have a public element or aspect but a categorial aspect as well, and even a private or solidaristic aspect or element, we should not wonder that supply of these values often requires some cooperation between government and associations, since these are by far the most important allocating mechanisms of more or less collective goods.

The main difference between government and associations is, that government supplies goods and services authoritatively for society as a whole, which implies a huge bureaucracy and control by force, whereas associations supply goods and services for their members and they know best what their members want so they are very flexible and expert organisations.

Government and associations are very often complementary so that one could speak of a 'third party government'. Both categories of organisations have their strong and weak points so that they can compensate each other.

Associations are flexible and expert, but they may lack funds and tend to be parochialistic and paternalistic. On the other hand, government is a bureaucracy that lacks the necessary knowledge about client groups. But government has the monopoly of power so that it can collect tax money and it is supposed to serve society as a whole as to compensate for parochialism, while the liberal democracy in particular guarantees rights to its citizens as to avoid paternalism in providing services for its citizens.

It is not always clear when and why government should do something and associations something else. There are service imperatives, but political arguments are important as well. Some cooperation between government and associations may enable them to supply more or less collective goods and services that could not be supplied otherwise because of severe political conflicts. Finally, ethical arguments may limit the powers of government or those of associations and conclude to some form of cooperation between these two types of allocating mechanisms.

The relation between government and associations is a very dynamic one. Existing arrangements can hardly be understood without historical knowledge. Service imperatives may change as our preferences and the balance of power do. All in all, the problem of government in interaction with associations is very complex and a simple solution cannot be provided now. The only thing we can do is to give some models of recent developments along these lines. A blueprint or recipe for future developments cannot be given so easily, we only offer a checklist of what is important in thinking about the system of governance of a society and the government of the collective sector.

INTRODUCTION TO PART IV

PROSPECTS FOR REFORM

These examples of 'co' governance are followed by four chapters, again of a somewhat more conceptual character. All four chapters concern the changing role of government in these new kinds of interactions between government and society.

Les Metcalfe considers a new role for Public Management in terms of managing and steering the development of interorganizational networks. In his opinion such capacities are the key to resolving public action problems. He defines this new Public Management primarily as a learning process.

In the second chapter of this part Walter Kickert continues this line of argumentation while discussing coordination and control of interorganizational networks. In theoretical terms he advocates shifting the attention of coordination and control from the intra-governmental level to the inter-governmental level in terms of interorganizational networks. He also (see chapter 1) takes issue with the fashionability of the auto-poietic solutions and outlines other ways of coordination and control at the boundaries of state and society.

Kyösti Pekonen develops an argumentation why in complex, dynamic and diverse modern societies new forms of (co) representation combined with politization are needed, even in public administration. In his opinion, tension, conflict and struggle between people may help governance. Some kind of mutual understanding between those concerned is needed. Pekonen's analysis shows that one of the conditions for such 'politicized' representation is a change in the way of understanding the audience of public administration. He sketches a model of such an interactive representation process.

Finally, Torben Beck Jørgensen advocates a situationally dependent reform strategy for public administration. The heterogeneity of public tasks calls for specialized reform strategies. These - again - are not given for all times. Different 'roles of the state' and different ideological emphasises make for changing governance modes. Some examples from the Danish Public Administration are given.

14

PUBLIC MANAGEMENT:
FROM IMITATION TO INNOVATION

LES METCALFE

Public Management in the 1990s

During the 1980s public management became a growth industry (Kapil and Kekkonen, 1990). There is now a world-wide movement to upgrade public administration by using management concepts, tools and techniques, many of which were originally developed in business. But public management will not flourish as a growth industry in the 1990s merely by extrapolating from the approach on which its initial successes were built. New and different problems of public management are emerging for which there are no ready-made answers. There is already a worrying tendency for solutions to be more predictable than the problems they are supposed to solve. Privatization, contracting out, formation of agencies, creation of internal markets and the use of a whole battery of specific management techniques are almost reflex responses to the problems of governmental underperformance. A fundamental reappraisal is urgently needed if reform is not to narrow into this self-limiting process of relying upon conventional business solutions. Before investigating alternative solutions we need to be sure that the key questions are correctly formulated. The agenda for reform must be revised to take account of distinctive features of public management. Public management reform is not just an apolitical quest for technical efficiency, within a given institutional framework. Public management in the 1990s will have to develop new concepts and models of governance which alter policy processes, redefine the criteria of policy effectiveness and transform the patterns and processes of public accountability as well as deploy more familiar management techniques.

The theme of this chapter is that we are reaching the limits of useful application of business management practices in government but we have hardly scratched the surface of public management proper. Public management cannot meet the needs of government if it remains little more than a collection of second-hand business management methods. The real challenge is a different one. Public management needs to be recognized as the main area for creative developments in the theory and practice of management. Governments, by accident or design, have far more difficult management problems than any business would attempt to tackle. If the basis of public management reform until now has been imitation of business management, the challenge for the 1990s is to move on to innovation; the development of new methods of management appropriate to the distinctive needs of government.

Managing Change: Managing Networks

The challenges facing public management stem from two interrelated features of contemporary government; the pace and type of change with which government must cope and the fact that government operates through networks of interdependent organizations rather than through independent organizations which simply pursue their own objectives. If there is a single contrast between the traditional concerns of public administration and public management modernization, it lies in the shift of emphasis from stability to change; from keeping the ship of state on an even keel, to ensuring that flotillas of organizations are equipped to steer a common course through rough and sometimes uncharted waters. Public managers must not only manage the work of their organizations efficiently, they must also participate in a more strategic and political process of managing large-scale structural transformations in the networks of organizations through which public policies are developed and delivered. It is a matter of personal preference whether one regards this as politicizing management or managing politics. Public management and politics are inextricably intertwined in the process of managing change at the interorganizational level. Dror (1990) coined the term 'reformcraft' to highlight the importance to government of developing new skills and capacities for governance appropriate to the difficult and demanding task of steering strategic changes. This chapter considers what reformcraft involves in contemporary government where the critical public management problems are interorganizational in scope, while many of the standard business management solutions are pitched at the level of the single organization.

The basis on which management modernization was launched in the 1980s is not obsolete. It still has some value. But it is inadequate to answer the crucial contemporary questions. The core values around which reform evolved in the 1980s are usually summarized as the 'three Es' - Economy, Efficiency, Effectiveness - denoting the eradication of waste, the streamlining of services and specification of objectives to ensure that resources are targeted on problems. Within this mind-set, imitation of business methods seems the rational management response. But in the 1990s the pace of change, and the complexity of the tasks facing governments mean that the 'three Es' are no longer a sufficient basis for reform. They presume a degree of constitutional and institutional stability that cannot be taken for granted. In the turbulent contexts of Eastern Europe and the Soviet Union, this is obvious. Less dramatically, but no less importantly, in the European Community and Canada where federalism is an issue for markedly different reasons, problems of large-scale institutional change are also prominent. But even where the basic framework of government is not an issue, the challenges of governance are severe. In many policy fields; the economy, the environment, education, health, welfare, transport, urban planning; the problems are outrunning the capacities of the organizations charged with dealing with them. The common underlying theme in these different situations is the need for new capacities to handle structural change and manage reforms at the interorganizational level. But 'reformcraft', at this level, is in short supply. Just when it is vital that organizations work together, crisis conditions undermine the trust and mutual confidence on which coordinated action depends.

Paradoxically, as the discussion below will show, the business management ethos may make things worse rather than better, by reinforcing go-it-alone attitudes and weakening incentives to coordinate. However, this is not an argument for throwing the management baby out with the bathwater. Rather, it points to theoretical shortcomings which it has been possible to gloss over until now, but which become an increasingly powerful constraint on reforms. Having borrowed heavily from business, public management lacks an adequate theoretical underpinning. It lacks a logic of its own. Filling this gap involves going back to basics and addressing a set of conceptual and theoretical issues which, for a variety of reasons, have been mishandled. These include some of the public choice assumptions on which advocacy of business management solutions ostensibly depends. Paradoxically, their reliance on market-oriented prescriptions has diverted the attention of management reformers away from the governance problems which public choice theory was originally developed to resolve.

Public and Private: Locus or Focus?

A pivotal issue in the public management debate is the meaning of the public-private distinction. Generally, this is regarded as a matter of specifying, on efficiency grounds, where the boundary should be between public and private sectors. While this has the appearance of objectivity, such distinctions are not mere products of empirical observation and technical analysis, they are socially constructed means of organizing experience and, in this case, guiding policy (Malkin and Wildavsky, 1991). They provide us with ways of perceiving the world and interpreting experience. They exert a powerful, but subtle, influence on how we see the world and seek to shape it. The reason for laying such stress on this is that imitation of business management practices rests on a particular way of making the public-private distinction which, on closer inspection, turns out to be seriously flawed.

The flaws have been brushed aside, not without some justification, by reformers in their haste to implement ready-made solutions. If the private sector has solutions to public sector problems, why not imitate them? Government presents such a large target for management reform that almost random attacks can quickly produce some positive results. In operational management and policy implementation, there is ample scope for a piecemeal approach and little reason to delay in taking action. However, the political attractions of early successes mask the danger of compromising longer term reform objectives. Sustained progress depends on something more than a succession of ad hoc interventions. At a minimum, public management requires a framework to guide and consolidate different contributions. Yet, this minimum condition has been regularly, if inadvertently, disregarded because of a widespread tendency to confuse and conflate two different ways of drawing the public-private distinction which are part of a broader debate in the public administration tradition. Henry (1975) distinguished between 'locus' and 'focus' starting points for reform and research in public administration; the one institutional, the other analytical.

> *'Locus is the institutional 'where' of the field. A recurring locus of public administration is the government bureaucracy, but this has not always been the case and often this traditional locus has been blurred. Focus is the specialized 'what' of the field. One focus of public administration has been the study of certain 'principles of administration' but again, the foci of the discipline have altered with the changing paradigms of public administration'* (Henry, 1975: 318).

The distinction between locus and focus is useful for analyzing different ways of conceptualizing management responses to public policy problems. For clarity of exposition, the term *public sector management* will be used for a locus approach and *public management* for a focus approach. The former is concerned with *government* in the structural sense of a grouping of institutions and the latter with *governance* in the functional sense of a process of steering and conducting policy. Reformers and researchers, have created confusion by assuming a locus approach embodies a consistent theoretical focus. Reformers, in particular, dogmatically assume that public sector management problems are sufficiently similar to those of business to apply the principles of private sector management. Researchers often adopt the more sceptical and, on the face of it, open-minded attitude that empirical studies will uncover the theoretically distinctive features of public sector management if there are any. In practice, investigations with a locus starting point are inconclusive. Efforts to identify empirical similarities and differences between management in the public and private sectors lead nowhere. The answers are not 'out there' waiting to be found. Any assumption of two distinct and homogeneous sectors rapidly evaporates. The boundary between public and private sectors, which the locus approach assumes, is blurred and ambiguous. Different criteria, such as ownership, legal status, use of public funds and profit motivation produce overlapping definitions of the scope of the public and private sectors. Introducing a voluntary sector; non-business and non-government adds to the confusion. To accommodate these disparities the initial sharp dichotomy between public sector and private sector management is often watered down into a spectrum or continuum embodying degrees of publicness. For some authors, 'all organizations are public' (Bozeman, 1987). The task of making comparisons is further confounded because many organizations do not fit neatly into one or other 'sector'. Marginal cases, intermediate types and hybrid organizations variously labelled as quangos or para-state organizations, proliferate haphazardly. Just to add to the confusion, there is clear evidence that the organizational diversity of the public 'sector' is as great, if not greater, than that of the private 'sector'.

Not surprisingly perhaps, in view the lack of coherence in public sector management, eclecticism rules. Surveying the literature, Gunn (1987) identified six contending attitudes which he summarised as:

- Public administration is unique.
- Public and business management are alike in unimportant respects.
- Public management is the integrative paradigm.
- Convergence between public and business management.
- Management is generic.
- Public management is a less efficient form of business management.

Advocacy of these different interpretations of the extent to which public and private management are alike or unlike has created a debating society atmosphere. Well-worn argument and counter-argument are arrayed against each other in ritual combat, without a basis for determining the importance of similarities and differences. The protagonists see little need to adjust to each other's point of view. It is symptomatic of the disordered state of the field that Perry and Kraemer (1983) entitled their compendium 'Public Management: Private and Public Perspectives'.

'Those who advocate that public management and private management are similar and their counterparts who argue that they are different approach this issue from vastly different perspectives or biases.' (Perry and Kraemer, 1983: 55).

Some may regard this as healthy academic pluralism. My own view is that it is an unnecessarily confused mess. Progress is blocked because basic concepts remain ambiguous. The same terms are used in diverse and inconsistent ways, providing no basis for cumulative theoretical progress. This leaves government dangerously vulnerable to ideological fads and business management fashions - and the public badly served. In short, the belief that there is a public sector in which public organizations have a clearly distinguishable set of management problems is undermined by those who seek to use it. The 'locus' approach to drawing the public/private distinction fails because the world does not fracture along a clear institutional fault-line, dividing the public sector from the private sector. Fortunately, the alternative starting point; treating the public/private distinction as an analytical 'focus' rather than an institutional fact; provides a much more fruitful way forward. Most of the remainder of this paper is devoted to outlining the set of problems and processes of public management which provide this theoretical focus. Some of the analysis is familiar in the sense that it starts from the problems of collective action or public choice which have had such an influence on the direction of

administrative reform. Where it takes a new direction is in developing
management solutions from those that have become conventional wisdom.

Management; Taking Responsibility for the Performance of a System

There is a prior question to be addressed before defining the differences
between public and private management. We need to consider what they
have in common and how, in turn, the common characteristics of management distinguish it from other images of the public policy process. This
is no more than an application of the basic logic of comparison (Sartori,
1970; 1991). Several definitions are possible but, to begin with, management will be defined as taking responsibility for the performance of a
system (Metcalfe and Richards, 1987). Responsibility is an essential
attribute of management. Getting things done through others, to quote
another definition of management, means that some individual or group
must be invested with the right and duty to ensure that group efforts are
coordinated.

This definition distinguishes a managerial conception of the public
policy process from the incremental and rational images which dominate
theoretical and practical discourse about governance. Neither gives central
importance to responsibility. On one side, in the incrementalist image of
the policy process no one is effectively responsible for the overall performance of systems governed by the interplay of different interests. Groups
and organizations pursue their own objectives in an organizational ecology.
The parts are managed; the whole is not. The performance of the system
is an unintended consequence of the interactions of the parts. Markets and
many political systems rely upon the disjointed incrementalism underlying
Lindblom's (1959) 'science of muddling through' to coordinate their
activities. On the other side, control rather than responsibility underlies
rationalist images of the policy process. A unitary model of governance
underpins rational decision-making with performance standards set at the
top and sub-units acting merely as agencies carrying out policies determined above. Rationalist prescriptions usually assume the feasibility of
hierarchical control as the precondition of shouldering responsibility.
Although management and control are often used as synonyms, there is
a vital distinction between them: to manage is not to control (Landau and
Stout, 1979). Control in a strict sense presumes an ability to determine
outcomes; control is possible if objectives are well-defined, well-ordered
and stable, and the techniques needed to achieve them are proven and
reliable. Predictability is the condition of control. Routine is the servant
of control. It is when non-routine responses are needed that control breaks
down and management qualities; ingenuity, creativity, risk-taking,
conflict-resolution; come into their own.

Management is an intermediate category. It involves acceptance of
responsibility for steering a system when control is not possible but

unguided ecological processes produce substandard results. Management is an adaptive process which proceeds by experimentation, learning and innovation in a changing environment. It is not the enactment of a preconceived programme or the enforcement of rules. Management is a more widely applicable concept than control in government precisely because public policies require intensive and sustained cooperation among many organizations. By the same token, it is difficult, because it requires common action where there are diverse and possibly divergent organized interests.

These comparisons suggest a first approximation to the distinctive character of public management. If management in general is getting things done through other people, public management is getting things done through other organizations. Public policies typically engage the efforts of many organizations. Public management usually involves the complex and delicate task of taking responsibility for steering an interorganizational network. Coordination among organizations which are formally autonomous but functionally interdependent is one of the keys to ensuring effectiveness in public management. The next section considers how the public-private distinction should be formulated to illuminate the problems of managing in a multi-organizational context, where goal consensus and unitary authority cannot be assumed.

The Public-Private Distinction: Macro and Micro Management

The challenge for public management is to bridge the gap created by the emergence of interorganizational tasks and public policy problems where central control is impossible but completely decentralized adjustment processes among organizations are too slow and reactive to achieve satisfactory performance. The problematique of public management is most starkly revealed in the logic of collective action or public choice, of which Olson's (1965) analysis is probably the best known. While the theoretical focus of this problem is quite familiar, the form of an effective solution is not. Reduced to essentials, the problem is that in certain situations private interests override public interests and individually rational actions produce collectively irrational outcomes. Rational, self-interested individuals will choose not to cooperate; first, because they do not expect others similarly motivated to cooperate and second, because if others do display cooperative behaviour, non-cooperative free riders will benefit without contributing. The pessimistic conclusion of the logic of collective action is the lack of collective action. All are worse off than they would have been if they had cooperated. Yet, given the circumstances, each does what seems the best for themselves by pursuing their private interests. The interests of each diverge from the interests of all.

Public Goods and Private Interests

The source of the problem of collective action resides in the nature of public goods. Public goods are often, wrongly, reified as goods and services produced by government. This reification is founded on, and sustains, a locus approach and therefore assumes the validity of the traditional distinction between public and private sectors which was discarded earlier. As Malkin and Wildavsky observed: 'If public goods *should* be provided by the government, then the answer to the question, 'what is a public good?' is the equivalent of deciding, 'what should the government do?' When to classify is to decide, definitions have powerful implications for public policy'. (Malkin and Wildavsky, 1991: 357-58).

Bearing these strictures in mind a clear theoretical focus is needed. At least in this chapter, what distinguishes public goods is not who produces them. It is the peculiarly difficult problems of producing them and the harsh consequences of failing to do so. Two characteristics distinguish public goods from private goods; jointness of supply and the impossibility of excluding others from benefitting from them if they are provided (Mueller, 1979). Joint action is necessary to produce public goods. Individuals cannot provide them for themselves. But, once produced, no-one can prevent free riders from benefitting. Stripped of all substantive content, this is the heart of the problem of governance; the delicate balance between shared public interests and individual private interests.

Public choice theorists, having posed this problem, show little real interest in finding constructive solutions to it. More often than not, they evade the issues it raises. Having established that individualistic pursuit of private interests does not satisfy the requirements for producing public goods, they use the intractability of public choice problems to justify their own preferences for reducing the scope of the public sector, rolling back the frontiers of the state and increasing the sphere in which competitive market forces and commercial incentives operate free of government regulation. They seek to absolve government of responsibility for dealing with these problems by shifting them from the public sector to the private sector. But in doing so they also shift from their original theoretical focus, which is clear, to a locus approach which is both unclear and misleading. Familiar 'trust the market' reform proposals like privatization, contracting out, deregulation and imitation of business practice in government are too narrowly conceived to provide solutions to the urgent and important problems of collective action such as environmental protection, economic reconstruction, regional development or the reform of major services of the welfare state like education or health. However, disregarding these very difficult problems does not make them disappear. The popularity of business management solutions of these kinds depends far more on ideological preconceptions than on logical inference. The conclusion that the remedies to collective action failures lie in more competition is quite at odds with the fact that the pathologies of public choice stem from unbridled competition in the first place. Simply assuming that a complex mixed-motive situation can be transformed into a straightforward zero-sum game in which purely competitive behaviour is socially beneficial, is as unsatisfactory as naively assuming that cooperation will emerge spontaneously in interorganizational networks where there are severe competitive pressures and acute political constraints.

The real question is whether collective action problems can be managed to further vital common interests. An affirmative answer to this question depends on formulating the public-private distinction in a new way. The most fruitful way of doing so is as a sharp analytical distinction between macro and micro levels of management rather than a fuzzy institutional distinction between ill-defined sectors. In these terms, public management at the macro level is concerned with the performance of a whole system and private management at the micro level with the performance of the parts. The analogy with the macro-micro distinction in economics is obvious but incomplete. Macroeconomic management, whatever its limitations, is basically a stabilization process. Public management as a macro-process is mainly concerned with change and especially with structural change. It is in phases of major reorganization that the balance between public and private interests is most precarious and a macro management process is most needed to steer the transition to a new institutional framework.

For clarity, it is useful to regard macro-management as concerned with steering interorganizational networks and micro-management as steering individual organizations. The more interdependent the functions of organizations become, the greater the probability that collective action problems will arise which are irresolvable at the micro level. When they do, a macro management process is required to ensure coordination. This does not mean that macro management should displace or supplant micro management. To a considerable degree, individual organizations can retain autonomy in dealing with other organizations within the existing institutional framework. The distinctive focus of public management is on achieving cooperation *among* organizations in circumstances where the basic framework of public policy and interorganizational cooperation comes into question. These circumstances must be defined more precisely.

The acute problems of achieving cooperation under adverse circumstances have been explored in several social science analyses conceptually equivalent to the logic of collective action. They highlight different facets of the problem and, indirectly, provide pointers towards their resolution. The tragedy of the commons (Hardin, 1968) is directly relevant to the over-exploitation of the physical and biological environment. The congestion of the social environment in cities and transport systems through the mal-adaptive ecology of micro-motives (Schelling, 1978) and the social limits to growth (Hirsch, 1977) centre on the problems which arise when there are macro problems but no macro competencies for dealing with them. The well known difficulties of establishing trust in a context of uncertainty and mutual dependence such as the prisoners' dilemma game and Mintz's (1951) analysis of the social psychology of panics and crises reveal how suspicion of others' intentions (whether or not it is well-founded) triggers a vicious circle of devil-take-the-hindmost competition and destructive conflict. Finally, and most directly relevant to public management, there is the problem of turbulent organizational environments (Emery and Trist, 1965; Metcalfe 1974, 1978). In contexts of high interdependence the performance and effectiveness of any organization depends to a large extent on how its activities mesh with those of other organizations. Go-it-alone strategies disrupt the framework of mutual expectations and undermine the institutional ground rules on which continuing cooperation depends. The more complex the causal texture of the organizational environment the greater the risk that individualistic actions will precipitate destructive conflict and disintegration.

These variations on the theme of individually rational actions combining to produce collectively irrational outcomes display important continuities which support the idea of a macro-micro distinction. First they make it clear that public goods are not merely private goods produced by governmental means; they are qualitatively different. They are of a higher logical type (Bateson, 1972; Watzlawick, Weakland and Fisch, 1974) than private goods. Second, more concretely, public goods provide the macro context of governance within which private goods are produced. They are necessary complements rather than competing alternatives. The distinction is akin to the relationship between the rules of a game and the strategies of individual players within the game. Third, changing the rules of the game is a different order of change from the mutual adaptation of individual organizations to each other in the normal run of business. It is structural change rather than incremental change and instead of contributing to the maintenance of an existing pattern of interorganizational relations precipitates a process of redefining the roles and redesigning the relationships among the participating organizations.

Incremental and Structural Change

This interorganizational perspective fixes the theoretical focus of public management innovation on the issues of structural change that the public choice approach tries to evade by reducing structural problems to incremental problems. These different orders of change must be clearly understood, because the consequences of failing to distinguish them in practice and manage them appropriately are extremely serious. Incremental change fits the 'muddling-through' model of the public policy process. It both assumes and maintains macro-stability. Structural change is change *of* a system rather than change *within* a system. It involves the modification of the rules of the game that frame organizational interaction, define organizational roles, responsibilities and relationships and regulate interorganizational competition and conflict. In government-business relations, macro management involves the design and operation of what are usually called regulatory regimes. The failure to construct and manage these regimes effectively underlies, for example, the US Savings and Loans catastrophe and the collapse of BCCI and the Maxwell empire. In each case the cumulative impact of commercial exploitation of a weak institutional framework precipitated an enormously costly and unmanageable crisis.

It is only at the macro level that it is possible to gain a full picture of structural problems and manage the transition to a new institutional framework. But who should take responsibility for the performance of the whole system? It is tempting, but mistaken, to see the solution as some form of central direction. But, structural change in pluralistic systems is not amenable to central control. Ascribing to public management the task of dealing with macro organizational problems is not a return to a master-minding synoptic decision-maker. Since individual organizations cannot resolve these problems by acting independently and solutions cannot be effectively imposed by outside interventions, ways must be found of *sharing responsibility* for managing structural change. An effective public management process must embody a capacity for joint decision-making and action specifically dedicated to the task of steering structural change at the macro level. Public choice theorists will resist this conclusion, which certainly implies more governance,though not necessarily more government. But it is artificial and arbitrary to exclude the possibility that the participants in the system can make collaborative efforts to resolve structural problems by remodelling the macro-environment in which micro-decisions are made (Buckley, Burns and Meeker, 1974).

Public Management as a Macro Process

The difference between imitation and innovation in public management is now clear. The imitative task of management reform in government is to adopt and adapt business or other management ideas to upgrade *micro-organizational* capacities. Individual organizations are then better able to cope with incremental change. The innovative task of public management as a macro process is to develop new and quite distinctive *macro-organizational* capacities to deal with structural change at the interorganizational level. The requisite macro-management capacities for steering large-scale reorganization and major reform have no counterpart in business. Public management as a macro process requires an interorganizational management process in which the various organizations and interests involved in a public policy system share responsibility for managing structural change while retaining their autonomy in managing incremental change. What is required to deal effectively with structural change is a participative process in which different organizations come together in a joint problem-solving, collective-decision process to redesign the rules of the game and redefine their mutual roles and responsibilities around an agreed definition of public interests.

Public management at the macro level is not a natural outgrowth of the relationships that evolve among organizations seeking to protect their own prerogatives and advance their separate interests. It will not emerge spontaneously. Managing structural change requires interorganizational dynamics which are the *reverse* of those that evolve from the politics of managing incremental change. Instead of working from micro to macro it starts from the macro level. Instead of aggregating predefined private interests and seeking allocative compromises within established structural parameters, public management begins by diagnosing and formulating systemic problems at the macro level and designing integrative solutions based on common interests and collective goals. After a new macro framework has been established individual organizations can once more focus on the pursuit of private interests within a new structure of governance.

The difficulty, as with all public goods problems, is that the public interest in the resolution of structural problems is everyone's concern and no one's responsibility. Part of the task of public management is to develop institutions and processes which ensure priority for formulating structural problems and managing structural change. Solutions cannot be imposed from outside. Attempts to do so are liable to trigger the disintegrative dynamics they are intended to avert. The willing cooperation, commitment and dedication which are essential to resolving structural problems must be developed from within. Macro-management solutions are needed which are, paradoxically, participative and top-down. They require extensive active involvement in diagnosing problems and designing solutions by those who will be involved in implementation. Their participation must be re-framed in terms of joint problem-solving rather than special pleading. Psychologically and politically this involves a risky shift from the defensive 'what-we-have-we-hold' postures of distributive bargaining to the more innovative reforming attitudes of integrative bargaining.

An important example of this process is the '1992' programme to complete the internal market of the EC, although, for political reasons it has been portrayed as a process of deregulation and removal of micro level obstacles to the operation of free markets. But the internal market will not operate in a political vacuum. Positive integration requires collective action by the Member States to restructure the economic environment of the EC. The European Commission has a key facilitating role in formulating common interests and integrating the efforts of the administrations in the Member States as participants in a macro-management process. But it can not undertake the macro management function alone. To be effective in managing structural change it should create the context in which the macro issues are collaboratively identified and a new basis of integration designed and developed.

Effectiveness; From Individual Optimising to Pluralistic Learning

The discussion of public management as a macro process raises important general issues about policy effectiveness and the contribution of reform to improving performance. Public management as the guiding theme of reform raises strong expectations of better performance. The primary motivation for administrative reform is improved performance. Improvements in performance may take different forms: better service, greater value for money, lower costs and so on. However, in practice, reform efforts which venture into large-scale structural reorganization often fail to produce the desired results. Reformers tend to concentrate on localised improvements which promise a quick payoff. Ministries are divisionalized and agencies are formed with sharply defined missions and presumed autonomy. Reform relies mainly on micro-management prescriptions, constrained by the conventional management-by-objectives model. The assumption underlying this 'look after the pennies' approach is that better management involves targeting resources at specific problems. However commonsensical this may seem, it is far too restrictive. It falls well short of providing a model of effectiveness for public management at the macro level.

Reformers have been reluctant to go further into the issues surrounding the meaning and measurement of effectiveness. This is because of the theoretical complexities of managing with multiple conflicting objectives and ill-defined shifting priorities. But to sustain the claims of public management as a macro process a broader concept of effectiveness than the attainment of predefined objectives is indispensable. Targeting resources at problems assumes the validity of a model of management based on individual rationality which equates effectiveness with optimising within constraints. But public management operates in a pluralistic context in which goal consensus cannot be assumed, in which authority is dispersed, in which conflict is legitimate and in which, nevertheless, the different constituents are interdependent and have common interests - however dimly perceived. The rational model provides no clear prescriptions when objectives uncertain and constraints alter - as they do in phases of structural change. Being based on 'the logic of individual rationality', it presupposes the existence of a unitary mind which is capable of ordering its preferences, of formulating non-contradictory goals and of evaluating alternative means and actual performance in the light of its integrated goal system' (Scharpf, 1978: 346). These conditions accord better with a model of hierarchical control than with the inter-organizational realities of governance.

Even in business, the rational model is being superseded as an ideal or standard of excellence. The stresses experienced by business in the 1970s and 1980s forced a reformulation of ideas about the meaning of managerial effectiveness. Ouchi's (1981) contrasts between Japanese and

American management practices is instructive because the qualities that he criticizes in American management closely resemble those that are being introduced into government. Flexibility and innovative capacities acquired much greater importance than they had had in a more stable environment. Ideas about management effectiveness are in flux (Goodman and Pennings, 1977; Cameron and Whetten, 1983) and criticisms of the rational model have been moving for some time towards a more general and inclusive concept of effectiveness. Effectiveness criteria are not givens. March (1962, 1978) observed that values and preferences are often formed in the course of policy development and implementation rather than being optimising criteria derived from a predetermined objective function. Vickers (1973) pointed out that, in the appreciative systems of policy makers, goals are subsidiary to norms and values. The orthodox model of rationality disregards the extent to which management involves problem-formulation as well as problem-solving as leaders confront the creative political task of developing new visions and generating new values from which future goals can be derived (Dror, 1988). The public management function of bank supervision depends on evaluating the private management of commercial banks against prudential norms and values defined within a macro level framework (Metcalfe, 1982). The BCCI disaster illustrates the consequences failing to establish an international regulatory framework for banking.

Landau (1973) criticized the conventional management wisdom that optimal effectiveness is achieved by eradicating organizational overlap and duplication in the execution of policies. Contrary to many popular critiques of public bureaucracy, overlap and duplication are not always wasted effort. They can increase reliability by providing a measure of insurance against the risks of human error and organizational failure. The interorganizational context of public management multiplies the sources of error and underscores the importance of strengthening the interfaces among organizations. An interorganizational network is only as strong as its weakest link, but often interdependence is undermanaged. A common characteristic of a succession of recent disasters in and around Britain which have taken their toll of human life - a passenger ship capsizing; trains crashing; an explosion on a North Sea oil rig; a fire at one football stadium and fatal overcrowding at another - has been the failure or breakdown of coordination among various authorities so that no-one saw the whole picture until too late. Safety, as a public good, was everyone's concern and no-one's responsibility.

These specific criticisms of the goal-seeking model of management have been accompanied by more thoroughgoing challenges. Weick (1977) advanced what may appear to be merely flippant proposals that; effective organizations are garrulous, clumsy, superstitious, hypocritical, monstrous, octopoid, wandering and grouchy. However, they have a definite theoretical underpinning; centred on a concern with adaptability, flexibility and resilience to meet unforeseen situations, as Pondy (1977) showed. Weick sought to shift the emphasis from conventional models that place the emphasis on specialization and optimal efficiency in dealing with a specific task in a given situation; models which inform current developments such as the formation of agencies in the UK and similar developments in the EC, Spain and other countries. Instead he underlined the need for generalized learning capacities to cope with an evolving set of problems in a changing environment. In the short run this may seem less efficient, but in the long run it is more effective.

Nystrom and Starbuck (1983) presented a positive case for an evolutionary rather than an optimizing view of organizational effectiveness.

> '*Judgements about organizational effectiveness generally undervalue information, discovery and learning. Effectiveness that falls below the best performance attainable is nevertheless desirable if it includes information about better criteria or better methods. Conversely, superficially optimal effectiveness is actually undesirable if it forecloses learning. The managers of successful organizations quite often inflict crises on their organizations by deciding that they have already attained optimal effectiveness or that they know how to attain it*' (Starbuck and Nystrom 1983: 153).

These contributions set a new agenda. They call for theory of effectiveness in public management as a pluralistic process of interorganizational learning. While few people would dispute the desirability of organizational learning as a useful adjunct to public management, the argument here is that organizational learning and interorganizational learning capacities are central to effectiveness in public management.

This is not as vague and ephemeral as it might seem. A rigorous and well-defined general concept of learning is contained in Ashby's (1960) exposition of the adaptive processes of ultrastable systems. Ultrastability is sometimes misunderstood as implying extreme rigidity. The opposite is true, it denotes an enhanced capacity for flexibility, along the lines of the discussion of incremental and structural change above. The distinguishing feature of an ultrastable system is a dual capacity for gradual, step-by-step adjustment in a given environment, backed up by a reserve capacity for major self- reorganization to match environmental discontinuity. An effective learning system displays this self-designing capacity for responding to major changes in policy objectives or environmental circumstances.

Learning Processes in Public Management

In the political environment of public management learning processes are especially difficult to create and maintain. Individual learning is a psychological process. Organizational learning is also a political process (Metcalfe, 1981). A critical task of public management is to build institutional learning capacities at the macro level to manage the environment in which private management operates. But, conventional political processes often block learning because ideology overrides evidence or vested interests resist policy evaluation and change. The practical difficulties of building learning capacities at the interorganizational level are enormous. But at least in concept, ultrastability provides a model which can guide the development of organizational learning capacities at the macro level. Managing structural change depends on the constituent organizations pooling their adaptive capacities and acting in concert as multistable system (Metcalfe, 1974) with what Dror (1984) has termed a central mind and what Deutsch (1963) called a learning network.

At this level, public management reforms are better regarded as management by design rather than by direction. It should be concerned with designing adaptable systems rather than producing blueprints for specific reforms. In a world of rapid and discontinuous change, reform is not a single isolated event, but a permanent responsibility for public learning. There is no need to try to improve upon a classic statement.

> *'If government is to learn to solve new public problems, it must also learn to create the systems for doing so and discard the structures and mechanisms grown up around old problems. The need is not merely to cope with a particular set of new problems, or even to discard the organizational vestiges of a particular form of governmental activity which happen at present to be particularly cumbersome. It is to design and bring into being the institutional process through which new problems can be continually be confronted and old structures continually discarded.'* (Schon, 1971).

While the design of individual organizations as adaptive, learning systems can draw on a growing body of work in organization theory, this is less true of the design of interorganizational networks which have so much importance in public management. The agenda of future research should focus on the problems of designing interorganizational networks which have macro-level capacities to learn and manage structural change as well as micro-level capacities to deliver services efficiently. In democratic systems of government this includes setting the framework of accountability. Private management operates within whatever accountability framework exists and exploits whatever opportunities and loopholes it offers. Public management should create incentives and accountability systems which align private interests with public purposes. In the past public accountability has been associated almost exclusively with the negative function of preventing abuse of power. In a democratic society, this is, of course, one of the essential bulwarks of constitutionalism. However, in addition to preventing the abuse of power, well-designed accountability processes can serve the positive function of promoting the effective use of power, by creating incentives for effective performance (Metcalfe, 1989). This substantially enlarges the scope of public management beyond the narrow limits of applying business methods in government, but it responds to strategic problems of governance at the interface of politics and administration where strategic decisions about forms of organization and accountability are made and broad issues about the design of regulatory regimes are decided.

Conclusions

If necessity is the mother of invention, public management reform will see the development of new and original theories of management in the near future. The problems facing government are such that it will become the forcing-house of management innovation. But to make the shift from imitation to innovation, public management needs new theoretical foundations. This article has proposed a theoretical focus on the distinctive problems of public management at the macro level. The function of public management is defined as dealing with structural problems at the macro level in contradistinction to private management concerned with managing incremental change at the micro level. The crucial task of public management is to recognize the emergence of these problems and initiate action at the macro level to remedy them and forestall the turbulence that otherwise occurs. Some of the most important implications that flow from this analysis have to do with the meaning of effectiveness and the requirements for achieving it. The conventional goal seeking model of effectiveness must be superseded by models based on a logic of learning which takes account of the pluralistic context of public management and accepts the integrative challenge of building interorganizational cooperation in the midst of structural change.

This concept of public management implies a very significant expansion of the role of management in government beyond the sphere where existing business management methods can be applied more or less directly. It proposes the extension of management into areas of strategic policy-making and large-scale reform. Creating the macro-management capacities necessary to handle structural change will require significant investments in human resources and organizational development; investments on a much greater scale than governments have made in the past. But the price is small compared with the costs of failing to resolve structural problems or the benefits that flow from overcoming them. In any case, wherever governments are facing the challenge of managing structural change, there is no viable option to developing macro-management capacities.

15

COMPLEXITY, GOVERNANCE AND DYNAMICS: CONCEPTUAL EXPLORATIONS OF PUBLIC NETWORK MANAGEMENT

WALTER KICKERT

Introduction: Public management

As stated by Metcalfe in the preceding chapter, public management should not be an indiscriminate imitation of business management. Although many of the generic organisation and management theories apply to both the private business sector and the public sector, it also seems desirable and necessary to obtain a specific public sector theory. The object specificity - public sector management - requires a methodological and theoretical specificity - public management (Denhardt, 1984; Harmon and Mayer, 1986; Metcalfe and Richards, 1987; Bozeman, 1987; Heffron, 1989; Flynn, 1990; Pollitt, 1990; Rainey, 1991).

Management in the public sector seems to be characterised by strong context-dependency, high complexity and a typical sort of governance.

Compared to the private business sector, public management is more strongly, and especially differently, related to the external socio-political environment. Even organisation and management processes that occur within government, cannot be properly understood without insight in their relations to the concerning societal sectors, to politics, to the numerous advisory and consultative instances, to social institutions, to the 'customers', the pressure and interest groups, etc. Moreover, the management by government of public policy-making processes explicitly is a form of 'external' management, that is, the directed influencing of political and societal processes outside the government. The management of complex policy processes is not an internal organisational activity, is not administration in a narrow sense, but is a complex and externally oriented activity, a way to handle the process of policy and institutional change in society.

Public management cannot be properly understood without an outside-in view, an approach starting from the outside world of societal fields, a reasoning backwards from this context towards the government system (c.f. Metcalfe's notion of macro-management, this volume).

The second characteristic of those mentioned before, is the complexity of the management. Public management is mainly the governance of complex networks of many different participants, such as governmental organisations, political and social groups, institutions, private and business organisations, etc. (Mandell, 1990). In such a multi-level network there is no single monolithic actor but many various actors, all of which have their own interests, goals and positions. None of the actors is dominant, none has the power to unilaterally force others. Power is dispersed. All actors are more or less autonomous. Decision-making is a negotiating process. In this view it is better to use the broader concept of 'governance' than the concept of 'management' which is interpreted more narrowly in business administration.[1]

The usual hierarchical management approach of top-down control in a pyramidal organisation, based on mono-rational and mono-centric modes of coordination and management, is not applicable in a complex network perspective.

Government itself is not a monolithic single entity but consists of a complex network of various bureaus (c.f. Allison's (1971) model of 'bureaucratic politics)'. Furthermore 'external' management of complex policy processes involves many different actors in the network, all with their own goals and rationales. The network is not only multi-actor but also multi-rational.

Public management is the managing, the governance, of complex inter-organisational networks. The interorganisational network approach therefore seems to offer a promising opening for the development of a theory on public management and organisation.

The Concept of Governance: Governance, Steuerung, Steering

Such a governance approach comes closer to the Dutch interpretation of public policy and administration in which political science plays a dominant role and which is not interpreted in the narrow sense of internal administration and control -running the business - of public policy and organisations. Although the American public administration also originally descends from political science, one cannot deny the impression that more general questions of governance and the state have not attracted so much attention there as e.g. in Germany - the debate on 'steuerung' (Mayntz, 1988 and this volume) - and the Netherlands - the limitations of government 'steering' (Kickert et al., 1985; Kooiman, 1988). A difference which presumably has to do with the different nature of the North American public administration and the strong public and political emphasis which are put upon effectiveness and efficiency of government, that is, upon 'management' in a narrow sense. In North-West-European countries, with their more legalistic tradition and their much stronger public and political

---

[1] As a matter of fact the Dutch equivalent for the scientific field of public administration 'bestuurskunde'— contains the term steering. The Dutch term is not restricted to a narrow cybernetic meaning. The term has a broader meaning (Kooiman, 1988). The presumably best Anglo-Saxon equivalent is the term 'governance'.

legitimacy of the state, general questions about (the limitations of) governance have attracted more attention, particularly at the end of the seventies and the beginning of the eighties (Kaufmann, 1986).

In a certain sense, one might state that the roots of the network management perspective in the States can be found in the search for practical solutions to problems in the management of difficult implementation programs, whereas its roots in North-West-Europe are to be found in the general debate on limitations of government steering.

The economic crisis of the seventies and the hard times of government budget cutbacks, have ended the euphoria about government planning and control in The Netherlands. The makeability and controllability of society turned out to be restricted. Government appeared not to be able to govern above and apart from society. Government appeared to be only one actor in a group of co-directing actors in societal networks. After an initial strong emphasis in research on the boundaries and limitations of government (Kickert et al., 1985), in the second half of the eighties more and more scientific attention was paid to the possibilities of government steering within the constraints of complexity. Not networks as a picture of governmental incompetence, but insight in networks as a possibility to improve government steering (Ringeling and Hufen, 1990).

The development of a theory on management in complex networks should begin with an exploration of the concept of governance. It is well known that management of networks cannot be characterised as top-down control from a central position (Hanf and Scharpf, 1978). That does not answer the question what form of governance it is, what the essential features of this type of governance actually are. What is the essential difference between governance in a network of more or less independent actors, and 'normal' governance? What is the essential difference between concepts and theories about processes and structures in 'normal' public organisations, and those about complex networks in the public sector?

In order to obtain conceptual clarity in a theory of management of networks, one had better begin with a thorough reflection on the constituting essences: the concepts of complexity and of governance.

Governance, Complexity and Dynamics

Cybernetics and Control

A search for new concepts of governance or steering, should evidently begin with a consideration of the basic idea about steering as it exists in cybernetics and systems theory, that is, the concept of 'control'.

The existing concepts about control that systems theory provides us with, are insufficient for public administration (Kooiman, 1988). In control systems a controlling entity is supposed to exist. A system is controlled by a controller. However, the criticism on the 'control centrism' is that government is not able to control above and apart from society from an 'Archimedal' position (Den Hoed et al., 1983). Governance is not only top-down steering in hierarchical conditions. Governance in complex networks is primarily self-control in autonomy. In classical cybernetics there is a separate controlling entity, control is rational and the system possesses little uncertainty and complexity. All these assumptions do not hold up in the field of public administration.

After this warming-up, let us gain some insight in the essences of 'normal' control theory. Despite all its limitations, the formal-mathematical theory about control, as used in systems and control theory, reveals the pure essences of the concept in its most clear and least concealed way.

In control systems theory, the following different types of control are distinguished.

The lowest type of control means that a certain value of a systems variable must be kept as constant as possible. The well-known feedback principle has proven to be particularly useful to this aim. Feedback of the output to the input, via a comparison with a fixed desired value, appeared to be a good instrument to reduce disturbances and to guarantee stability. This is called 'servomechanism' in control engineering, and 'homeostasis' in general cybernetics.

Control on the next level means that a system has to be transformed from a certain initial state to another 'desired end state'. This is controlled transformation of the system's state. The notion of 'desired end state' is equivalent to what we would call 'objective'. Finding the optimum of a utility function is the mathematical translation of goal-oriented rational behaviour. Control is called 'optimising'.

At the next level 'adaptive' control also means transformation from one state to another, but moreover, the parameters of the controlled system also change. Control while the system's structure changes. During the control, the changes have to be detected and the control has to be adapted. Modelling and parameter-identification complement the control.

'Normal' control in systems theory should therefore not be misinterpreted to be only a dull simple form of rule and command. Control is not only guarding, maintaining. Control in systems theory is also the dynamic transformation of one state to another. Control also encompasses the notions of goal and optimality. Control also deals with dynamics in the structure of the system. Not only the systems vary, their structures can also be dynamic.

Starting with this 'normal' concept of control, let us now further investigate two aspects and arrive at new concepts. First the complexity, then its dynamics (Kooiman, 1991 and this volume).

Complex Balance of Forces

Let us consider the complexity of network management in administrative reality. Control has before been interpreted as 'the' control of 'a' system.

Such a system can consist of a multitude of variables and parameters. In a mathematical sense this might be complex, in a conceptual sense the system still remains a strongly coherent, strictly ordered set of elements. The system remains a single unity with one single controlling entity. Administrative practice is not that simple, however. Public governance is in reality control in complex networks. In systems theoretical terms, not only the controlled system is complex and multiple, the controller itself is too, for the complex system consists of a multitude of actors, each of which is a controlling subcomplex, with a high degree of self-control of the own complex subsystem and mutual control between the subsystems. The distinction between controller and controlled system does not hold here.

This yields an essentially different image of the concept of control. Control in a complex network is not something of a 'third' party, an influence from outside and above, but an influence which the actors exert on each other and themselves. Firstly, the control system is not singular but complex, composed of controlling parts. Secondly, control in such a complex is a form of self-control. The parts control each other and thus themselves.

control   control of   self-control
               complex   of complex

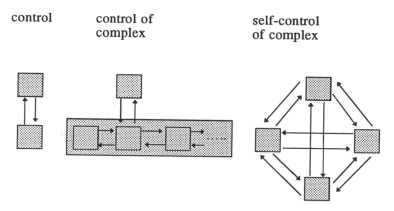

Control and complexity

Governance is the achievement of a balance between governing actors. Control is the balance of controls, a balance in a field of different, often opposing forces (see Dunsire, this volume). Let us take a closer look at this image, this metaphor of balance of forces. In analogy with classical mechanics, an equilibrium of forces occurs when, on all relevant dimensions, the sum of all their projections adds up to zero. Governance is pushing and pulling on the many subjects that are at stake. Getting the sum of all forces on all these dimensions to zero, is balance. Attaining and maintaining an equilibrium in a complex of forces is quite different from a homeostat which keeps a variable constant via a feedback mechanism.

Concepts of stability and equilibrium in the case of a composite complex balance of forces, have a meaning qualitatively differing from the case of the usual simple feedback controller in cybernetics.

Dynamic Balance

Let us now, after discussing the subject of complexity, turn to the next subject, that is, dynamics and stability. Up till now the balance of forces was a static equilibrium. Let us pursue the metaphor, increase the amount of dynamics and consider the picture of a dynamic equilibrium. Not only attaining and maintaining equilibria, but dynamic transformation of equilibria. According to the picture of balance of forces, changes then have to occur in the various forces, both in direction and size, or new forces have to rise or old ones to disappear. However, as one might remember from secondary school physics, a force implies an acceleration. A system in constant acceleration ultimately shoots like an arrow into the universe. An image which can be recognized in many practical examples of disturbance of sensitive political social balances. In order to return to a balance, the sum of the forces again has to be neutralised. However, in our administrative practice there exist no natural laws and neither does a god, not even a 'deus ex machina'. According to this metaphor it is a miracle that in complex administrative reality with its many actors and forces, so little derailments happen.

The foregoing metaphor of a balance of forces can be recognized in strategic policy operations. The difficulty in neutralizing the sum of forces on all relevant dimensions makes adequate policy making such a hard task. Similarly, the distinction between static and dynamic balance can be recognized. For it is many times more difficult to get such a complex sensitive balance of forces in movement then it is to keep it moving without too many disruptions, frictions and explosions. Changing a complex policy is many times more difficult than maintaining it.

Order Out of Chaos

Let us further increase the degree of difficulty and introduce more dynamics, more instability and move further away from the equilibrium. Let us explore an extremely dynamic image of governance with little balance and much chaos.

Chaos theory has become very popular in general (Gleick, 1988; Prigogine and Stengers, 1985) and particularly in our fields of science (Gersick, 1991; Loye and Eisler, 1987; De Vree, 1991; Van Dijkum and De Tombe, 1992). Massive popularity causes suspicion. Will the fashion last? Do the new clothes of the emperor exist? The term 'chaos' seems to seduce many people to various creative and far-reaching associations.

Some enthusiastic epigenists do not seem to be hindered by too much knowledge about its 'hard science' aspects. The term 'chaos theory' seems rather misleading for a study into the dynamics of non-linear, non-equilibrium, instable systems. This might be due to the intriguing perspectives which Prigogine (1985) sketched.

In order to avoid the impression of dilettantism, a short overview of the natural scientific origins of chaos theory will first be presented.

'The' chaos theory does not exist. The various developments in several fields of natural sciences - such as meteorology, biology, chemistry etc. - have as a common denominator the fact that they all use formal models in which non-linear dynamics play a central role. Dynamic systems are studied in mathematics by means of differential equations. The main characteristic of non-linear differential equations is that they are much more difficult to analyze than linear ones. Those equations are hardly or not at all solvable in an analytical way. Research is then only possible by producing long-time series of computer simulations. Hence the beautiful graphics which are displayed in books on chaos theory. Only a few specific categories of non-linear differential equations actually have analytical solutions. Such as e.g. the simple quadratic function which forms the population-biological model of a predator-prey situation. This function is known to result, depending on the parameter value, either in an extinction of the population, or in an equilibrium, or to alternate between two equilibria, or between four, or eight, or sixteen, etcetera, or to result in instability, that is, in no equilibria at all. This doubling of equilibrium states is meant by the term 'bifurcation' which is frequently used in chaos theory. Another characteristic of non-linear differential equation is that, contrary to linear ones, deviations do not work out proportionally. Very small changes in initial conditions of such an equation can result in tremendous ultimate deviations. This is meant by the popular term 'butterfly effect'. The wing movement of a butterfly on one continent can in the long run cause a hurricane on another continent. Apparently some mathematicians do not lack prosaic imagination.

Various efforts have been made to apply chaos theory to the social sciences. Loye and Eisler (1987) attempted to apply chaos and non-equilibrium to social sciences and social reality. Their systems theoretical approach is general and normative. Likewise De Vree (1991) reveals little practical applications. Gersick (1991) has investigated several scientific subfields theories where revolutionary change is alternated with stable periods of rest. Wamsley and Bruce (1991) reviewed the implications of chaos theory for policy subsystems and policy development. In Van Dijkum and De Tombe (1992) a collection of applications of chaos theory to various fields of social science - particularly also management and organisation - is presented.

My use of chaos theory will be modest. No far-reaching sweeping remarks about revolutionary consequences for public administration. Interest is in the conceptual added value for a better insight in the governance of complexity. The following conceptual image will be borrowed from chaos theory.

Previously a climbing series of images of governance has been presented with the picture of a dynamic change in balance as its preliminary high point. Let us now introduce the picture of dynamics far from equilibrium states, far away from stability, in a state of dominant instability, that is, in chaos. The idea in chaos theory is the pattern, the order is chaos. Systems which at first sight seem to behave completely unordered, at random, unbalanced, irregular, may on second sight appear to possess certain patterns, regularities, order.

This differs from a system which is accidentally disturbed, shows irregular outbalanced behaviour for a short period of time and subsequently returns to its stable equilibrium. Instable far-from-equilibrium systems do not show short temporary irregularity but possess dominant if not permanent imbalance. In this last metaphor irregularity and fluctuation are considered as sources of change of order and structure (Jantsch, 1980). Equilibrium then means stagnation, the dying of the system. Order originates from fluctuations. The system reinforces its imbalance till a certain threshold of instability is passed and then arrives at a new structure, another order. Order arises from disequilibrium.

This presents a fundamentally different view on dynamics, stability and on governance.

Firstly, in such a view order, regularity and pattern apply to higher meta-levels of the system. Only at an analytically higher level of consideration does a regularity emerge in the instability. Order and structure occur at the meta-level.

A second essential characteristic is that the question whether and which eventual regularity will arise in the chaos, highly depends on small factors subject to chance. Very small changes in initial conditions of non-linear dynamics can ultimately lead to wholly different end results. Due to the imbalance such small changes will be highly accidental.

Thirdly, the notion of governance is essentially different. Control is not exerted by a 'third' separated from the system. The dynamics of an irregular chaotic system are intrinsic. Under certain far-from-equilibrium conditions the system can reach some new form of order at a high meta-level. On its own, not influenced from outside, autonomous, self-controlling. The new order organises itself.

Balance is stagnation, is death. Order arises from imbalance. Increase of chaos leads to new order. It all sounds very strange. Such metaphors can, however, be recognized in the practice of government functioning. The image of a complex balance of administrative, political and societal actors, that can only be set to move by extreme efforts, shows that the intricate balance in such a network forms the stagnating inhibition for change and renewal.

The sensitivity of complex balances implies stagnation. In such a situation the system indeed has to move rather far away from its equilibrium before any structural reform can take place. Only when the degree and nature of the policy changes reach some qualitative threshold, can the stagnation be broken through, does the system move and does a new order originate. Much dynamics and disorder are necessary for a social complex to cross the threshold and change.

The further parallel holds as well. The new order, the structural change, applies to the meta-level. The real structural change does not apply to the many specific concrete policy issues at stake but mostly exceeds them. The emergent new order exceeds the daily practice of public policy making by far; it even exceeds the imagination of the rare strategic forecaster. The meaning of governance is then of course relative. The influence of a single politician on the course of history is small. Small, more or less accidental, unconscious disturbances during complex policy processes can have far-reaching consequences, which overshadow the planned, intended and predicted outcomes. Whether, how and which pattern will arise in the chaos is not controllable by one actor, is hardly predictable at all and seems to depend on chance.

All things considered, the metaphor of 'order out of chaos' does seem to be an appropriate image of government practice.

Self Organisation

A next step in the conceptual exploration of governance in complex networks is to consider the theory on self-organisation and self-referential systems. The systems theoretical ideas on self-organisation have been influenced by an interesting invention in the field of biology, especially genetics, that is, the model of a living system called 'autopoiesis' (Varela et al., 1974). The origin of its increasing popularity in the social sciences can be found in the publications on self-referential systems by the renowned sociologist Luhmann (1984). In the organisation sciences the term 'autopoiesis' became known mainly because Morgan (1986) used it as one of his metaphors on organisations.

The biological model of autopoiesis pictures a living system being able not only to produce and reproduce its elements but particularly to generate and reproduce its organisation, the interactions between the elements that compose the systems. The capacity of a system to generate its own organisation and to reproduce it, characterises it as living. We will not dwell upon the elaborations of the model in its field of origin, biology and systems theory, but rather proceed with its application in social science (In 't Veld et al., 1991).

Luhmann (1984) speaks of a paradigmatic shift in systems theory. Systems theory started with the holistic notions of parts and whole, proceeded with the distinction between system and environment and subsequently ended up with a theory on self-referential systems. In the development of their elements systems refer to themselves. They are self referentially closed. Communication is not effectuated by external influences and forces, but by the communication network itself. Maintenance of social systems is self-referential reproduction.

In the organisation sciences, autopoiesis became known because of its use by Morgan (1986). He contrasted autopoiesis to the traditional approach in organisation science. Traditionally the emphasis is on the interaction between the adapting organisation and the changing environment. In the contingency approach of organisations the basic line of reasoning is that the environmental situation determines what organisation structure is adequate. The organisation has to adapt to the environment. In an autopoietic system environmental relations will on the contrary be internally determined. The order is reversed, not outside-in but inside-out.

The concept of autopoiesis led Morgan (1986) to three creative interpretations. The first is 'selfreferential closure', the attempt of organisations to handle their environments as if they were self-projections. The second he called 'egocentrism': organisations try to maintain their own identity in the face of a threatening outside world, they become preoccupied with their own importance and underestimate the meaning of the wider context. The third is 'self-reflective evolution': organisational change as an evolution of the own identity in relation to the wider world. Morgan also warned for its dubious implications. Egocentric 'corporate cultures' can harm their environment in the long run. Morgan advocated more self-reflection and less self-centrism.

Autopoiesis models a system which generates and regenerates its organisation. It models stability at the meta-level of the organisation of the system. Whatever the disturbances are at the object-level of the elements of the system, at the meta-level the system maintains its organisation. Chaos can reign in an organisationally stable system. Chaos theory studies the possible structure, order and regularity at the meta-level of a system which seems unstable and chaotic at the object-level. Autopoiesis is an example of that.

Such a model of self-organisation can be used as a model for autonomy and self-control in complex networks. The possibility of a network of autonomous subsystems to maintain itself and its organisation when confronted with external disturbances, its capacity to survive in a turbulent and complex environment, is a vital quality in an administrative situation where direct top-down governmental control is more and more replaced by autonomy and self-regulation of social institutions.

At the same time, a warning for this model seems to be appropriate. Elsewhere (Kickert, 1991), I indicated that a literal translation of autopoiesis can lead to a model of extreme conservatism of a governmental organisation, to 'dynamic conservatism'. The maintenance of the institution, the organisation, as the ultimate and only goal. Whatever happens, government organisations are immortal (Kaufmann, 1976). Autopoiesis pictures that dynamic conservatism. This objection resembles Morgan's warnings against ego-centrism and an overemphasis on self-identity. The objection is that systems can be so full of their own identity and self-image, that the societal environment is not only ignored but even harmed.

A different interpretation with a considerably more positive connotation, arises when connecting self-organisation and self-referentiality to chaos (Jantsch, 1980). Self-organisation can be considered as a condition for self-renewal, for the dynamic process of evolution which in continuous exchange with the environment leads to structural innovations of systems. Contrary to a structure-conserving system an evolutionary system is capable to generate so much change and fluctuations that a threshold is crossed towards a new structure, to another order. In such a context of a far-from-equilibrium, strongly fluctuating, highly chaotic, threshold surpassing system, the idea of self-organisation gets an entirely different connotation from the afore-mentioned ego-centrism and conservatism. It then becomes an indispensable link to prevent such an evolutionary system from the 'big bang', the explosion and destruction. In an image where balance is considered as stagnation, and where order arises from chaos, the self-organising capacity of such a system does definitely not amount to introvert conservatism. When the threshold of the stagnating conservatism is crossed by the increasing pressure for change, by much dynamics and imbalance, it is rather reassuring to know that a new order can be generated and regenerated, that indeed from chaos order will arise.

Lessons for Governance

Theoretical perspectives

In the last section about self-organisation the two main issues of complexity and governance have been synthesised. Self-organisation refers to a complex system which maintains its identity amidst a hostile outside world. In the situation of high complexity and dynamics there is no separate 'third' controller, but rather self-control, particularly the specific type called self-organisation. This creates a conceptual basis for a theory about governance in situations of high complexity and dynamics.

It is time now to assess the results of the explorative search for new conceptions about management of complex networks. What did the abstract reflections on complexity and governance contribute to the further development of a theory of management and governance in complex public sector networks?

The ideas about self-control in complexity, about self-organisation in far-from-balanced situations, offer the perspective of a quite different theory on public management. Difficult complex relations and strategic drastic changes are no longer considered as problems and difficulties which have to be mastered, but rather as sources of innovation. Much complexity and dynamics in such a theory are not considered nasty problems which are hard to deal with, but rather the positive fundaments for innovative self-control. Management of complex networks is then not the maintenance of sensitive intricate balances but the deliberate use of imbalance for the sake of renewal. The notions about self-organisation in far-from-equili-brium situations open quite different perspectives on management and governance. Such a theory must be an appealing perspective for innovative public policy makers who have experienced how long it takes before complex policy networks start moving at all and how extremely difficult it is to obtain any fundamental renewal. Complexity is not considered as something in which to obtain and maintain balance. Imbalance is not a danger to be avoided. Stability and order get a new meaning.. The aim is to get a system so far out of balance that a jump to a new order is made. Not the governance of situations of relative calm and quiet, not the governance of marginal alterations, but periods of fundamental transforma-tions of the system. Not the maintenance of an existing system, but its abolition is the objective of such a theory.

Notice that this differs quite from what is normally meant by the term 'management'.

The second perspective on self-organisation, particularly that of autopoiesis and self-referentiality, is therefore reassuring. This entails the notion that a system which finds itself in a state of high complexity and dynamics, even chaos, possesses the capacity to maintain its structure, its organisation. The notions of self-referential closure and self-centrism, which can have the negative connotation of ultimate dynamic conser-vatism, obtain a different connotation when placed in the situation of governance of fundamental order renewal. If innovation consists of the abolition of an old order, it is not irrelevant that the system is capable to generate and reproduce a new order, that the system is capable of self-governance.

In summary, the ideas of chaos theory and self-organisation do not con-tribute to a general theory on 'normal' management of networks. Rather, they deal with an extraordinary and very specific case, that is, fundamental changes in complex, dynamic networks, and with a very specific type of governance, that is, self-governance of the network.

Let us conclude this section on theoretical perspectives with some remarks about a possible future perspective. As indicated before, one of the characteristics in which the Dutch (and German) science of public administration differs from the North-American, is its broader inter-pretation of 'management' in terms of 'governance'. Research into network management does not primarily stem form the desire to solve specific concrete implementation problems, but rather from the general debate on limitations of government steering. The period of belief in government control made way for a period of aversion of government planning at the end of the seventies. In the beginning of the eighties, the emphasis was on the boundaries and limitations of government steering. In the mid-eighties this negative orientation made way for a more positive orientation on the possibilities of government steering in complexity. In such an evolutionary macro-series of periods, it might be that this is the beginning of a period of attention for self-governance in the public sector.

sixties and seventies	beginning eighties	end of the eighties	nineties
belief in governance	aversion of governance	possibilities of governance	self-governance

The evolution of views on governance

Not only does one see theoretical indications of such a trend towards self-governance, but also practical ones.

Practical Implications

Self-governance has a large and growing significance both within government and in the administrative relationships between government and social actors on various policy areas.

Within Dutch government a process has been going on of privatisation, self-management, independent administrative bodies, autonomous agencies, etc., in other words, various forms of 'autonomising' of government tasks, that is, increasing the distance, the independence, the autonomy, the self-governance of the particular agency vis-a-vis the core of government. In the early eighties government has primarily emphasized privatisation, the transformation of public to private tasks. In the mid-eighties forms of 'internal' autonomising such as self-management and contract-management were created. At the end of the eighties attention revived for functional decentralisation of public tasks in the form of so-called 'independent administrative bodies'. In the beginning of the nineties the idea of autonomous agencies, more or less resembling the British 'next steps' agencies, was added to the Dutch governmental landscape.

Apart from obvious political reasons of economising and withdrawal of government, the 'autonomising' of government organisations is related to the administrative argument of improvement of management. The organisational line of reasoning is as follows. In a complex and dynamic environment an organisation which strongly interacts with its environment - such as government - has to be adaptive and flexible. Adaptivity and flexibility do not relate very well to hierarchical central steering and bureaucratic procedures. The parts of the organisation have to become more autonomous. More autonomy leads to more flexibility and adaptivity, and this means more self-governance.

The relationship between government and societal fields has changed as well. The administrative relations between government and other social, public and private actors have changed in many policy fields. In other words, the complex policy networks and policy communities in the public sector have changed. Withdrawal of government took place in a series of so-called 'great operations': decentralization, deregulation and privatisation.

Apart from these 'great operations' specific changes have occurred at each ministry with different causes, forms and results in the different policy areas. Although it is impossible to point out one common denominator in all these alterations, most changes in the policy networks indicate an increase in the distance between government and the other network participants, a decrease in the unilateral steering by government, and hence an increase in the self-governance of the networks.

So both within government and in the wider public sector networks, the practical significance of self-governance is becoming increasingly important, although the 'real' work of consolidation, operationalisation and empirical validation has yet to begin. Only the ouverture of the conceptual exploration has sounded.

Discussion

One of the many possible criticisms against the previous considerations about control and complexity is that it rather raises questions than it solves problems. The introduction of a very high degree of dynamics, of chaos, raises the question what residual meaning can be attached to governance. Is there any notion of control left at all in such a situation? Likewise the introduction of the concept of self-referential (autopoietic) systems, raises a similar question. If the complex network consists of various self-referential subsystems with their inherent form of closure and self-organisation, what notion of governance of the network then remains? Is it not fair to conclude from the viewpoint of a practically applicable theory on management of public networks, that these images refer to uncontrollable situations? What could be management there, what could be identified as the managing social entity? From that empirical and application-oriented viewpoint serious doubts can be casted upon the abstract conceptual ideas presented before.

It is indeed undeniable that the previous explorative conceptual journey has only resulted in impressionistic vistas. However, it must strongly be denied that it resulted in the conceptual perspective of non-governance. My starting point was the existing theoretical body of knowledge on the coordination of interorganisational networks. Out of a feeling of discomfort, a reflective exploration of the notion of governance in complexity was started. Gradually the explorative journey moved away from 'moderate' complexity and ended up in situations of 'extreme' complexity and dynamics. Actually a situation where normative opinions and ethics enter the scene, that is, a situation where the complexity and chaos of the policy networks at stake have reached such heights that nothing seems to be possible at all. Does one have to acquiesce in the unchangeability and uncontrollability of such an extreme complex? Is stagnation and the impossibility of structural innovation inevitable then?

My personal belief in the values of government makes me refuse to ever admit the impossibility of public government, to resign governance.

16

GOVERNANCE AND THE PROBLEM OF REPRESENTATION IN PUBLIC ADMINISTRATION: THE CASE OF FINLAND

KYÖSTI PEKONEN

The Problem of Representation in Public Administration

According to Kooiman, governance concerns the interaction between government and society. By 'governing' he means 'all those activities of social, political and administrative actors together that can be seen as purposeful efforts to guide, steer, control or manage (sectors or facets of) societies'. He also puts forward the hypothesis that 'governing is not primarily what governments do by themselves (the official point of view), but a continuous process of interaction between social groups and public or semi-public institutions and authorities' (Kooiman, 1990: 2).

In politics, representation is a classical concept in the analysis of the interaction between government and society. We are accustomed to thinking and demanding that politics and a government must, in one way or another, represent society.

In the actual representative apparatus, i.e. government, we can, of course, draw the customary distinction between politics (politicians) and administration (civil servants). These groups have traditionally had different roles and functions in the process of representation. In recent times however, the problem of what public administration represents and how it represents, has become particularly actual and acute. This requires a more penetrating analysis of the representative process.

During the past few decades we have been witnessing lively discussion and research on the strengthening of the political role of administration. 'By 1970, civil servants throughout the West were deciding how to restructure the steel industry, how to design an actuarially sound pension scheme, where to locate airports, how to break inflation, and a thousand other such issues. Throughout this century the tendency toward governmental omnicompetence has accelerated virtually everywhere in the West' (Aberbach, Putnam and Rockman, 1981: 2). This strengthening of the political role of administration brings the problem of the basis of administrative action compellingly to the fore. Whom or what does administration represent? Whose problems, or what kind of problems, is administration trying to tackle?

There are many ways in which one may try to approach the representative role of administration. The classical point of departure has been the argument that the civil servants should not act in accordance with their own interests but with those of society. In official documents the interests of the society are usually equated with that of the state. For the civil servants this usually means carrying out orders of the state employer. In official documents this often is stated as follows (an example characteristic to Finnish official documents): *'with regard to different interests, civil servants should have an objective, state representing attitude and should not identify themselves with any other parties involved'* (Keskushall-intokomitean II osamietintö, 1978: 308). The problem of this kind of viewpoint is that the state is not a homogenous structure. Instead, we have, in fact, a 'plurality of states' which may even struggle with each other (of which governmental departments provide a notorious example). Therefore, the above mentioned 'objective' attitude does not necessarily become equated with the state. Even representing the 'will' of the state may prove difficult because there may exist a 'plurality of states' and, therefore, many 'wills' which may strive to achieve conflicting aims.

Another widely known approach to the problem of representation is to argue that the representative administrative apparatus should constitute a cross-section of the people. However, as many studies have shown, this is seldom the case: as a rule, civil servants' social background differs clearly both from that of the people as well as from that of the MPs (Aberbach, Putnam and Rockman: 46-83; Laegreid and Olsen, 1978: 259-60; on the situation in Finland, see Alestalo and Uusitalo, 1972). Moreover, in many studies it has been emphasized that an organization or an institution is more 'powerful' than an individual. This implies, among other things, that the social background of the administrative personnel has less influence on administrative activity than does e.g. their position within the organizational hierarchy. In other words, in their actions, administrative personnel do not so much represent their social backgrounds as their status in the hierarchy of an organization. With regard to the problem of representation in public administration, this means that the interests of the state would outstrip other interests in the actions of administrative personnel. (On these kind of conclusions, see e.g. Laegreid and Olsen (1978: 259-60) who emphasize the significance of 'administrative biography' and the power of the organization; Bourdieu, 1981, with the focus on the power of the institution with respect to the symbolic capital of the administrative personnel; Pekonen, 1985, who emphasize the significance of the phase of a political cycle).

If these are not sufficient solutions to the problem of representation in public administration (and it seems to me that they are not), where should we try to look for them? What would be a 'more constructive' viewpoint? One way to approach the problem of representation might be to analyze it from the viewpoint of language and rhetoric.

Administrative action may be both described and analyzed through the language used in administration. From the language (vocabulary) of the administration and from the way it uses language (its rhetoric), we may try to deduce e.g. to whom the administration addresses itself, what its real audience is, i.e. whom and what it actually tries to represent. On the other hand, we can also draw conclusions from the language used how successful the administration is in its governing endeavours.

The Problem of 'Representative Language and Rhetoric'

Both politics and public administration must 'represent' somebody and something in their language (e.g. in the vocabulary used) and rhetoric (in the actual use of language). How should this 'representative language and rhetoric' be understood knowing that language itself does not exhaustively represent or express reality? Or to put it differently: language should be seen 'as a historical contingency rather than as a medium which is gradually taking on the true shape of the true world or the true self' (Rorty, 1989: 50). If language cannot take us to the objective truth or to the true description of society, to what reality really is, how can language and rhetoric then help us solve the problem of representation?

Language, however, still has at least one very important function in this respect; it is the medium of communication, a medium by which one can create ties. Can these ties be understood as the basis of representation? To my mind the answer seems to be: yes and no. Yes, when we understand language as the expression of the forms of life. Here, we can follow Ludwig Wittgenstein's well-known statements in his Philosophical Investigations: 'And to imagine a language means to imagine a form of life' (19) [...] 'The speaking of language is part of an activity, or of a form of life.' (23). Different forms of life have their own languages and language games and, therefore, we can 'see' the connection between life and language. And then the second answer: no. These languages can be only transitory phases of representation. Transitory, because languages should also be seen 'as new forms of life constantly killing off old forms' (Rorty, 1989: 19) and because these ties in fact do not form a common vocabulary on which almost all should agree; rather, it is a matter of 'overlapping words' (ibid.: 93).

If we deal with the connection between language and forms of life only, we necessarily get too static a picture. The problem is not that such a connection does not exist. It is introduced by the inevitable change which is constantly taking place both in languages and in forms of life. With respect to language, a change can mean a new way of describing the past.

If our main interest is not the close relationship between language and a form of life, which is in a way self-evident, but the much more dynamic problem of their necessary change, we must also find a more dynamic concept than that of language to describe the process of representation. I argue that the concept of audience, referring to the group of people which the language user actually 'speaks' to and which he or she is trying to persuade with his or her arguments, may be useful in this respect.

Following Perelman's idea of 'new rhetoric', we could discuss the 'rhetoric of representation'. We may find connections between rhetoric as a way of using language and the problem of representation. This becomes clear e.g. in Perelman's definition of audience. He defines (1982: 48) it as the ensemble of those the speaker wishes to influence by his argumentation. The speaker wishes to reach some kind of consensus with this ensemble. This means e.g. that language using is always addressed to some audience, and that the speaker must always take his or her audience into account. This language-addressing may be seen as an attempt to establish a tie, which, again, may be understood as signifying an attempt to institute a representative relationship. However, in the end the addressed listeners are in the position to decide whether or not the speaker's re-presentation of some aspect of reality is worth anything.

The Problem of 'Representative Language and Rhetoric' in Politics and Public Administration

The strengthening of the social and political role of administration has made the classical 'Weberian' picture of the division of labour between politics and administration problematic. Traditionally, this picture implies that politicians 'make politics', whereas civil servants do the administering. Politicians make decisions; bureaucrats merely implement them. However, the modern West has produced a situation which has been described as a 'pure hybrid'. 'The last quarter of this century is witnessing the virtual disappearance of the Weberian distinction between the roles of the politician and the bureaucrat, producing what may be labelled 'pure hybrid' ' (Aberbach, Putnam and Rockman: 16).

The speculation (which, it should be added, is not mere speculation) about the emergence of the 'pure hybrid' poses at least two questions for us. Firstly, now that the trends towards the emergence of the hybrid situation are evident, have the political and administrative organizations undergone organizational restructuring? What conclusions can we draw from the analysis of language in this respect? Secondly, how should public administration be organized in order to enable the administration to use the representative language and rhetoric which this new situation would seem to require? I will consider these issues briefly in the following. Moreover, I will venture to put forward some tentative answers.

At first we must briefly describe the role that language plays in politics and administration: When one talks about the substance of politics and about politics as dealing with 'public affairs', one must first define those 'affairs'. *'On the one hand, politics constitutes the transformation of physical confrontation into verbal ones, and on the other, the resolution or accommodation of these confrontations involves the use of political rhetoric...'* (Hall, 1972: 51). This definition implies much more than stating facts which would have the same meaning for everyone; the question is of naming those facts, and, along with it, the provision of meaning. In the definition of the situation *'language is [...] not simply an instrument for describing events but itself a part of events, shaping their meaning'*

(Edelman, 1977: 4). *'[...] It is language about political events rather than the events themselves that everyone experiences [...]'* (ibid.: 142).

If modern politics is seen as a struggle for words and language by which reality is in fact defined, the relationship of modern politics to reality is seen as being realized through the struggle concerning the nature of reality itself. Accordingly, we can define representation in politics as a struggle revolving around the reality-principle itself; and this struggle is realized through a struggle over what kinds of language and rhetoric are understandable, plausible and significant.

Politics, politicians and politicizers may, in the struggle over the definition of the reality-principle, i.e. in the representative process, play a more or less active part. From the point of view of the problem of governance, the question should be about the ability of politics, politicians and politicizers to introduce into public discourse the most relevant problems and points of view.

On the part of civil servants, the articulation and representation of interests, values, etc. is even more problematic: as a rule they have no immediate relationship with, responsibility for or dependence on citizens or the electorate. Because public administration and civil servants have no immediate and imperative relationship with the electorate, they have, therefore, limits in their capability of representing and articulating interests that are, for example, unorganized, broad (bridging the divisions between functional sectors in the administration), strongly politicized, ideological or simply novel.

Accordingly, we may propose a hypothesis: in a situation which is not strongly politicized, and which exhibits no intensive political competition and struggle for political leadership, we may define the traditional (Weberian) role of administration to be in its 'essence' a definition of the situation, a definition which conforms to the existing balance of social and political forces. This kind of administrative action may be described as follows: civil servants' policy-making role and ability lie, above all, in their role as arbitrators of organized clientele interests in their specific functional sector, the objective being to establish the balance of forces, a status quo and a consensus and, accordingly, to minimize conflicts and to seek technically appropriate solutions to the more accurately defined problems (Aberbach, Putnam and Rockman: 13-14, 241-48, 256).

When we emphasize the special role of language and rhetoric in the process of representation, we must also analyze the division of labour between politics (politicians and politicizers) and the administration (civil servants) with respect to language and rhetoric. On the level of language, we may further differentiate between political and technocratic modes of action. The technocratic mode is often, when we follow the Weberian model, identical with the administrative one.

We have at our disposal at least two ways to describe the specificity of political language and rhetoric with respect to the problem of representation. Firstly, we may talk about 'politicizing language'. This 'politicizing language' may be understood as an attempt to find a new way to describe the past and the present (usually, of course, a specific aspect of the past). Here, we are dealing with a change in a 'form of life' and, accordingly, a change in language. This kind of new and in its effect politicizing, language in a way breaks 'silence' (unquestioned self-evidence) which the past and 'frozen' power structure so easily produce (by means of sedimented language and dead metaphors). In 'silence' everything goes on without questioning. The 'function' of criticism, in the form of politicizing language, is to bring the undiscussed under discussion.

The second specificity of political language can be described by the friend-enemy metaphor. When the question is about a political mode of action, a political actor usually presupposes that somewhere out there he or she has an 'opponent'. It is understood that this opponent also has the role of a political speaker. In a way the speaker tries, by the aid of language, to influence the opponent and also otherwise to mobilize people 'behind his or her language', in other words, to take seriously the reality principle which is communicated by his language.

In a technocratic mode of action, the opponent is reified; in a way one 'loses sight of' the opponent because the 'aspect of consciousness', the social and political nature of action, has no directive role in this type of action. Opponents are no longer other people (with their languages), but facts and regularities in society, or people as 'things'. Accordingly, the social and political role of language is more or less excluded -or attempts are made to exclude it- from the domain of technocratic action. An apolitical administrative action often tries to simulate this kind of action: its use of language may be such that it tries to 'say' that administrative action is not directed against anybody, but is value-free, neutral and for general welfare or the common good. Therefore, we can say that official language strives above all to determine 'the rules of the game', and this determining is in most cases realized through existing power relationships.

Accordingly, the administration may gradually develop an orientation in which willing, knowing, opinions of what can be done, the representation of interests, etc. are perceived and evaluated from the standpoint of existing 'necessities'. Now we can propose an ideal-typical definition with regard to the problem of representation in public administration. By the following definition I try to describe the most common way to approach the problem of representation. Generally speaking, representation in administration means a definition of the situation in such a way that this definition conforms to the existing balance of social and political forces. This definition of the situation is usually accomplished through leaning on 'facts', 'regularities' and 'necessities' which, so it is argued, exist in society. The most common form of administrative legitimating language seems to be language which I have elsewhere called the 'necessity-language and rhetoric' (Pekonen, 1985). The way of acting is legitimated by saying that there were no alternatives to what was done. Furthermore, these 'necessities' are typically justified by reference to economic requirements.

I have tried to show how administrative 'facts' may be formed from the perspectives and needs of an organization or abstract 'necessities' which are supposed to guide societal development. Technical apolitical facts which have been separated from their social contexts may become the real facts on which administrative action is based.

This may indicate the possibility that an attempt is made to persuade audience by appealing to impersonal and nonsubjective organizational or social necessities and needs. Accordingly, administrative documentation may also reveal the technical nature of language and language use. An administrative text is supposed to be objective and impersonal, void of any personal style or expression of values.

I want to argue that this kind of language, the way of using it, and the corresponding 'form of life' (the way of organizing activity), do not represent a fruitful approach to the establishment of an active role and the social and political significance administration has. This kind of language implies problems and perhaps a failure in the attempts to govern.

Next I will show some examples which concern failures of governance in public administration. In these I have especially in mind how failures may be studied from the viewpoint of the rhetoric used.

Examples of the Forms of Administrative Language with Respect to the Problem of Governance

The ability of administration to govern social processes may be evaluated on the basis of the language that administrative actors use. In the following I will give examples of some language-usages; examples which, I hope, reveal something about the problem of governance. To my mind, we can render this problem more concrete by focusing on the role of the audience in the different ways of using language in public administration.

Administrative Language as a Situation Dependent Definition of the 'Rules of the Game'

When we considered the political and representative role of administration and the ways in which administration tries to deal with this role that 'felt so dangerous', we defined that role ideal-typically as a language and the use of language with the idea of trying to define a situation by revising the respective 'rules of the game' on the basis of existing power relations. How does this happen? How is the audience constructed in this kind of action?

When we try to understand why administration functions in a certain way, we must focus on the problem of the horizon of orientation in administration. Murray Edelman emphasizes the significance of 'mutual role-taking' (taking the role of one another) for both social action and the creation of the self. Role-taking is action, finding and constructing a relevant audience; and through this role-taking, significant symbols which 'direct' our action, and in terms of which we rank values, are created (Edelman, 1964: 49-50). The 'choice' of language and the way of speaking, then, provide the means of role-taking. This mutual role-taking is necessary because organizations survive only in so far as they represent the interests of those who may serve or damage the organization.

However, mutual role-taking in a situation in which it is necessary to follow existing social and political power-relations may produce at least three problematic ways of using language: Sometimes the language used reflects, following the course of action, the balance between different interests and social forces. Conflicting expectations and goals may 'compel' one into a vague usage of language. With this kind of vague language, administration avoids taking and expressing firm loyalties to anyone concerned. However, the result may be a 'state of indecision' expressed by the vagueness of language. Administration may have too many audiences which it tries to please.

On the other hand, administrative language and rhetoric are not usually designed for the common people but for 'real customers' whose interests it primarily serves. This may mean that administrative language is characterized by language which is understood by their users in highly pragmatic terms. This language is often affectively and cognitively insignificant outside the confines of this small circle (see Edelman, 1964: 50). Therefore, there may emerge an insiders' way of using language which, again, may tie those working within the organization to this insiders' language. Edelman states (1977: 98) in this connection that 'resort to jargon in any organization can be understood as an implicit expression of loyalty to the values that are dominant in that organization'. In the cases discussed above, audiences are either too 'small', or (as in the latter case) identical with the hierarchy of the organization.

Changes in the construction of the audience usually follow changes in social and political power relations. 'Strong politics' naturally defines the audience construction in public administration. However, when politics are 'weak', as was the case in Finland in the first part of the 1980s (see Pekonen, 1985), the audience may change from politics and civil society to more 'abstract' audiences. In a dissertation (Summa, 1989) analyzing housing policy in Finland, the author shows that the hypothetical audience of the planning texts has changed from universal political audience to the Ministry of Finance. The change in audience has also changed the way of using language. 'The planning system has lead to the formation of an abstract and suppressive rhetoric which dominates the political, administrative and civil discussion on housing questions, and prevents rather than generates action in this field' (Summa: 221-22). 'The result of this is that the argumentative value of moral and political claims concerning the state's role or duties in housing, has decreased, while the value of technical arguments directly supporting the budgetary share of the housing sector as well as arguments drawing on state financial justifications, have increased. The change in the audience of the planning argumentation is at the same time reflected in a depolitization of a political question.' (ibid.: 222)

Bureaucratic Way of Using Language

When one takes into account the increasingly important role of administration, it is evident that if administration purports to be rational, it must also be politically rational. The question is about this political rationality when administration tries to tie the most important social interests to itself, to assimilate them as a part of itself (see e.g. Wassenberg and Kooiman, 1980). This can be seen, for example, in the increase of outside representation at different levels of administration and in party political nominations in the filling of administrative posts. Consequently, administration becomes in a way more 'politicized' and, at the same time, it becomes easier (or safer) for parliamentary politics to realize party interests (to make politics through policy-decisions) within the administration than in an open struggle before the public. However, the danger in this kind of corporative politics may be the actualization of the problem of bureaucracy.

A bureaucratic way of using language, which discloses the actualization of the problem of bureaucracy, communicates the failure of representation between government and society. It is the question of a phase of a political cycle characterized by the strengthening of the political role of administration so that administration has the possibility, need, will, and perhaps even the 'necessity' to step into the sphere of significations (political language). However, without adequate social contacts, the creation of social and political meanings cannot be realized representatively (for an analysis of this kind of political cycle in Finland, see Pekonen, 1985). This kind of situation of 'indetermination' may be seen in the actualization of the problem of official language in the latter part of the 1970s in Finland. (A state committee was set up to improve official language, as if the real problem was a mere language problem.) As an expression of this 'state thinking', it has been characteristic of this official language that it is highly formal, rigid, and difficult to read and understand. In this sense, official language is an expression of the bureaucratic form of 'state thinking', an expression of the actualization of the problem of bureaucracy in the political system. (For a more detailed analysis, Pekonen, 1983.)

In this kind of bureaucratic mode of 'speaking', the audience addressed is as large and general as possible, but exactly because it is so 'abstract', the discourse does not really address anyone. This general audience lacks an empirical basis. Society and its members do not receive concrete answers to their concrete problems.

Bureaucratic 'silence' may also be seen as a form of bureaucratic rhetoric. Silence means an ability, possibility, and will to remain quiet even when speaking is required. Here, the audience is identical with the hierarchical organization itself.

Conclusions and the Model of Governance as an Interactive Representative Process

The strengthening of the ways of using language described above and of this kind of administrative-technical language and rhetoric in social and political practice, and in relations between government and society, raise a challenge to the representative roles of both politics and administration. This challenge means the possibility of ungovernability which was first manifested in the creation and management of meanings.

The traditional rigid division of labour between administration and politics and the underestimation of the political role of administration no longer meet the requirements of the representative role of administration. To uphold these would only strengthen the administrative-technical rhetoric viewpoint, as a result of which the power of a 'one-dimensional fact' based on argued necessities in society or on needs of a hierarchical organization might grow to such an extent that it may start to authorize politics. Therefore, one should not be fearful of the political role of administration but try to develop new relevant institutional practices which would strengthen the role of politicizers (today especially citizens and social movements) in the governing process. The confrontation between the different languages and rhetorics and their struggle over the legitimacy of language should at least prove that facts are only 'facts'. In this way, administration might find new strategies to properly realize its political and representative role.

To my mind, this would mean that in Finland, whose politico-administrative systems are characterized by a deep-seated tradition of maintaining distance and an attitude of 'looking down on' citizens, a tradition still very much alive today, such new ways of organizing representation as e.g. the strengthening of the social and political role of administration. This will require that administration 'steps out into society'. 'Stepping out into society' could mean: diminishing the excessive number of the sectors of administration; bringing administration closer to 'clients'; citizens' participation in the production of goods and services which could mean a step towards decentralization of authority when citizens are seen as co-governors and co-decision makers, not simply as consumers or providers of services; breaking up the rigid hierarchical line organization and creating teams of liability as well as making the most important offices periodic. These kind of changes would, perhaps, mean a change in the principle of organization; the change from the organization of hierarchical control to that of liability and accountability, the shift from hierarchical to team control in organizations. Liability and accountability should be understood in the sense that they could no longer be understood as a responsibility to such 'abstractions' as the organization and necessities in society, but as liability and accountability to concrete audiences, to those concerned. These concrete forms of liability would result in social and political dialogue. The 'result' might be described as an agreement: 'Thus we willed it'.

In sum, the governability of modern society requires representative interaction between the actors. It seems to me that the concept of representative interaction can perhaps bridge the sharp dichotomies between politics and administration and between the public and private sectors; the dichotomies which have become in many ways obstacles to governance in modern society.

In this chapter I have been particularly interested in the problem of how representative interaction should be understood and organized in order to guarantee the best possible success in governance, remembering that successful interaction both requires and should create good learning capacities, flexibility and accountability.

The fundamental task implied by the idea of representation based on interaction is creating a common ground (which, of course, is destined to be relative and transitory) where value issues can be discussed. The problem is that of creating a situation and an arena where those concerned can begin a reality-constructing conversation. We might describe public administration as an arena where different aims, values, motives and interests can meet. What, then, is the use of all this for public administrators themselves? It facilitates, among other things, what White calls 'interpretive reasoning' (White, J.D., 1990: 133). Interpretive reasoning describes the type of thought and action involved in understanding what values and criteria are preferred and what means and ends are available to a decision maker.

Now I would like to present my model of interactive representation. With the model I try to describe the role of representation with respect to governance and emphasize representation as a learning process which should be based on interaction. The basic arguments here are: Diversity, understood as increasing differences between subjects to be governed, necessarily requires 'more' representation. Representation based on politicization and interaction at first furthers diversity, but, however, in the decision making process it should temporarily 'reduce' this diversity. In complexity the question is about the relationship between the parts and the whole. The whole is here understood as a 'temporary result' of political struggle between the parts. Governance may be understood here as the creation of the 'whole'. This creation naturally requires that the structural complexity of the system to be governed must be represented. Breaks and ruptures are characteristic to dynamic circumstances. Forces of the 'new' usually 'represent' these non-linear changes.

Governance as an Interactive Representative Process

In the model presented here, all arrows represent communicative action and arrows with two arrow heads tell about tensions and conflicts.

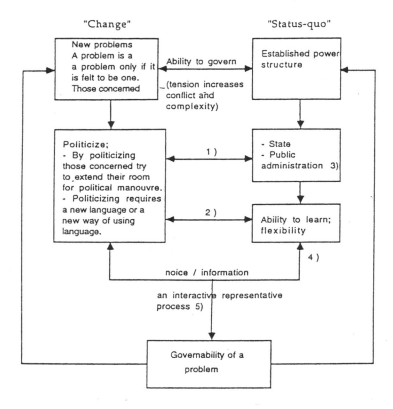

My starting point in the diagram is the idea that particularly the introduction of new problems, the 'change', poses the real challenge to
governance. I regard regeneration as the ideal-typical situation of governance. The success of the system in modern society is measured by its
ability to adapt. This is almost always a problem for the established power
structure because governing bodies have great difficulty in leaving behind
the 'old' image once this has been formed together with applied instruments and a chosen action path.

1) The basic argument here is that politicization, too, should be under-
    stood as one capacity among others. By means of politicizing, those
    concerned try to alter the image main actors and other people have
    of the problem in question and through this modify their social
    position.

2) By altering the images actors have acquired, those concerned try to
    create willingness to act in a given way, to do something. According-
    ly, politicizing provides those concerned with the means of enlarging
    their room for political manoeuvre.

3) The role of public administration in the representative process has
    traditionally been described, following the traditional Weberian model,
    as a nonpolitical system where the contacts of administrators with

society are 'distant', few and 'poor'. This model tries to take a new viewpoint towards politics which especially is understood as politicization.

4) It is very important for the learning ability of state and political institutions and public administration (civil servants) that they should get as 'close' to those represented as possible so that they 'hear' the 'speech' of represented, or perhaps even better: so 'close' that a representative would be capable to re-present, i.e., to move a little bit ex ante than ex post. In this respect I claimed that public administration 'needs' new kinds of mediation mechanisms. Social and political learning, in order to be successful, require organizational learning and the building up of new institutional learning capacities. Learning capacities, in turn, require flexibility, innovative capacities, and accountability.

5) The question here is one of a social and political learning process - which, of course, 'flows' also towards citizens. The special learning capacity of this kind of new interaction lies in learning by doing. In this process it is in fact 'decided' whether or to what extent the effects of politicizing are judged as either noise or information.

    The interaction between those concerned is a precondition for practical wisdom, i.e. the ability to relate principles to practice and practice to another practice. Practical wisdom requires practical discourse. Decisions about what ends to pursue and what means to use are the subject matter of this practical discourse. Practical discourse involves discussion, debate, deliberation, and argumentation over what is true or false, good or bad, right or wrong, and what should be desired. Dialogue involves communication, argumentation, deliberation, persuasion, and choice. The goal of practical discourse is the attainment of a mutual understanding of peoples' beliefs and values (White, J.D., 1990:143).

17

MODES OF GOVERNANCE
AND ADMINISTRATIVE CHANGE[1]

TORBEN BECK JØRGENSEN

Modes of Governance: A Typology of Public Sector Organisations

In this chapter we will discuss the heterogeneity of the public sector and its implications for public management. Starting point is the assumption that public management has to cope with growing diversity, dynamics and complexity *within* the public sector. In doing so, it is a prerequisite to acknowledge and conceptualize public sector heterogeneity. For that purpose, a typology of modes of governance will be presented below. In the following sections this typology will be related to the concepts of diversity, dynamics and complexity. In the concluding sections some implications for public management will be touched upon.

A typology can be developed in several, well-known, ways. The public sector can be categorized according to function (service, regulation), administrative level (department/agency; central government/local government), policy subsystem (agriculture, labour market etc.), and organisational type (bureaucratic/non-bureaucratic).

In the typology to be presented, focus is on the value orientation, by which is meant the political aspects of public organisations. In general, the basic orientation of a public organisation can be fourfold: public organisations can serve one of the following:

• the politicians,
• general principles or values,
• organized actors other than politicians,
• the primary users.

Based on this simple categorisation, four modes of governance will be presented. Each model specifies interactions between key actors in the state and within society, including the general role of the state and the citizens,

---

[1] This article is part of a multidisciplinary research project on organization and management of public organizations. Five state organizations were selected as cases and studied in detail. Based on the experiences from the case studies a database was established in 1990. It contains information on 120 state organizations on 1156 variables. Information on the state organizations mentioned in this article is drawn from the project archive and project reports. The author is indebted to comments from A. Dunsire.

the normative basis of public organizations and the organizational context (interorganizational networks) within which they are embedded.[2] Moreover, the typology emphasizes key aspects of internal operating principles, including control and decision-making forms and basic organizing principles. The models are summarized in figure 1.

The *hierarchial state* is the classical parliamentary model of most Western European states. It is characterized by the constitutional rules for election, parliament, and government. According to this model, the role of the state is to govern society on the basis of political preferences. The elected parliamentarians are viewed as 'the architects of society' (March and Olsen, 1989: 113). The role of the citizens is to elect the politicians and, between elections, to act as subjects.

Public organisations are organized in such a way that the political control of the administration's loyalty is made efficient and (equal) citizens are treated alike. Thus, the ideal model is the neutral bureaucracy that pursues no independent values in relation to either the citizens or the politicians. Dunleavy and O'Leary (1987: 185) label this model 'the externally controlled machine model'. Consequently, the orientation of public organizations is upwards to 'the owners' and the basic organizing principle is a vertical top-down relation. Control is carried out as 'comptrol' (Hood and Schuppert, 1988), using hierarchy and rules internally as well as externally.

In the model of the *autonomous state* the role of the state is one of safeguarding values. The role of public organisations is *not* neutral. On the contrary, they are expected to actively guarantee and sustain certain values and in this way to serve the abstract 'public-at-large'. They are *'carriers of cultures, missions, values, and identities'* (March and Olsen, 1989: 114) and the citizen is guaranteed law and order, is guided, and socialized. The orientation is introvert - towards the central mission of the organisation - and the basic organizing principle is almost one of short-circuiting vertical relations, i.e. to protect the organisational core from politicians and users, as both groups are to be considered ignorant laymen that possess no insight into what is essential; e.i. the production and development of professional and moral values.

---

[2]   Several theoretical ideas and models from organization theory, control theory, political science and state theory have been useful while constructing the typology (Beck Jørgensen and Larsen, 1987; Blau and Scott, 1963; Dunleavy and O'Leary, 1987; Hood and Schuppert, 1988, March and Olsen, 1989; Olsen, 1986; Rothstein, 1987).

Mode	The Roles of Public Organisations	The Roles of Citizens	Control Forms	Normative Bases	Organizational Context
The hierarchial state	Neutral implementation on the basis of political preferences	Voter and subject	'Comptrol' Hierarchy, rules	Political loyalty, 'the will of the people'	Parliament, Cabinet, Parental Department, Ministry of Finance, General Audit Bureau
The autonomous state	The safeguarding of rights and moral and professional values	Legally protected, guided and socialized individual	Peer group control, socialization, institutional rivalry	Legality, moral and professional standards	Professional associations, non-economic interest groups, 'duplicate organisations' in other countries
The negotiating state	Mediator in corporate structures	Member of interest organisations	Negotiations, Countervailing powers	Consensus and compromise, political stability	Industrial interest organisations, labour market organisations, employee organisations
The responsive state: • supermarket state	Act as a business firm	Consumer	Competition	Efficiency	Competitors
• service state	Act as a 'listening monopoly'	Client	Dialogue	Service	None (perhaps user groups)
• self-governing state	Setting frames for self-governing	Citizen, co-producer	Selfregulation	Selfdevelopment, participatory democracy	None

Figure 1 Modes of Governance

Autonomy can be brought about in several ways. Firstly, autonomy can be secured through *legal rules*. The ideal types here are the court and court-like bodies. Neither politicians nor citizens can intervene. Secondly, autonomy can be secured by an active subscribing to *basic values*. The ideal type is 'the normative organisation (Etzioni, 1968) or 'the missionary organisation' (Mintzberg, 1983), both of which recruit employees on the basis of attitudes, values held or a certain life experience. This type has a cause, and pursues the values held to the extent of almost preaching those values. Thirdly, autonomy can be secured by *expertise*. The idealtype is 'the professional organisation' (Mintzberg, 1983), which either recruits professionals from universities or trains its staff itself (or a combination of the two).

Quite often, these remedies are combined in practice. The growing use of professionals and semi-professionals in many public organisations is a striking feature of the development of the public sector. A profession is very often marked not only by expertise but also by certain values (ethical codex).

Organisations belonging to the autonomous state are not entirely left without external control. Control can be carried out through socialisation and peer-group evaluations (Hood and Schuppert, 1988), based on norms and knowledge (Beck Jørgensen and Larsen, 1987). In some cases external control can also be carried out through institutional rivalry.

The *negotiating state* builds on the idea of 'realpolitik'. The state cannot be regarded as an autocratic agent that has a free hand to impose all its decisions on citizens. The state is up against many interests such as industrial organisations, labour-market organisations and employee organisations. The role of the state is to negotiate between different interests. In this model the citizen acts as a member of one or several interest organisations.

The public organisation is located in arenas of dense but organized conflicts and its role is that of a mediator. This mediating role comprises attempts to act as a weathervane, balance interests in an impartial way, but also to actively create a balance based on the interests of the public organisation (Dunleavy and O'Leary, 1987: 43-49). Apart from the concrete tasks that have to be performed, an important aspect of the negotiating state is that of reproducing and developing patterns of influence which can facilitate political integration and stability.

Public organisations may be organized in multiple ways, but are specifically characterized by their location in an institutional structure, comprising different fora/channels of negotiation such as hearing procedures, networks of corporatively composed councils, boards, committees, commissions, etc., to which authority has been delegated (March and Olsen, 1989: 112). Thus, the orientation is lateral-extrovert and the basic organizing principle is characterized by horizontal relations between the public organisation and various organized interests. Control can be said to be carried out through the necessity to reach an agreement among a number of autonomous parties (Hood and Schuppert, 1988).

The Responsive State

The model builds on the idea of the single individual's recognized demand for concrete goods and services. Basically, the task of the state is to see to it that the system is responsive to the concrete 'here and now' needs of the citizens. Although the public organisation can be structured in many ways, the basic orientation is downwards to the user and the basic organizing principle is vertical bottom-up, i.e. the opposite of that of the hierarchial state.

The responsive state has three variants. These can be distinguished by the mechanisms which ensure responsiveness.

The *supermarket state* is characterized by internal incentives related to productivity measures, competition between public organisations and by user fee systems affecting demand and other market-like mechanisms. The general role of the state is basically to ensure that public organisations enter into a fair competition, and that equal market conditions exist for all users (i.e. function as a kind of an Anti Trust Agency). This role of public organisations corresponds to one of a firm in a market, with the citizen acting as the consumer. The internal organisation of the administration may vary, but the key values for assessing organisational forms are survival, flexibility, economy, and efficiency (March and Olsen, 1989: 115). In its extreme form this involves privatisation, and the state is nothing more than an aggregate, an 'automatic' resultant of citizen demand. This variant is rooted in market economics and control is obtained through competitive processes in product or capital markets (Hood and Schuppert, 1988).

The *service state* is characterized by being generally service-oriented towards the citizen; this orientation is not, however, created by market-like mechanisms, but is rather to be viewed as an intrinsic part of the staff's professional code and the organisational culture. The public organisation may enjoy monopoly status but it has learned to function as a 'listening monopoly'. The citizen's role is a mixture of being client and consumer. This variant is rooted in consumerism as 'an officially-approved fashion' (Pollitt, 1987: 43) and in the corporate-culture tradition (Rhodes, 1987). The variant is close to the weak variant of the autonomous state, and the main control forms are similar to these mentioned in describing the autonomous state.

The *self-governing state* assumes that contrary to the above-mentioned variants the citizens not only have an essential impact on the services which the administration offers, but take part in the production process itself, not only as co-producers but also as citizens deciding what is to be produced and under what circumstances. Control can be carried out in several ways, for example by establishing user-group representation in public organisations (Hood and Schuppert, 1988) or by transferring grants directly to citizens, who in their turn organize the production themselves. This variant is mainly rooted in the tradition of participatory democracy (Pateman, 1970). While the two former models belong to the school of the 'new right normative state' (Dunleavy and O'Leary, 1987) the third model does not. Normatively speaking it is rather a typical leftist model. Analytically the crucial difference lies in the distinction between 'consumer' and 'citizen' (Rhodes, 1987).

Diversity

The simplest but perhaps also most important observation is that the public sector is characterized by a striking diversity. The typology helps to clarify this diversity and thereby to allow us to acknowledge the possibility that at one and the same time different parts of the public sector - their internal working and social-political interactions - may function or be guided according to different principles inherent in the types.

Although the modes of governance should be regarded as ideal types in the Weberian sense - i.e. we cannot expect to meet them as pure forms in reality - it is possible to identify examples that typify traits of each model. The hierarchial state is represented in all ministries, although to a varying degree, and especially in such areas as fiscal policy, transferring tasks, and regulation. The autonomous state is represented in many cultural institutions, hospitals as well as research and educational institutions. Examples include courts and similar bodies. The negotiating state is illustrated by such policy subsystems as labour market and industrial policy. The responsive state is represented within service areas such as institutions for children and elderly people and health service.

Looking at the historical development it is fair to hypothesize that this diversity has been increasing for quite some time. The primary features of the hierarchial state were already evident in Denmark in the middle of the nineteenth century due to the political development and especially the bureaucratization of public administration. Since that time, the model has been developed in practice as well as discussed and commented upon by many commissions and committees.

In contrast to this, the origin of the autonomous state is more diffuse. Cultural institutions and research and educational institutions can be traced far back in history. But this mode of governance has grown significantly during this century, partly as a result of the development of the 'rechtstaat', partly as a result of the strong development of all forms of professional expertise.

The negotiating state was developed after the Second World War, and the idea has been discussed in the theoretical literature in terms of the corporatist state and pluralist state. Some political scientists hold it as the distinctive feature of modern West European states (March and Olsen, 1989), but here and there it was actually introduced much earlier. The regulated economy in Denmark during the First World War shows clear features of the negotiating state and if we specifically focus on the agricultural sector, it goes as far back as the late nineteenth century.

The responsive state is a 'newcomer'. It is to be regarded as a feature of the political debate of the eighties. This does not exclude, however, that its historical roots may originate from an earlier time or that we might be able to find earlier waves of user orientation. The Danish 'free-school tradition', going back to the nineteenth century, is an example.

This brief - and admittedly incomplete - discussion leads to one important point: although it is possible to some extent to link different modes of governance to different historical periods, it is not likely that one model is definitively replaced by another. Rather, the development is characterized by a growing number of sedimentarily arranged administrative practices and ideologies. Therefore, diversity has been increasing, not constant. A possible explanation of this particular development will be discussed in the next section.

Some effects of increasing diversity can be pointed at. The central control of the public sector on behalf of the Cabinet, the Ministry of Finance, and the General Audit Bureau, is problematic. The imposement of budgetary constraints and general administrative reform policies initiated from the top will have different effects on different parts of the public sector. In many cases, the objective of central control is to reduce diversity or to homogenize the public sector. Ironically, the result might be the opposite. Concerning the implementation of political objectives, a similar problem can be pointed out. The implementation process will be influenced, opposed or enhanced by the functioning of the model in operation. On the other hand, the possibility remains that public-sector diversity may lead to better coping with societal diversity.

Dynamics

The modes of governance offer us a number of ways to analyze and interpret dynamics and the time dimension. One hypothesis is that change is a natural and inevitable feature of any social system. Let us put it more precisely: Any social system in itself contains the embryo or the seeds of its own destruction and is hence in danger of internal deterioration. The same thesis can be applied to the modes of governance. Two types of reaction can be distinguished:

- attempts to revive the essence of the individual mode of governance,
- the incorporation of elements of one or more of the other modes.

According to the first type of reaction, intervention in a social system can often be interpreted as an attempt to *prevent* changes in that particular system. No divine law ensures the basic principles in the individual mode. It represents a choice which may erode unless it is constantly renewed. Times and tasks change, and for that reason alone it is necessary to confront it with new challenges. Changing staff and politicians implies that newcomers have to be *educated* to understand the basic principle.

The vertical relation of the hierarchial state will, for example, get silted up if it is not continuously reproduced through action. Consequently, the discussion of whether or not the department/directorate model or the 'modern' business-like corporate management model is the most appropriate model, is of less importance. What is decisive is to keep the discussion about the vertical organizing principle alive and to illuminate it by adding new words and facets. In day-to-day interactions on a micro level we might observe change and disturbance. On a macro level we can observe stability. Thus, so-called administrative renewal programs are not about creating dynamics but rather, at the most, about creating a dynamic equilibrium.

If we review the whole spectrum of various administrative reform remedies, they appear to be intrinsic parts of the respective models. They group themselves according to the decisive organizing principle of each model that is the focus of administrative renewal.

In *the hierarchial state*, the focus is on vertical top-down relations. Typical reform ideas are the 'generalist' department-'specialist' directorate model which was popular in Norway and Denmark in the sixties, the unitary organisation, business-like corporate management, and arrangements to transfer personnel between department and directorate. Budget systems like PPBS and ZBB should also be mentioned. Although these reform ideas are expressions of different forms of renewal which are more or less 'modern', they deal with the same problem: how to construct vertical relations that ensure a general downward impact in the system.

In *the autonomous state*, the focus is on the professional core. Reform ideas concentrate on either the development or the protection of this core. Thus, renewal is expressed through a strengthening of the professional characteristics through new recruitment policies, strengthening of the professional network, influencing education (new vocational training, upgrading of existing training, further training, internal training) and different ways of buffering the professional core from the unprofessional environment. In this model discussions about whether the organisation (e.g. an university or a hospital) should be headed by an appointed administrator or by an elected representative from the profession itself (a scientist or a doctor), are settled in favour of the profession.

The negotiating state focuses on horizontal decision-making structures. Reform is confined to changes in the extent of these structures, their competence and recruitment patterns. Establishment or abolition of corporate bodies, such as boards and committees, changes the access structure and thus has a decisive effect on the stream of premises on which the administration has to base its decisions. In *the responsive state*, reform focuses on the customer. Manifestations of renewal are, bluntly, the catchwords of the eighties: make the client visible, turn the pyramid upside-down, service-management, reward employees making extra effort, initiate user surveys, introduce user fees, abolish district boundaries to ensure competition between schools or hospitals, and self-government. All have in common that they register the need and/or the demand of the citizen and take street-level bureaucrats seriously.

Referring to our starting hypothesis, administrative reform may now be seen as an attempt to revitalize the discussion of the basic organizing principle of each model, *not* to create changes but to secure the purity of the individual model.

However, the internal deterioration may follow a different path than described above. The hierarchal state may, for example, in time transform itself to numerous bureaucratic rigidities; the autonomous state may become technocratic, the negotiating state can develop patterns of oligarchy serving only the private interests of the participants; and the responsive state may adopt the worst advertising practices known from the private sector.

In those cases, it could be argued, there is no need to vitalize the basic principles of the individual model. On the contrary, exactly those principles are already overspelled. Consequently, in order to avoid this, elements taken from the other models may be applied (Beck Jørgensen and Larsen, 1987; Hernes, 1978).

Educational and research institutions are traditional examples of organisations belonging to the autonomous state. Their basic value is that of searching for the truth, independent of religious, economic, and political interests. During the sixties, this independence was a problem, not only in Denmark but in many other European countries as well. The basic criticism seemed to be that these institutions did not serve 'the public-at-large' (e.g. 'Science for the people, not for profit' or 'Science for society, not for the scientists'). The Danish reaction was to reduce the autonomy of the professional core. The means were to furnish the institutions with elements from the negotiating state. A bill in 1973 introduced a range of new boards incorporating representatives of students and non-academic staff in departmental and faculty decision- making.

Secondly, politicians and administrators have interfered with the institutions: the Directorate of Education and Research has gained increased influence on admission, allocation of resources, and the contents of research and teaching. Elements from the hierarchial state have been introduced. This is furthermore illustrated by the simultaneous growth in the size and number of sectoral institutions for applied research that are subject to the jurisdiction of various ministries. Here, the possibility for autonomous research is considerably reduced and the hierarchial state is correspondingly stronger.

Furthermore, the growing number of sectoral research institutions has resulted in a different and more competitive population of institutions. This development and recent developments during the eighties (e.g. open education, charging fees) even introduces the responsive state. Thus a group of institutions, traditionally organized according to the principles of the autonomous state, has had elements added from three other models.

Another example is The Royal Theatre in Copenhagen. Compared to private theatres, this theatre is committed to the cultural heritage of Danish theatre. One of its most important goals is to reproduce and develop this cultural heritage. As a secondary, informal goal, it is expected to maintain and develop technical and craft theatrical traditions. Furthermore, being the largest and most complex stage in Denmark (comprising play, opera, ballet, and a full-scale symphony orchestra), The Royal Theatre also functions as a kind of theatre university. Viewed in this way, The Royal Theatre is part of the autonomous state.

Two new trends break with this tradition. One trend is the idea that the theatre is part of a cultural policy, implying that its frame of reference is not only 'theatre values' but culture as such. The relevant environments become different from and larger than those of other theatres. The other trend represents the idea that performance for the sake of art and artistic development should be combined with the attempt to deal seriously with the problems of society. The audience role is not just to respond to artistic performance. The audience is the direct purchaser of the performance, implying that elements from the responsive state are being introduced.

The interesting dilemma of The Royal Theatre is how to establish a tighter link with the audience (market) and the ministry (policy) without simultaneously creating a dependency that might result in artistic vapidity. Universities face the same problem. In both cases it remains an open question whether or not the joint development has reached the point of threatening the basic orientation. We shall return to that in section 5.

In the above-mentioned cases one might interpret the purpose of changes as one of challenging a deteriorating public organisation or of preventing such a deterioration by creating dynamic forces which might take the organisation to a new dynamic equilibrium. One mode of governance can be seen as a countervailing power to another, i.e. altering an existing balance of interests or - metaphorically speaking -by letting the acidity of one model balance the alkalinity of another. These examples of combining modes of governance are close to what Dunsire (this volume) labels *collibration*.

The implicit assumption in the discussion so far has been that changes in combinations of the modes of governance as dynamic forces are rationally planned. However, changes may also reflect a shift in political and administrative ideologies or belief systems and thus be of a more symbolic nature.

Consider the eighties. This decade was specifically characterized by catchwords such as: decentralization, user orientation, service, privatization and individualization. As part of the 'New Right'-vocabulary this development is well-known in many other countries. In Britain we find it in the guise of New Public Management (Hood, 1990). The litany has been monotonous: all public organisations, regardless of what they produce, must be service-oriented and geared to meeting users needs.

In this case administrative reform can be perceived as a signal and symbol (cf. Feldman and March, 1981). This leads us to consider dynamics as expressing *the spirit of the time*; i.e. current ideas of what seem to be reasonable and rational starting points in discussing the public sector's tasks, organisation and ways of functioning. Conceptually, the spirit of time is part of the institutional environment of an organisation, but also forms and alters it (Scott, 1987).

To regard administrative reform as the spirit of the time does not imply, then, that it is irrelevant to discuss the empirical effects. Firstly, administrative fashion can be used extrovertly by public organisations, the ostensible implementation of new practices as a buffer against hostile parts of the organisational environment (Meyer and Rowan, 1977). Secondly, we are made more aware of the dimension of time. The key hypothesis is that organisations are not equally vulnerable to environmental pressures all the time. On the contrary, it is obvious that an organisation is more sensitive to externals influence in some situations than in others. One could point to two such situations, organisational birth and change in top management.

The most important situation is probably organisational birth. Naturally, at this time the organisation has not yet developed its own routines, own culture, and own institutionalized interests. Consequently, new organisations can be expected to be strongly influenced by the spirit of the time embedded in administrative reform ideas. The Ministry of Environmental Affairs in Denmark is an example of this. It was established in 1973 and compared to other ministries has most successfully been able to execute the recommendations of the Committee of Administrative Affairs of 1960 (Administrationsudvalget af 1960, 1962) and the Korsbæk Commission (Korsbækudvalget, 1971), both of which expressed the administrative reform ideas of the sixties and the seventies: the department/directorate model. This cannot be explained by this model being especially suitable for environmental issues compared to e.g. defense, and cultural affairs. It is more likely to be an effect of the time of organisational birth.

Consequently, one would sooner expect public organisations established in the eighties to bear the stamp of the responsive state, than organisations established earlier, which are far more resistant to what they may define as 'modern twaddle'. Thus, we are left with a somewhat different perception of administrative development; public administration is seen as a number of temporal sediments.

Complexity

Diversity and dynamics seem to add to the complexity of public organisations by the interlocking of several modes of governance. Each model can be described by its characteristic organisational context. The organisational context displays the typical external organisations the public organisation in question will be in contact with, i.e. an interorganisational network. The combination of more than one mode of governance to a public organisation therefore has as a simple consequence that the structural differentiation of the environment increases.

We will illustrate this with an example: The Danish Seed Testing Station (DSTS). The task of the DSTS is first and foremost to test seed samples delivered by Danish seed-growers and distributors. For example, the seed quality is tested for water content, oil content, authenticity, purity, and germination capacity. The documented seed quality is important to the trade in general and specifically to exports. Denmark is the world's largest seed exporter.

The DSTS is subject to strict control by methods derived from all four models. Firstly, as a state institution, DSTS is controlled through the appropriations system and public auditing. More important, the tasks are to a large degree determined by Government regulations. As DSTS exerts control over an industry, relations between DSTS and the private firms are distinctly defined. Secondly, what is to be tested, how it is to be done and the quality norms to be applied, are all specified in legal rules. Thus, here we find strong traits of the hierarchial state.

The autonomous state in the DSTS case is represented by its methods of working which are strongly influenced by the methodology and thinking of the natural sciences. All experiments and tests are carried out according to standard guidelines, and all results are strictly formulated. Furthermore, some methodological research is carried out, and DSTS has a long tradition of close contact with agronomic research outside of the institution and of participation in international professional networks. Moreover, several of the managers at DSTS hold a doctoral degree in agronomy.

The negotiating state is illustrated by certain 'attached' decision-making structures. The Seed Testing Commission is an advisory organ in which interested groups have a seat, i.e. agricultural and industrial organisations. Under the jurisdiction of the Seed Testing Commission, various sub-commissions have been appointed in which the interest organisations are also represented.

Finally, DSTS is characterized by the responsive state: 85% of its costs are covered by user fees, the remaining part being covered by appropriations. The demand is highly seasonal and the capacity is regulated by laying off/hiring a significant proportion of the staff.

Summarizing, the DSTS is engaged in at least four interorganisational networks, each of which specifies certain values and principles to be followed. This might create internal tensions and blocking effects. Nevertheless, the DSTS seems to be a highly efficient organisation. In 1990 it was elected as one of the 5 most excellent public organisations in Denmark. How can we explain that? We will address this question in the following section.

Handling the Interplays of Modes of Governance: Technical and Political Implications for Public Management

The problem of the public manager could be stated as follows: the public manager has to combine politics and production or macro management and micro management (Metcalfe, this volume), i.e. he or she has to reflect and act upon different and conflicting demands, values, and norms, while at the same time being able to protect the operational core of the organisation from those conflicting demands which otherwise would tend to threaten organisational efficiency. Both legitimacy and efficiency must be obtained. Clearly, this confronts the public manager with a dilemma. A dilemma cannot be solved. It can only be handled (Brunsson, 1989). It is easy to see that a combination of several modes of governance - all other things being equal - increases the importance of macro management and the handling of dilemmas.

This does not necessary lead to the avoidance of a joint combination of several modes. On the contrary, it could be argued that there are certain disadvantages to applying only one of the modes. Each mode has its blind spots as well as its strong points. Thus, it is only natural to draw from the other modes to improve the functioning of the mode in question. To combine traits from all modes may seem to be the optimal approach. An organisation characterized by all modes of governance can be expected to be sensitive to a diversity of societal demands. But the tensions created by a multiplicity of principles might also lead to situations of stalemate. A joint combination of all modes may lead to organisational confusion and unclear ideas about the primary mission of the institution. This is probably the case if each of the modes simultaneously demands primacy on the same organisational aspect. Thus, it is important to focus on the conditions under which such a combination is effective.

From the description of The Danish Seed Testing Station it seems to follow that a dilemma has been handled. We will therefore take a closer look at this organisation and compare it with another public organisation to see whether we can find some explanations.

Firstly, if the interplay between the individual models is not to have a blocking effect, they probably have to be either separated or decoupled; controlling efforts should, for example, be directed towards different parts of the organisation, of its work process or should be separated in time (Brunsson, 1989). In the case of DSTS an organisational decoupling of the modes is a likely structural property. The principle features are: the responsive state determines the production volume, the hierarchial state determines tasks and procedures, the autonomous state determines methods and 'impartial' scientific standards, and the negotiating state assures the basic relations to the industry and institutional legitimation. In other words, the successful combination seems to be a result of non-competitive application of control forms embedded in the individual modes. Each of them aim at different aspects of DSTS.

In contrast, this was not the case with The Danish School of Public Administration. In the beginning of the eighties, a previous employee at the school characterized it as 'a Byzantine hotchpotch of a directorate and a university'. This description was not intended to be positive, and at the time the organisation diagram of the school was indeed confusing. Translated into the language of models, the school was composed of elements from the hierarchial state, the negotiating state, and the autonomous state, each model fighting for primacy.

Secondly, the interorganisational networks of the DSTS are not completely separated. They do overlap in terms of memberships and values. Agriculture representatives, the seed growers and dealers, meet Veterinarian University representatives, who meet Ministry of Agriculture representatives, who meet interest organisations representatives, not only at meetings at the DSTS but also outside the DSTS. Together with a rather slow and stable development in technology and within the industry, this facilitates the unfolding of common values and shared understandings which criss-cross the boundaries of the networks. As a consequence, and despite external structural complexity, diversity in terms of tensions and conflicting demands tends to be reduced.

Thirdly, the networks are not entirely equal in strength. Although the responsive state appears to be quite strong (very few public organisations are financed for 85% by user fees) it should be noted that the demand for the services of the DSTS is not 'natural'. It is a regulated and law-enforced demand. Therefore the hierarchial state seems to have primacy over the responsive state. A perhaps more striking feature is that the DSTS has highly valued the engagement in national and, not the least, in international networks (the International Association of Seed Testing Stations and the EC) concerning the development and application of control methods (i.e. the autonomous state). This involvement has given the DSTS an expertise monopoly and made the private firms as well as the ministry dependent on DSTS.

Fourthly, despite the joint combination of all four models, the internal structure is a simple hierarchy which centralizes power in the hands of management. Taken together, this gives the DSTS an autonomy in handling and balancing possible conflicting demands from the different networks. In other words, room for managerial manoeuvring has been created.

It seems fair to conclude that a joint combination of several modes of governance can be made effective. We have discussed under which conditions multiplicity of conflicting organizing principles and demands can be handled. But since the handling of the interplay of modes also implies balancing conflicting values or setting priorities between conflicting values - e.g. political loyalty, legality, professional commitment, interest organisation preferences, efficiency and user needs - we point to the inherent political nature of public management. It is political in terms of the *design* of the interplay of the different modes of governance as well as in terms of the *handling* of conflicting demands imposed on management. This raises questions not only of the training and socialisation of public managers but also, and perhaps more important, to what extent and in what sense public organisations can be held democratically accountable.

INTRODUCTION TO PART V

EVALUATIONS

The final part consists of two chapters. Roger Duclaud-Williams takes a critical view of the social-political governance and governing approach. He formulates a number of central dimensions (level of abstraction, generalizability and normative presuppositions) by means of which we can evaluate experiences. In a case-study of the governance of education in France and the UK he shows some of the limits of the approach discussed in this book. In the final chapter the editor broadens points made by Duclaud (and others) in terms of some general statements on the 'state of the approach as such'. To a large extent, these remarks are based on our discussions during the collaborative sessions. We regard these remarks as 'self-critical' observations on the subject of our common interest. By working on it and discussing it, its basic complexity, dynamics and diversity become more and more clear.

In the final chapter, the editor and his associates collect some outcomes of the project as a whole in terms of theoretical contributions, of some generalizations which might be drawn from empirical illustrations and of some methodological implications. What the chapter basically tries to do is to sketch, in a rough and somewhat speculative way, based upon the conceptual and empirical contributions, a possible theoretical underpinning of what we see in new forms of interaction between the public and private sector. In short, this can be seen as a first effort in theorizing on what we call social-political governance in this project.

We present our results in the expectation that others may have comparable interests and that the thoughts developed in this book may form the basis of an interactive process between scholars and practitioners.

18

THE GOVERNANCE OF EDUCATION: BRITAIN AND FRANCE

ROGER DUCLAUD-WILLIAMS

Introduction

The discussion in this chapter is presented in four parts. The aim in the first of these will be to examine a number of difficulties which arise when the attempt is made to apply the concept of governance to a particular area of social/governmental interaction. The purpose of this discussion is not to show that the approach described in the first part of this volume is unworkable, the aim is rather to sound a note of warning in order that certain traps can be avoided. The result of this discussion is to conclude that, in order to test the governance approach in practice, it is necessary to distil from the concept a number of more limited but more definite propositions.

The first of these concerns the concentration or dispersion of power measured on the vertical axis. The proposition to be examined in the second part of this chapter, which derives from the governance perspective, is that new structures which relate society and government are evolving under modern conditions and that within such structures the institutions which deliver public services are permitted to assume some of the features of sub-governments and to enjoy a limited but increased degree of autonomy. We shall use the education services in Britain and France as our empirical testing ground. The assumption underlying the governance perspective is that modern governments will find it more convenient to rid themselves of certain responsibilities and powers in order to govern in partnership with those institutions which were formerly treated as more strictly subordinate. Whereas formerly a realistic analysis of political life might have adopted the maxim that a government divided is a government weakened, the governance perspective holds on the contrary that a proper degree of fragmentation, in this case in the vertical dimension, strengthens government and makes it more effective. The third part of this chapter tests a similar proposition but in the horizontal rather than the vertical dimensions, examining in particular the change in relationships in education between public authority and various centres of private power. The fourth and final part of the chapter draws the discussion together, in order to formulate a number of conclusions.

The Governance Perspective: Some Problems

The Problem of Abstraction

Kooiman insists in his contribution to this volume that the appropriate structures within which society and government can relate under modern conditions must be complex, dynamic and varied. The difficulty which seems to emerge at this point in the argument is that of translating this description and prescription into more specific political or administrative terms. We may illustrate this point by a discussion of the second of the three characteristics on which Kooiman insists.

If we wish to promote a system of governance which is dynamic then we are necessarily involved in avoiding anything which is too rigid. Should a government therefore always refuse to offer formal and legal recognition to a representative association on the grounds that, once such recognition has been conceded, it is likely to be difficult to withdraw? Should informal, inter-personal means of coordination always be preferred to inter-organisational forms of coordination because the latter are almost certainly more rigid, that is less dynamic? Must legally enforceable individual rights to the receipt of particular public services be eschewed as an approach to service delivery because of the rigidities which such arrangements inevitably involve? Common sense would seem to suggest that the proper answer to these questions is that in certain circumstances the more flexible approach is appropriate, whilst in other circumstances greater rigidity, or should we say solidity, is to be preferred. To reiterate constantly that the dynamic is preferable to the static or the rigid, does not help us to distinguish between those cases in which this is genuinely so and others in which greater formality and permanence seem advantageous. In other words, the level of abstraction at which the governance propositions are enunciated is such that it is often difficult to translate them unambiguously into the kinds of political or administrative propositions which might be tested or tried. The same kind of point might well be illustrated with respect to the criteria of complexity. Is the more complex of two alternative arrangements or policies always to be preferred to the more simple?

The Problem of Generality

It may appear at first sight that the problem of generality is very similar to, or the same as, the problem of abstraction. This is not so and we shall therefore begin by clarifying this distinction. The problem of abstraction is the problem of translating theoretical propositions into propositions which are sufficiently concrete to be tested empirically. The problem is essentially one of imprecision of meaning. The problem of generality arises at a later stage in the analysis. We may have decided that it is proper to translate the governance perspective into a particular proposition for testing but at this stage we may be unsure whether the proposition is intended to apply without discrimination between national political systems, sub-systems within nations, or regardless of the governmental task under examination. On this point there is some diversity of approach between the different contributors to the first part of this volume. The chapters by Kooiman and Kickert operate at the level of the political system as a whole whereas the contributions by Mayntz and Aquina seem more reluctant to theorise at this level and suggest the need to introduce distinctions between policy sub-systems or broad areas of government responsibility. My preference is for the second of these approaches. It is difficult not to agree with these writers that convincing recommendations for the most appropriate forms of government/society relations ought to take account of the variability of policy problems and environments. An approach which elaborates a theory of governance at the system level seems to ignore these difficulties when the essence of good government lies precisely in finding structures which are appropriate to the task in hand.

Explaining or Improving

As Mayntz points out in her contribution, the meaning to be given to the concept of governance when discussing how government and society interact under modern conditions, is different from the meaning to be attached to this concept when our purpose is to recommend improvements in government/society relations. The concept of governance as employed by Kooiman and Kickert seems best confined to attempts to understand the way in which the modern state is evolving. When we move from explanation to recommendation it seems more appropriate to employ terms which refer to a particular actor and his/her attempts to achieve more effective control. Here the more appropriate concept seems to be that of governability. When assessing the usefulness of the governance perspective we must be careful to separate these two modes of analysis. It might, for example, be the case that, in some nations and in some political sub-systems, the form taken by government/ society relations was evolving in the direction described in the governance literature. This would not necessarily imply that the newly emerging structures were any more effective than those structures which they were replacing. Alternatively, it might be possible to make a persuasive case for the adoption of the governance approach as a means to more effective government but to observe that most governments and government departments were not persuaded by this analysis and were neither attempting nor succeeding in moving in this direction.

Unexamined, Underlying Value Assumptions

The case for the adoption of the governance perspective would be greatly strengthened if it was given a clearer political content and in the process compared with alternative political approaches with a view to showing the superiority of the governance perspective. If asked to situate the governance approach on the conventional left right spectrum, we would surely have to indicate its centrist position. Advocates of the governance perspective seem to assume, without defending the proposition in any great detail, that the market recipes of the new right and the bureaucratic recipes of more traditionally minded administrators are equally inappropriate. Much of the appeal of the governance perspective derives from and depends on those lines of argument which might best be summarised as describing the failure of the state. The discussion of education which follows is intended to show, amongst other things, that this perspective, although it may appeal in some policy arenas, is not universally applicable. There is much to be said in favour of markets and traditional bureaucratic administrative arrangements in their proper place and there is no doubt also a proper place for systems of governance which lie between command and market. To argue then that the descriptive analysis associated with the concept of governance is more and more observable in modern European government is in fact to argue some kind of convergence thesis in which different European systems and different policy arenas are assumed to be moving away from the extremes of bureaucracy and market provision towards something which lies between these two. Once expressed in these more political terms the boldness of the propositions contained within the governance approach becomes more evident.

We can go further in our examination of underlying value assumptions by briefly contrasting traditional British adversarial political practice with the political practice of those smaller European democracies once described as consociational (Lijphart, 1975). We might even describe governance as the new consociationalism. Kooiman and Kickert argue convincingly that the older Dutch consociationalism contained all kinds of rigidities which were not conducive to good government. Many of the pillars which were accorded an important role in the process of government did not in fact enjoy the kind of genuine social support which they claimed. These authors argue then that the old consociationalism must give way to new forms of partnership or governance in which the old rivalries between public and private, left and right, give way and these distinctions are no longer taken quite so seriously. The governance perspective is clearly recommending a consensual rather than an adversarial approach to the problem of government. For this reason it is open to the objection that the insistence on devolution and on power shared between public and private sectors may create conditions in which particular professions or interests acquire unjustified privileges which are difficult to challenge. In such circumstances there is something to be said for a less consensual more top down approach to the problems of government.

The intention behind these remarks has not been to express a preference for an adversarial rather than a consensual approach to government. My intention has simply been to situate a governance perspective historically and politically so as to be in a position to understand more accurately its strengths and weaknesses.

We are now in a position to examine the propositions about the vertical and horizontal diffusion of power within education which were stated at the outset. In this examination care will be taken to separate the identification of trends from the evaluation of results. In order that the task remain manageable, only two relatively specific propositions derived from the governance approach will be examined and with respect to only one area of government activity in only two countries.

Decentralisation in Education: Loosening the Reins

We shall argue in this section of the chapter that the recent development of the governance of education in England and France provides little support for the governance perspective. There is general agreement amongst observers that centralisation has been on the increase in the government of English education from well before 1979 (Ranson, 1980; Salter and Tapper, 1985; Jones, 1989). There is some slight movement towards a greater degree of decentralisation in the French case (Perrier, 1991) and these moves have sometimes been prompted by an analysis which is rather close to that to be found in the first part of this volume. With respect to the normative side of the argument we shall argue that developments in both systems, although opposite in character, are likely to correct some of the more obvious faults of inherited practices and to provide a more satisfactory system of governance than that enjoyed in the recent past.

France

There are a number of developments in the 1980s in the French case which, taken together, do amount to a small step in the direction of greater decentralisation. Local authorities now have an important part to play in decisions about the location of new schools and are responsible for construction and maintenance. Provision was made in the 1989 orientation law for each secondary establishment to produce a school plan after a consultative process which, it was hoped, would involve staff, parents and pupils. The plan would be a statement of pedagogic objectives and the means to be employed in reaching them. Socialist legislation early in the decade also indicated a prominent role for the regional authorities in the finance and organisation of vocational training for young people and adults. The processes through which university courses are now approved as elements in national qualifications seem now less prescriptive than was the case before 1981.

No-one can pretend that these are dramatic developments. A national curriculum prescribed in considerable detail still exists despite the pleas for relaxation forcefully stated in the Prost report in 1983 (Prost, 1983). Processes for the recruitment and promotion of teachers are still organised purely by the administration without reference to the particular character or wishes of individual schools. Most departments of most universities still enjoy no discretion with respect to the selection of their students but must do their best to provide for all school leavers with a baccalaureate who decide to register with them. There is no variation in educational structure between regions and departments apart from the greater density of catholic schools in those areas where the faith is more widely practised.

At first sight one is surprised at the rather meagre results of much agitation in favour of greater decentralisation. The anti-bureaucratic themes, which are an important part of the governance perspective, which were first given academic and political prominence by Michel Crozier in France, have been echoed in many subsequent more specialist educational reports (Crozier, 1964; Legrand, 1982). At the intellectual level, therefore, there seems considerable sympathy for important parts of the governance analysis. It is a truism of contemporary French journalistic and academic discussion of educational provision that there is a need to move away from the over-bureaucratic and over-centralised French educational legacy.

Although all parties involved advocate decentralisation, little progress has been made sofar. It is worth trying to understand why this is so because in doing so we may go some way towards understanding why an approach which is intellectually appealing has had so little impact in practice. An examination of the principle obstacles to change in the desired direction helps us to understand why the governance concepts have not had the impact on educational practice which we might expect. We may summarise the most important obstacles to change under four headings.

a) *The World of Higher Education.* French students, and to a lesser degree the teaching staff in French universities, are notoriously hostile to any measures of decentralisation in higher education which might adversely affect the conditions of access which they currently enjoy. More broadly, there seems to be a general fear that any attempt to promote differentiation would inevitably lead to advantages for some, and more pertinently, to disadvantages for others.

b) *The Teacher Unions.* Teacher unions are still strongly committed to the maintenance of existing arrangements in which individual teachers are governed by impersonal rules administered by a distant and rather innocuous bureaucratic authority. These unions are opposed to any form of decentralisation which might threaten the erection of a more real authority at the level of the school, which might be more discretionary, and would certainly be better informed. These unions have certainly lost large numbers of members in recent years, but this does not yet seem to have deprived them of their role as legitimate spokesmen for those employed in the public educational service.

c) *Parents.* Parents, through organisations which are most visible at the national level, seek to advance their conception of education through modifications of nationally prescribed rules. They are much more accustomed to acting politically in this way than attempting less formally at the local or school level, to obtain what they want.

d) *Failure of the State.* Finally, although there is much loose talk of a crisis in education, it is my impression that the kind of 'failure of the state' analysis which is a necessary support to any widespread adoption of the remedies favoured by theorists of governance, does not command very wide support in France. Far from believing in a failure of the state, many students, staff and parents still believe in the old and tried remedies of state guarantees of quality, fairness and minimum standards. There is no widespread perception of such a fundamental failure of inherited centralised educational arrangements as to justify a radical shift away from more conventional approaches to the problem of government. We may conclude that, although some important aspects of the governance perspective have won intellectual support amongst observers of French educational practice, this analysis, as it affects decentralisation, has not yet had very much impact and, given the obstacles to change briefly described above, does not seem likely to have much impact in the immediate future.

England and Wales

An examination of the English case does not produce evidence which provides any support for the applicability of the governance perspective. One of the assumptions underlying the governance perspective is that we have experienced in recent years a 'failure of the state', and that a greater degree of effectiveness in government can only be restored by a move away from hierarchy and command towards systems of regulation in which self government plays a more important part. The evolutionary processes which have been at work in English education since the mid 1970s seem to be moving in quite the opposite direction. There has existed a widespread dissatisfaction with the lack of coordination and absence of sense of direction found in a system which was formerly very loosely coordinated. It does not seem exaggerated to say that political/social governance identifies problems of over-organisation and rigidity and seeks to remedy them by moving away from an over-reliance on top down control whereas, in English education, observers from a variety of political perspectives have identified a problem of under-organisation and sought to remedy these difficulties by increasing the degree of government intervention and centralisation.

We can illustrate the general case stated above by describing some of the sources of dissatisfaction and the centralising remedies to which they have given rise. The curriculum was one such area. Under the 1944 Education Act responsibility in this area was delegated to local authorities who in turn frequently delegated their responsibilities to head teachers and their staff. Critics of this lack of organisation point to what they see as the tendency of teachers and pupils to prefer easy to more challenging options, and the over-extension of pupil choice of subjects for study which can lead to imbalance and the neglect of subjects, the study of which is regarded as useful in the promotion of economic growth. These criticisms have stimulated two particularly centralising initiatives in the 1980s, the technical and vocational educational initiative in 1982, and the creation of a highly prescriptive national curriculum in 1988.

The most impressive monument to increased centralisation in English education is undoubtedly the creation in 1988 of a national curriculum for all pupils between the ages of 5 and 16. Subjects to be studied in each year and the topics within these subjects and the way in which progress is made from one level to the next are carefully specified. Nationwide testing of the extent to which children have acquired the skills and knowledge specified in the national curriculum is to occur at ages 7, 11, 14 and 16. School results will be published, league tables comparing schools in the same district created, and it is clearly intended that this testing and publication apparatus should provide powerful sanctions to ensure that the prescribed curriculum is indeed taught. The government has clearly stated that it expects pupils to leave those schools which obtain bad results and, since the funding arrangements are such that the money follows the pupil, such schools will be financially penalised. A sharper contrast between these arrangements and those which prevailed in English education in the first 30 years after the war can hardly be imagined. It would be quite wrong to dismiss these initiatives, and others which there is not space to discuss, as merely the product of the views of a particular prime minister or particular party in power. The moves, although at first slow and hesitant, towards greater centralisation and tighter organisation began before the Conservative Party was elected to government in 1979, and many subsequent initiatives have been broadly supported by spokesmen for the Labour and Liberal Democratic parties.

In summing up our discussion of the vertical dimension of change we must conclude that there is no evidence of developments taking the form described by the concept of governance in the English case, and only slightly more support for the applicability of this perspective in the French case. We might almost go further. In describing the English case we have concentrated on the most striking instances of increased centralisation because they are the most dramatic recent developments and contradict the hypothesis enunciated at the outset and drawn from the governance perspective but we might also have examined developments in the 1980s to illustrate the growing importance of the market as a means of regulating educational provision. In other words, whereas the governance perspective seems to anticipate the increasing importance of those forms of regulation which lie between market and state or between market and bureaucracy, the English case has seen an increased polarisation at both the market and bureaucratic ends of this dimension. The French case does supply some small degree of support for the governance perspective but the changes described here are much less dramatic and there seems no likelihood of any radical initiatives in a decentralising direction.

Diffusion on the Horizontal Axis

France

We are concerned here with the co-existence of public and private forms of provision or with forms of partnership in which both are involved or possibly the development of new hybrid institutions which are not easily classified as either private or public. Three areas of provision deserve our attention: the confessional schools, private higher education, and the new institutions of employer controlled vocational education.

There seems nothing in the position of the confessional schools which might be used to provide support for the governance perspective. It is true that these establishments have a private legal status and that the teachers employed in them are not civil servants. But educational structure, the curriculum, and examinations are nationally determined. In these circumstances the amount of flexibility or competition which exists between the two sectors, public and confessional, is rather limited. When parental choice of establishment within the public sector was more limited than it is slowly becoming today, the existence of a confessional alternative did offer parents, in some areas, a genuine choice. But this seems of relatively little significance when we bear in mind the weight of nationally uniform rules under which these confessional establishments must operate. If the confessional sector enjoyed a more genuine degree of independence and if, as a result, educational policy making at the national level was rendered more complex by this independence and by the relationship between the confessional and public sectors, then we might have the kind of dynamic and complex relationship which we are looking for. This does not seem to be what we find, the church and catholic parents have successfully defended what they rather exaggeratedly regard as their independence, but it seems hard to represent existing relations between public and confessional sectors as productive of that dynamism and complexity which are so valued in the governance perspective. The same negative conclusions emerge if we take a longer term perspective. Confessional schools undoubtedly enjoy much less genuine independence today than they did in the period before 1959 when they were substantially financially independent. The long term development has therefore been towards the emergence of a much more tightly regulated and integrated national system and not towards more loosely integrated structures.

When we turn to higher education we immediately encounter a rather different situation. Here many of the Grandes Ecoles, whether private or public, enjoy a genuine degree of independence. There is also a plethora of less well-known private institutions which compete with the universities in the public sector. We certainly cannot say that this coexistence and competition has been consciously organised by policy makers who see in it a more effective mode of governance. But it is possible to argue that such results have been achieved if unintentionally. Those who see considerable merit in the existing rather confused condition of higher education in France argue that, the Grandes Ecoles selective sector provides admirably for the recruitment necessary to the business, political and cultural elite of the country, whilst the democratically inspired demand for greater access can be satisfied through much less costly and prestigious public university provision. In this way, it is sometimes argued, contradictory demands are met through the application of policies riddled with contradiction. If this point of view is adopted it is possible to see provision in this area as fitting in rather neatly with the governance perspective. We find this conclusion ingenious but unconvincing.

The radical opposition between the selective principles operated by the Grandes Ecoles and the much greater ease of access provided through the university system has created a system of provision which is polarised in status and degrees of selectivity. There is not space to argue the point in detail here but it seems to this author that less money would be wasted and more satisfaction obtained by teachers and students if a continuous hierarchy of institutions competing with one another existed. My preference is for a house with many floors and with many staircases which lead from one level to another, rather than a construction in which there are only two levels, each at an enormous distance from the other, in which many of those who failed to reach the upper level seemed to find no intermediate resting place but instead fall painfully to the lower level. More educational competition between institutions and less political rivalry between categories of institution would produce a form of regulation more likely to give satisfaction. If such a system were to exist perhaps it would demonstrate the viability of a complex dynamic and varied institutional arrangement; but it does not.

A third area in which there is a plausible case for a form of horizontal diffusion consistent with the governance approach is that of vocational education and training (Commissariat general du plan, 1988). Of all the sectors or sub-sectors so far examined, this is probably the one in which we can see most clearly the collapse of a clear distinction between the private and the public. For example, employers in France have been compelled since 1971 to devote a minimum percentage of their wage bill to training. Thus there is a publicly imposed legal obligation to spend, but very wide discretion left to the private actor as to the objects of that spending. Many of the organisations to whom employers choose to pay the training levy are employer associations specialising in the training function whilst others are simple profit-making concerns. Yet others exist within the public sector but have a separate budget with which to offer training on a cost-covering basis to those willing to pay for it.

Another area of vocational education and training in which some of the same features appear might be described as the new apprenticeship sector. Governments of the right and left in the 1980s, in an attempt to respond to the problems of youth unemployment, and also to encourage young people discouraged at school to continue training in some form, have negotiated with the representatives of employers new forms of publicly-regulated apprenticeship in which trainees are given some time at college for general and vocational study and spend some time on the job learning and working. The trainees in these programmes spend most of their time on private premises and under employer supervision but the system as a whole is heavily publicly subsidised and inspected. There has been some tendency in recent years for governments to rely more on the firm and less on levels of employer organisation which are intermediate between the firm and the state, but even if this tendency were to develop further, it would still leave us with a system which is neither market nor bureaucracy, and in which the private/public distinction seems difficult to establish.

The striking point about this sector of educational provision in France is that it meets the criteria of the governance perspective at a number of points. At the level of intention and design it is clear that the system has been constructed in its present form quite deliberately. The 1971 law on vocational education and training was a deliberate attempt to manoeuvre around the heavy bureaucracy of the national educational system by the creation of new structures. The new training contracts or apprenticeships of the 1980s represent a conscious rejection of the laissez faire philosophy of leaving employers to make training decisions in the light of their own financial interests. These traineeships were developed as an alternative to simply prolonging conventional schooling in the public sector. At a second level which goes beyond intention to realisation, we can see that genuinely novel forms of governance have been created. Thirdly, and finally, there seems every reason to believe that these structures do provide greater satisfaction than the market and bureaucratic alternatives on offer. The public goods aspects of training and the mobility of the labour force make it clear that market solutions to training questions will almost certainly lead to under-investment. At the other end of the spectrum, it is all too evident that some young people cannot be usefully kept in school beyond the age of 16 but are quite ready to learn outside the public sector in structures which come nearer to recognising their adult status and which are more closely linked with the world of work. It would seem then that at the levels of intention, realisation and evaluation we find here developments entirely consonant with the governance perspective.

We shall return to the case of vocational training again in our conclusion because it may provide us with some clues as to the kinds of services or policy arenas in which political/social governance is most likely to emerge.

England and Wales

In the universities and the independent schools we find two areas of English educational provision where institutional autonomy has traditionally been high but this degree of self-government, which is still very real and substantial, does not give rise to structures which can be described as representing political/social governance. These are forms of autonomy which are longstanding and have in no sense been devised to meet peculiar modern conditions. But, if the case cannot be established at the level of intention it might be plausibly argued at the level of evaluation. One might well argue that the existence of these self-governing structures produces governmental arrangements which are generally more satisfactory than any much more bureaucratic system might offer. But here we find ourselves very much entangled in the fourth of the four problems described in the first section of this chapter. Anyone who is an enthusiastic advocate of wider access to higher education and who believes that such educational expansion is a genuine response to social need would have to condemn the autonomy of the English university and the social irresponsibility to which it has given rise. On the other hand, an observer more concerned with intellectual freedom, quality of educational provision and the satisfaction of individual rather than social need, might well applaud the existence of these relatively autonomous structures as providing a sophisticated system of governance. In other words, the normative evaluative aspect of governance theory is difficult to cash because judgements depend entirely on policy preferences. It does not seem possible to establish criteria for the assessment of the relative effectiveness of different governance structures which are independent of the policy options of the observer. In a discussion earlier in this paper of arrangements for vocational education and training in France a favourable judgement on the evaluative plane was offered. Such a judgement must necessarily be conditional on the approval of particular policy options, and although it was possible to produce some arguments in favour of these options, there will always remain many who are not convinced.

The picture in English vocational education and training appears at first sight rather different from that in France but on closer inspection emerges as very similar. The rhetoric of policy making in this sector since 1979 has been very much that of a preference for vouchers and market provision as a way of escaping from the wastefulness and unresponsiveness of public services. In practice, however, we find the same blurring of the public/private boundary and the same complicated intermingling of public and private provision that we found in the French case. The local committees of businessmen, the technical and enterprise councils, who now control vocational provision in each locality, are spending public money not their own. There is no need to repeat here what was said earlier in discussing the French case, which has been created because of similarities between the French and English experience. The English system of certification is much more complicated, less uniform and more privatised than the

French but English funding arrangements rely more heavily on the public purse, and the training system as a whole allows less influence to employer associations and trade unions than is the case in France. Although these differences exist, a governance perspective finds equal support in both the English and French cases.

With respect to horizontal diffusion we may conclude that we have found more evidence which supports the governance perspective than was available in discussing vertical diffusion. It is also apparent that this support is heavily concentrated in the area of recently developed vocational provision for young people and that the longer established parts of both educational systems seemed to have proved immune to the attraction of new styles of governance.

Conclusion

We have seen that it is possible to examine the governance perspective at any or all of three levels. There is firstly the level of intention. Here we are concerned with the character of the rationale which policy makers develop as a justification for new structures. Secondly there is the level of newly created institutions and practices. Here we have been concerned to discover whether genuinely new practices arise, whether for example power is genuinely decentralised or shared between public and private sectors. Thirdly there is the normative or evaluative level. Here we are concerned, to decide, with great difficulty, whether the newly created structures do indeed provide something which is more effective than their more traditional rivals.

We have concluded that there is relatively little support for the governance approach in the recent development of structures of governance in education in Britain and France. At the level of rationale there is certainly more support in the French than the English case. The more exaggeratedly bureaucratic and centralised character of the French state, especially in its educational manifestation, did lead to a widespread perception, especially after 1968, of a state which was failing its citizens. There was an active and successful search by those in the centre of the political spectrum for new structures of government which avoided the vices of bureaucracy and free market provision. This line of action and thought is most clearly represented in the law of 16th July 1971 on vocational education. At the level of intention and theorisation there is much less support for this approach in England than France but in practice, at least in the area of vocational provision, many rather similar structures have evolved. The English rhetoric is very adversarial and traditional but the reality of provision is more complex and does not correspond to the left and right ideologies in which the debate is conducted.

What may we infer from the observation that most of the evidence favourable to our thesis relates to the very specific area of vocational education and training and is found in both England and France? We should certainly conclude that the governance approach ought to be used at a level below that of national systems. It would seem that this approach has been adopted in this very specific area in part because we are dealing with newly assumed state responsibilities. Where public structures of provision already exist political/social governance seems to have much greater difficulty in making headway. It would also seem that in vocational training for young people who might otherwise be unemployed we are dealing with a service whose provision is of peculiar importance to the young people themselves, to the maintenance of harmonious social relations in society at large, to the future of the economy, and to future employers. This service is one which is of peculiar importance therefore to both private and public actors and therefore unlikely to be satisfactorily provided through any structure which excludes either of them. We ought therefore to conclude that this is a particular illustration of the point made by Mayntz in her contribution to this volume, namely that the applicability of the governance perspective is likely to vary sharply from one area of provision to another. We have successfully identified, in two very different national settings, a case whose nature helps us identify those service characteristics whose presence increases the likelihood of the creation of structures of governance similar to those described in the first part of this volume. We may conclude this discussion by returning to the second of the four problems of analysis described in the first part of this chapter. Our concern there was with the problem of generality. If we have success-fully identified some of the characteristics which predispose to the adop-tion of structures of political/social governance, then we have gone some way towards a clarification of those areas in which the theory is likely to be applied and those in which it is not. We may usefully summarise our findings concerning the areas in which the governance perspective is most likely to be applied as follows:

1) Application is more likely in a newly established area of state respon-sibility than in an area where the exercise of public responsibility is traditional.
2) Application is more likely where intense public and private concerns converge, in other words, where the service to be provided has mixed public goods and private goods characteristics.
3) The diffusion of power associated with the approach is more likely to occur in the horizontal than the vertical or territorial axis. Much more research in a variety of policy and national settings would, of course, be necessary in order to establish more firmly these and other propositions.

19

FINDINGS, SPECULATIONS AND RECOMMENDATIONS

JAN KOOIMAN[1]

Introduction

This book is not primarily about failures such as 'failures of the state' or 'market failures'. We do not look upon ourselves as participating in a 'failures discussion', although, of course, there are many shortcomings in this respect. Incidental and structural shortcomings, mistakes and unsolved problems are discussed at great length in this book.

However, we do look upon ourselves as 'signalizers', pointing at recent developments in forms, styles or even models of governance, which aim at overcoming such shortcomings; which try to learn from mistakes and which try to improve the way in which major social-political problems are solved. The tendencies we signalize focus on a variety of forms of interaction between government and society, between the social and the political. Some of them are new, others build on already existing patterns of interaction. We call efforts such as these 'social-political governance' (note: although governance has a special meaning, we will use the term social-political governance for the approach as such).

In our opinion, the shortcomings to which these new tendencies may be an answer, are situated in the insufficient awareness that our societies change so much that traditional ways and means of governance are no longer adequate. Social, technological, economic and all other kinds of 'partial' worlds, change towards more dynamics, towards higher complexity and towards greater diversity. A shortcoming of our governors is that they show little feeling for these changes. The weakness of the scientific community is that it has not made them sufficiently aware of these changes.

We simply do not know enough about these changes and we have spent too little scholarly effort and energy in trying to discover what the significance of these changes is and what their meaning is for those governing and for those governed. How can we come to grips with these basic changes and their interpretations in such ways that a new interaction between the scientific community, our governors and others, might help in finding answers to quite severe, complex, dynamic and diverse prob-

---

[1] To the substance and ideas in this chapter all authors of this book have contributed in one way or another; that is the reason I speak of 'we'; but 'we' have no responsibility for the text as a whole, only 'I' have. (J. Kooiman)

lems? Several authors in this volume hint at these problems but Metcalfe states this as follows: *'The willing cooperation, commitment and dedication which are essential to resolving structural problems must be developed from within'*.[2]

By approaching social-political governance in the way we do and as is reported in this volume, we hope not to make the mistakes Mayntz points to when she criticises others who neglect methodological principles and jump to conclusions: *'the relation between diagnosis and solution remains implicit or is not scrutinized itself'*.

Empirically, we are looking for two kinds of findings. In the first place we look for the appearance in practice of new or changing forms of interaction between government and society; secondly, we look for clues and hints which support our point of view that changes may be 'caused' by the awareness of growing complexity, dynamics and diversity. Conceptually we will try to contribute to an analytical understanding and theoretical interpretation of what these new forms of interaction might be.

Findings on Interaction

Can social/political interaction be observed in new or renewed forms? From the contributions which (also) have an empirical basis, the following summary can be made.

Most of the contributors describe the emergence of new forms of social-political interaction: Dunsire, Aquina/Bekke, Kouwenhoven, Van Vliet, Bouckaert, Breuillard, Raab, Beck Jørgensen. Royall and Duclaud Williams see the emergence of new forms as well as the application of more traditional forms. Prins and Stenvall see no emergence of new forms in their studies.

The image we receive from this short survey certainly shows new and renewing forms of social-political interaction, albeit in quite differing substantive forms. The most outspoken examples are: Dunsire with collibration, Aquina/Bekke with co-allocation, Kouwenhoven with co-entrepreneuring, van Vliet and Raab with new forms of co-regulation, Bouckaert with co-production and Breuillard with co-activation.

Within the chapters of this volume a variety of forms of social-political interaction is presented, in which 'co'-arrangements, in the sense of co-ordination and, if possible, of co-operation between different social and political actors, are central.

These new and renewed forms can be separated from, for example, (neo-)corporatist forms of interest-mediation, because they are issue-oriented. Interests are not 'given' but are moulded - as are the structures of interest - in the process of governance itself. Social-political interactions

---

[2] Unless otherwise indicated, when authors are mentioned, we are referring to chapters in this book.

are organized and become more and more 'stable' forms of governance, but they are not as fixed as in neo-corporatist and (other) more classical forms of interest representation.

When we order the results of the various chapters, we find the following: The existence of '(functional) interdependence' between formally and/or relatively autonomous (non-hierarchically ordered) political and social actors, is of the essence.

By 'interdependence' we mean that no single actor has the possibilities of 'doing the job' (solving a problem or grasping an opportunity) unilaterally. No actor is so dominant as to be able to enforce a certain line of behaviour, or to place the costs of social problem-solving on others and take the revenues himself. And all actors can be severely hindered in reaching their own objectives by other actors. 'Interdependence' in itself, however, is not enough. The realization of the opportunities within interdependence is the central assignment of social-political governance.

In practice, certain conditions seem to be favourable to the emergence of social-political governance (Duclaud Williams):

- Existing and traditional structures of authority, methods and instruments, have failed or are eroded.
- New fields of social-political activities exist in which organisational forms and patterns of interest-mediation are not (yet) strongly established.
- There are issues that are of great concern to the (public and private) actors that involved.
- There must be sufficient convergence of objectives and interests to make it possible to reach a synergetic effect or a 'win-win' situation.

Apart from these more or less 'objective' conditions, some other, 'subjective', factors, regarding the 'state of mind' of the involved actors, have a positive influence on the development of social-political governance:

- a certain amount of mutual trust or mutual understanding;
- a certain preparedness to take (common) responsibility;
- a certain degree of political involvement and social support.

For the emergence of social-political governance (or efforts in that direction) it seems to be necessary that these 'objective' and 'subjective' conditions are 'linked' by a 'trigger' or a 'broker'. It must be realized that there is a grave situation in which traditional structures of authority and of problem-solving processes have failed but that, at the same time, a new approach gives hope for new opportunities.

Behind the veil of complexity, dynamics and diversity (see next paragraph) it is possible that, not yet visible, positive-sum solutions exists (complexity, Van Vliet), that new interaction-patterns with new 'exchange-packages' and coalitions are possible (dynamics, Raab and Breuillard) and that fresh insights, ideas and ideals are formed as a result of using a multitude of social contacts (diversity, Pekonen).

Instead of relying on the state or the market, social-political governance is directed at the creation of patterns of interaction in which political and traditional hierarchical governing and social self-organisation are complementary, in which responsibility and accountability for interventions is spread over public and private actors, but leaves enough autonomy on the micro level (Mayntz, Metcalfe, Raab and others).

Findings on Complexity, Dynamics and Diversity

A central assumption in looking at new or renewed forms of social-political interaction is that they have to do with the growth of and variety in complexity, dynamics and diversity of all the partial worlds we live in and which we create and recreate as ungoing processes. In our opinion the (implicit and explicit) awareness of these fundamental changes is an important source and inspiration for searching new forms of interactive governance 'between' government and society. Although other ideological and pragmatic reasons are also at the basis of the experiments we report, we emphasize these structural developments, because they seem to call for new methodologies and innovative actions. Several authors in this book have elaborated on this assumption, either on a conceptual or an empirical level. From a conceptual perspective, in particular Kooiman asks for a much more important role for complexity, dynamics and diversity in the analysis of problems with governability. According to Kooiman, problems of governability arise when the increase in complexity, dynamics and diversity in modern societies is not accounted for in governance theories and practice.

Complexity

Kooiman distinguishes three approaches to deal with complexity: complexity as a hierarchy, complexity reduction at the system level and situational operationalisation of the complexity concept (such as in the number and intensity of relations between sub-systems). Kickert follows the 'complexity as hierarchy'-approach and Dunsire applies the 'operational' approach.

Both Mayntz and Kooiman point at increasing complexity in the economic, political and administrative sub-systems of modern societies. Raab presents a case in which an increase in technological complexity is evident. Van Vliet argues that governing actors have difficulty to come to grips with complex problems because of troubles in sufficiently disentangling cause-effect mechanisms. Several authors point at the complexity of interactions between government and society. Aquina and Mayntz refer to the complex character of resource transfer and allocation processes and Raab refers to interdependences in the regulatory space.

Aquina, Kickert, Raab and Metcalfe refer to the complex character of networks. And, of course, several authors point at the consequences of increasing complexity for governance itself. Mayntz discusses the relation between political governing and self-organization, whereas Van Vliet points at the consequences of complexity for finding solutions and applying instruments.

Dynamics

Most of the authors discuss dynamics in relation to interactions and other forms of governance. At a conceptual level, Kooiman emphasizes the balance of tensions expressed in dynamics. According to Dunsire, it may be possible to bring about change in this balance of tensions through 'collibration'. In similar terms Kickert argues for destabilizing network arrangements that have become too stable.

These three authors consider dynamics to be of central importance to governance. On the basis of (cybernetic) concepts such as positive and negative feedback, principles of governing can be developed that fit certain dynamic situations. According to Mayntz governance should be aimed at internal dynamic properties of a system. Such dynamic properties are either characteristic for certain sectors of society or are the result of political processes.

Metcalfe, Kouwenhoven and Mayntz also discuss aspects of dynamics, for instance the dynamics of structural change. According to Metcalfe, macro and micro dynamics should be coordinated and it ought to be a special task of public management to focus on macro dynamics. Kouwenhoven distinguishes elements of dynamics in the interaction between government and business and he elaborates on societal factors which play a role in exploiting those dynamics.

Examples are given of specific forms of dynamics that can be important to new forms of governance. Jørgensen argues that, due to dynamics, public organizations increasingly resemble private ones. In order to survive, public organizations become more and more dependent of interactions with the environment which provides the legitimacy of their function, task or service. Dynamics can also have an effect upon the relation between government bodies. Breuillard shows how the dynamics of building the Channel tunnel work out differently in the British and in the French system of governance dealing with this development at different levels of government.

Diversity

There are four aspects of diversity. Firstly, increasing diversity in society at large. This happens at every level: individual and differentiated in organizations, sectors and state forms. It has been pointed out that tensions may rise because of simultaneous tendencies towards a decrease in scale (Dunsire). Secondly, this increase in differentiation, heterogeneity and diversity can be related to governing and public management. Aquina refers to the consequences of allocation mechanisms having to deal with diversity. Both Mayntz and Aquina show that because of this, the inter-actions between government and society become more complex. Thirdly, attention is paid to the consequences for direct interventions at the increa-singly diverse micro level. Duclaud points at increasing direct interaction at the lowest level in all kinds of new forms of governance in areas such as vocational training. The increase in public private partnerships can also be explained from an increase in diversity (Kouwenhoven). Both government and trade and industry prefer a diversity of project-like arrangements instead of long term commitments on broad subjects. Finally, it should be mentioned that diversity implies that broad and generally accepted 'interpretations of reality' are less and less available. This implies that problem definitions are becoming more and more subjective. As a result it is increasingly difficult to define a 'general interest'. This means, in short, that more attention must be paid to 1) ways in which a diversity of· social views and interests are represented in decision-making on problem definitions and potential solutions (Pekonen), and 2) ways in which learning/dialogue/communication can occur between the (increa-singly) diverse actors (Van Vliet, Prins).

Summary of Findings on Complexity, Dynamics and Diversity

	'do-it-alone' (government)	'co'-arrangements
complexity	cause-effect relations	wholes and parts
	unilateral dependencies	multidimensional interdepen-dences
	divide in units or disci-plines	handle in communication networks
dynamics	linearity and predictability	non-linearity and chaotic pat-terns
	continuity and reversi-bility	discontinuity and irreversi-bility
	use of feed-forward mechanisms	use of feed-while/ feed-back mechanisms
diversity	approaches/ analyses based on averages	situational and discrete analysis
	from rules to exceptions	from exceptions to rules

Outline of a Theory of Social-political Governance

Based on the empirical findings as summarized in the forgoing sections and the conceptual notions as developed in some of the chapters in this volume, we now will develop the three concepts of governing, governance and governability and the relation between them, as building blocks for a theory of social-political governance. The kind of theory we have in mind is directed at the understanding of modern societal developments, and especially (the nature of) modern modes of governance and forms of social-political interaction. The character of this theory (in statu nascendi) is normative and prescriptive; it is a search for a coherent set of statements about the organization of interactive governance processes for social-political problems with a complex, dynamic and diverse character. Our aim is to strike an effective and legitimate balance between social self-organization and political-administrative intervention with the coherence in these statements.

Governing

In a world which is characterized by increasing complexity, dynamics and diversity, we can observe that:

- social problems are, for a large part, the result of various interacting factors (which are not always entirely known) and can not be regarded as being caused by a single factor,
- technical and political knowledge about problems and possible solutions is dispersed over many actors,
- objectives of public policy are not easy to define and are often submitted to revision: uncertainty is the rule and not the exception.

As a result of this, in contemporary society, activities which are related to governing efforts are by definition interaction processes between public actors and involved target groups or individuals. Modes of governing are necessarily interactive in a complex and mixed hierarchical and non-hierarchical society: *'In other words, the outcomes of administrative action are in many areas not the outcomes of authoritative implementation of pre-established rules, but rather the result of a 'co-production' of the administration and its clients'*, (Offe, 1985: 310).

Governing in contemporary society is mainly a process of coordination, steering, influencing and 'balancing' these interactions. In our view, this means new governing forms are necessary. The recognition of the inter-active nature of modern government means traditional forms of governing based on a top-down perspective or a rational-central-rule approach, lose their attractiveness in many, but not all, circumstances. It does not mean the government is left without any instruments for intervening in social-subsystems (as proposed by some of the more radical members of the autopoiesis-school). Many of the foregoing chapters have shown the emergence of a variety of new ways of intervening and governing in practice. However, the theoretical underpinnings of these new forms are very limited.

The interactive quality of modern society can cause problems but it can also give new possibilities (Mayntz, Raab and others).

Governing in an interactive perspective is directed to 'balancing' social forces and social interests and to 'enabling' social actors and systems to organize themselves. So the question whether and how cooperation can be deliberately directed at further vital common interests, is a key one, in which the various organizations and interests that are involved share the responsibility for managing structural change while retaining their autonomy in managing incremental change (Metcalfe). In particular, Dunsire's concept of collibration is a governmental intervention directed to influencing the existing relations of forces between social actors while manoeuvring these actors in a desired direction in such a way that a new, more desirable 'balance' is reached. Kickert adds to this that the management of social-political networks is not always the rotten of balance but also the willing application of 'ratione' for the sake of renewal and change and directed at the aversion and danger of dynamic conservatism within organizations and interorganizational networks.

Increasing complexity, diversity and dynamics mean a decrease in the possibilities to govern societal developments from a single point. As a result, unilateral state interventions based on the conception of an omnipotent state have lost most of their attractiveness. However, in our opinion, this does not necessarily or automatically mean the best thing to be done is to create a state that leaves society to its own dynamics and leaves societal organization to the 'free flow' of social and, especially, market forces. On many issues social problems and the risks associated with modern society are growing (Dunsire, Bouckaert). The need for collective problem solving, in new and more interactive ways, remains the same or even increases (Metcalfe). Balancing and enabling have nothing to do with a withdrawal of the state or with the state disconnecting itself from society, but with a state that governs in other, more apt, ways. In many cases 'other' will mean more connecting than disconnecting. The task of governments in contemporary, complex societies is to influence social interactions in such ways that political governing and social self-organisation are made complementary.

How do these new ways of governing occur? Which general forms of social-political governing are signalized? We suggest these new forms have to take into account the basic characteristics of modern, contemporary society. These characteristics constitute challenges for governing. Therefore we propose the following rather hypothetic classification - as a subject for debate:

- complexity: form of governing: coordination and composition;
- dynamics: form of governing: steering and collibration;
- diversity: form of governing: regulation and integration.

Complexity is the expression of increasing, but often diffuse and difficult to trace, interdependences between social-political systems and social sectors. Regarding complexity, the governing challenges are 'coordination' (the fine-tuning of separate but interdependent elements and actors within a system (Kickert)) on the one hand, and '(de)composition' (the way in which the interrelated parts within a 'complex' system and a complex problem situation are defined and divided) on the other hand.

Dynamics is the expression of increasing tensions as a result of changes, speed and cybernetic principles. Regarding dynamics, the governing challenge can be phrased in terms of 'steering' (Mayntz) aimed at direction and in terms of 'collibration' as the balancing of social forces (Dunsire).

Diversity is the expression of processes to substantiate (materially and culturally) richer social-political forms. The governing challenge regarding diversity can be separated by 'regulation' (Raab) on the one hand, and 'integration' (the more substantial coordination and (fine-)tuning of the growing diversity of objectives, wishes, ideals, ideas and interests as result of growing diversity and specialization) on the other hand.

Related to all three characteristics of the modern world is the 'politicizing' of the administrative apparatus as a strategy, as suggested by Pekonen. In a modern society with modern problems and needs, the usual 'Weberian' differentiation between the political system and the administrative apparatus, forms an obstacle to governance. In a society in which policy making and implementation are interactive and can be regarded as a co-production between government and target groups, the role of the administration becomes more and more a political one.

Therefore it is better to acknowledge this political role of the administration in order to enable not only highly organized and strong actors but also individual citizens and social movements to infiltrate within the administration and to be represented within the policy making process. In this way more justice is done to the diversity within modern society, and these groups can function as countervailing powers and the learning potential or processes of governing are broadened, causing, in our view, a restriction of the risk of self-referentiality or organisational/network closing.

To sum it up: 'governing' can be regarded as (goal-oriented) interventions of political or social actors with the intention to create a more or less predictable and somewhat stable pattern of interaction within a (social-political) system that is as much as possible in accordance with the wishes or objectives of the intervening actor(s).

Governance

Governance can be seen as the pattern or structure that emerges in a social-political system as 'common' result or outcome of the interacting intervention efforts of all involved actors. This pattern cannot be reduced to one actor or group of actors in particular: *'political governance in modern societies can no longer be conceived in terms of external governmental control of society but emerges from a plurality of governing actors.'* (Marin and Mayntz, eds, 1991: backflap) This emerging pattern forms the 'rules of the game' within a particular system or, in other words, the medium through which actors can act and try to use these rules in accordance with their own objectives and interests.

The governance concept is primarily a descriptive and analytical tool (1). It is a means through which we can search the pattern in which a particular social and/or political (sub-) system works and in which social forces are at work. But with the degree in which a pattern of governance can be seen as a result of actor-related interventions, there is also a normative aspect to it (2). It is possible to ask, then, which interaction pattern would be desired (by whom) for what purpose? Which actors should play a role in these problem solving arrangements? And which constraints have to be taken into account?

It is easy to see both applications of the governance concept are particularly relevant and interesting to our topic.

(1) By defining governance as the 'emerging pattern (or order) of a system' that is both the outcome of social processes (interactions) as well as the medium through which actors can act and can interpret this pattern, this interpretation of the governance concept gives a 'clue' to defining the relationship between 'governing' and 'governance'. With it, it is possible to construct a concept of 'governability' in terms of a balance between needs and potentials in a meaningful way.

A pattern or order should not be seen as a system based on unchangeable social laws (as in a 'natural sciences way') but as 'rules' or 'structures' which are interpreted, reinterpreted, formulated and reformulated in the process of social (human) action (compare Giddens, 1979 and Burns et al., 1985).

If we look at the 'duality of structure' approach in which a pattern of governance is not only the unintended outcome of social (inter)action but also the mechanism through which actors have the capability to act and to govern, we can see that governing and governance are subjected to a permanent process of mutual interaction. Actors who govern, or try to govern, also influence the governance structure of a subsystem. Some (more powerful) actors have the possibility to rewrite some 'rules of the game' but no one has complete control. There is always some intended and unintended change, which creates manoeuvring space for actors willing to change the existing pattern. Within this 'manoeuvring space' lies the possibility to 'create order' and to bring governing needs and potentials in balance, but also the possibility that such attempts will fail.

(2) Governance is strongly linked to the concepts of interaction and system. Governance is system specific. Interactions are in fact the definition of a system: namely parts interacting together more intensively than with others ('the environment') and governance is the normative expression of an interactional arrangement: how do we want to interact, what will be the main direction of the interactional arrangement and what will be the main substance of this interactive arrangement? Will it be primarily based on cooperation (common direction), trust (common order) and mutual understanding (common meaning)? Or will it be primarily based on conflict, power and contention (direction order meaning basically and permanently divided)?

Both extremes produce a more or less stable and predictable pattern but of a different type. Both can be seen as 'styles' of governance, without a qualification as to their 'aptness'. In practice, they will be mixed in terms of coexistence with a certain dominance. But there may be periods (or crises) in which complexity, dynamics and diversity can only be, or seem to be, handled by one style or the other.

Governability

As the third, and last, concept in this theoretical proposal, we introduce governability. By governability we mean the total quality of a social-political system to govern itself within the context of broader systems of which it is part. (This expresses the basic proposition of the systems approach.) Governability combines qualities of governing and of governance (in interaction).

Closer investigation tells us we can distinguish three main tasks in governability, which we regard as joined responsibility for social and political processes (although not formally organized for that purpose). These three tasks aim at structure, process and substance or, more specified to our perspective, handling complexity, dynamics and diversity of governability. (These include matters concerning ungovernability.)

The question of how social-political systems are structured, relates firstly to the positioning of the system 'between state and market', in other words, to the system as related to others in terms of interdependences. In the preceding chapters at least two tendencies are indicated. One is 'Verselbstandigung' (tendency towards autonomy - Mayntz), the opposite of colonization (drawn into the orbit of bureaucracy - Aquina/Bekke). What could be called the *external structuring task*, is the sailing between these scylla and charibdis.

As a part from the external task there is an *internal structuring task*. In the contributions to this book, several aspects of internal structuring are specified: structuring of 'communication and learning' (Van Vliet, Raab), structuring of (new forms of) representation (Pekonen) and structuring of management responsibility (Bouckaert, Beck Jørgensen, Breuillard). These aspects of course are closely related (Metcalfe).

The second governability task aims at *process* or *dynamics*. Here we can point at what Kooiman calls the tension between needs and potentials. This task points to the necessity to keep this tension in a sort of dynamic equilibrium (Kooiman, Kickert, Dunsire). We could also consider the dealing with this tension a model of the relation between the characteristics of 'collective action problems' and 'collective action solutions'. Several authors give indications in this direction.

The third governability task we mention is *substantive*, and may be the most difficult one. At this level this task can probably be best operationalized in terms of formulating criteria or setting standards. What matters, is that in the context of governability (of the system as a whole, but also the system-parts relations) substantive grounds for balancing governance and governing are formulated and applied. From the contributions the 'pair' effectiveness and legitimacy come forward most profoundly. In the last ten years or so the emphasis has been on higher efficiency and effectiveness; now the balance seems to move towards an emphasis on greater legitimacy (Bouckaert).

Recommendations for Design

According to Scharpf the co-existence of hierarchical and horizontal forms of politics should not only be notified but also used in a design perspective (1991) In the last part of this volume we will respond to this request in the form offering a few indications for design. These apply especially to the capability of the (modern) state to act as partner in social-political governance.

As is shown in this volume, in modern society the 'state' and the 'market' approach are becoming unattractive in many important issues of collective and societal concern. There is no place for 'standard' solutions traditionally being tailor-made by one-sided bureaucratic top-down systems of governance but neither for a unilateral withdrawal of the state and leaving societies to their own 'dynamic laws'. In a complex-mixed, partly hierarchical, partly non-hierarchical society (by Scharpf titled ' the new middle ages') new tasks of governments (or public tasks) could be summarized as follows:

- The enabling of social-political interactions. This may mean withdrawal at some point but often (and at the same time) this means taking the responsibility for organizing social-political interactions which enables social-political systems to organize themselves.

- The creation and sustaining of differing and varying kinds of 'co-arrangements' in which responsibilities or collective-action problems are shared.

Doing this means:

- Using knowledge and information and other means or instruments related to problems and solutions of modern society, that are scattered in the public and private sectors;
- Creating common responsibilities for the functioning of (maybe cross-cutting) wholes related to the problems and potential solutions;
- The realization of coordination and cooperation ...
- If and when necessary apply sanctions (certainly as a stick to beat with).

The question we finally want to address in this context is whether any general recommendation can be formulated in design terms on the basis of the diagnoses and analyses presented in this book. Our basic point of view is that the social-political arrangements themselves are quite situationally dependent, and a 'blue print approach' is certainly not appropriate. However, as far as the role and function of governmental organization in this respect is concerned we think we can formulate a limited number of guidelines:

- An external and interactive orientation of governmental organizations is essential;
- Public administration has to pay attention to a variety of administrative, political, scientific and social points of view and to operated definitions of collective action problems and collective action solutions, within the public adminstration itself;
- The government should try to disperse macro responsibilities to social actors and at the same time encourage those actors to take and carry those responsibilities;
- Striving for self-organization and self-reliance has its limitations in the tendencies of social-political arrangements to display ' dynamic conservatism'. One of the governmental responsibilities is to finally, or in the last resort/instance, reserve for itself the possibility to break through vested interests and other blockades in social-political arrangements.

The interdependence between non- hierarchical ordered political and social actors can be considered as problematic, but, in our view, it is also possible to regard these as a starting-point for finding solutions to social-political problems. Governing in contemporary society is about mobilizing and coordinating the social and political governing capabilities (potentials) that lie hidden in these interdependences (see also Dryzek, 1987). However, the presence alone of interdependences is a necessary but not a sufficient condition for successful social-political governance.

In this volume most theoretical elaborations and case-studies apply to the sector or intersectoral level. This level seems, for the time being, to be the most appropriate level for doing research and making suggestions for design. At the macro (state) level the interactions probably are too established, too organized and procedures too stable and 'interest loaded'. The micro interaction level probably is too limited in scope to make governance effective and legitimate at the same time. On the sectoral level, where social issues (problems and opportunities) are being 'governed' such as in education, pollution, regional and urban development, the labour market and data protection, interdependence between social and political actors seems to be almost by definition a realized condition. Therefore, the sectoral level seems to be the most appropriate level on which students and practitioners of public management and others can ask relevant questions such as: is there (really) a need for new forms of governance or are existing forms sufficient to cope with the problems and opportunities facing us? Which conditions favour the emergence of new patterns of governance and are these new forms in themselves and under which conditions successful, effective and legitimate?

Beck Jørgensen argues for a situational approach to reform and designs proposals within and for public management. In his opinion these proposals often reflect the 'spirit of time'. Reform proposals are not so much technical-administrative advices but foremost manifestations of a dominant political-administrative ideology. Although others have to decide whether the ideological dimension in our proposals reflect the 'spirit of time' and can be considered to be 'dominant', we do not deny that our ideas and suggestions are an ideological basis. In his chapter Roger Duclaud-Williams has also pointed to those values being implicitly or explicitly expressed in this volume. We wholeheartedly agree with him on this point.

ABOUT THE AUTHORS

Herman J. Aquina finished his Ph.D. dissertation in Political Science in 1974. He is an associate professor in policy science at the University of Nijmegen, the Netherlands. He has carried out extensive research activities in policy processes and problems of government-society policy relations. He served as a member of advisory committees to the Dutch Department of the Interior, studying problems of policy implementation and cooperation between public and private organisations.

Hans A.J.G.M. Bekke is professor of Public Administration at the University of Leiden and the Erasmus University of Rotterdam. He is also active as a policy and organisation consultant. Among his numerous publications are books on *Organization-development: Confrontation of individual, public administration and society* (1976), *Isolation of Public Administration* on the societal nesting of government (1984) and *The reliable bureaucracy* about changes of bureaucracies and developments in society.

Geert Bouckaert is a senior researcher at the Public Management Centre of the Katholieke Universiteit Leuven and a senior lecturer at the Universitaire Instelling Antwerpen in Belgium. His field of research is public sector productivity and related topics of financial management.

Michèle Breuillard is a Politics Research Fellow from the Centre National de la Recherche Scientifique, Member of the Centre de Recherches administratives, politiques et sociales de l'Université de Lille II, France.

Andrew Dunsire is an Emeritus Professor at the University of York in England. He taught administrative theory at LSE, Exeter and York and retired from the headship of the Department of Politics at York in 1989. His publications include *Administration, the Word and the Science* (1973), *Control in a bureaucracy* (1978) and, with Christopher Hood, *Bureaumetrics* (1983) and *Cutback Management in Public Bureaucracies* (1989).

Roger Duclaud-Williams teaches in the Department of Politics and International Studies at the University of Warwick, England. He has worked particularly in the areas of comparative housing and educational policy and has published in *Western European Politics*, *The European Journal of Political Research* and the *British Journal of Political Science*.

Torben Beck Jørgensen is Professor of Public Administration and Organisation Theory since 1987. He is currently affiliated to the Department of Political Science of the University of Copenhagen, Denmark, and Centre for Public Organisation and Management. He has published on *Models of Retrenchment Behaviour*, *Financial Management* *in the Public Sector, Control - an Attempt at Forming a Theory, Relations between Public Organizations and their Customers, Theory of Public Organisations - Demands and Possibilities of Development* and *The Giaconda Smile of Organisations: An Essay on Fictional Pictures of Public Administration and Citizens.*

Walter J.M. Kickert graduated in Experimental Physics at Utrecht University and worked in control engineering and fuzzy theory at London University. He finished his dissertation in organisation theory at the Technological University of Eindhoven (1979). Afterward he joined the Department of Public Administration at Nijmegen University. Since 1984 he has been a councillor at the Ministry of Education and Science. In 1990 he was appointed Professor of Government Management at the Erasmus University of Rotterdam, the Netherlands.

Jan Kooiman is Professor of Public Administration and Management at the Business School of the Erasmus University of Rotterdam, the Netherlands. He is a political scientist by training, worked at the Universities of Amsterdam and Leyden, was Secretary to the Dutch Labour Party in Parliament and served in several advisory functions to the national government. He wrote books on local decision-making in the US, on Parliament in the Netherlands and on the relation between politicians and civil servants in the Netherlands. Recently he is involved in a large scale research project on what in this book is called Social-Political Governance.

Vincent P. Kouwenhoven graduated in Business Administration at the Business Faculty of the Erasmus University of Rotterdam. His field of interest is the management of business-government interaction. He has published on Public Affairs, a comparison between European and American practice, and Public-Private Partnership. He currently works as a consultant with Van de Bunt Management Consultants, Amsterdam.

Renate Mayntz obtained a B.A. at Wellesley College (USA), a doctorate in sociology at the Free University of Berlin and honorary doctorates from the universities of Uppsala and Paris. She has held chairs at the Free University of Berlin and the Hochschule für Verwaltungswissenschaften at Speyer. She taught at Columbia University and the New School for Social Research in New York, at the University of Edinburgh, at the FLASCO (Facultad Latino-Americana de Cienzas Sociales), Santiago de Chile and at Stanford University, before becoming Director at the Max-Planck-Institut für angewandte Sozialforschung. She still holds a honorary professorship at the University of Cologne. Her research interests include sociological macro-theory, comparative social and political research, organizational sociology and sociology of technology.

Kyösti Pekonen is Assistant Professor at the University of Jyväskylä, Finland. Among his publications are *Bureaucracy from the Viewpoint of Politics* (1983) and *Symbols in the Modern Politics* (1991).

Marijke Prins graduated in Political Science at the University of Amsterdam, the Netherlands. She has been an assistant at the Department of Political Science. In 1984 she was appointed at the Department of Public Administration at the Erasmus University of Rotterdam. Currently she is associated to the University for Humanist Studies in Utrecht, which was founded in 1989.

Charles D. Raab is Senior Lecturer in the Department of Politics, University of Edinburgh. With Colin Bennett (University of Victoria, Canada), he is conducting research into data protection in Britain and data protection and information aspects of police co-operation in Europe. He also researched on education policy and he is the co-author (with Andrew McPherson) of Governing Education: A Sociology of Policy Since 1945 (Edinburgh, 1988), which was awarded the 1989 annual book prize of the Standing Conference on Studies in Education.

Frédéric Royall lectures in French Studies at the Department of Languages and Cultural Studies, University of Limerick, Ireland. He is at present undertaking research for a Ph.D. in the area of European integration and public administration.

Kirsti Stenvall is currently working as an assistant at the Research Institute for Social Sciences at the University of Tampere, Finland. Her interests include politics of education, constructions of welfare, and planning education and science in public administration. She is carrying out research for a Ph.D. thesis on the planning of the welfare state.

Martijn van Vliet lectures in management of change in non-profit organizations at the Business School of the Erasmus University Rotterdam. His fields of interests are environmental regulation of business and management of common pool resources.

BIBLIOGRAPHY

Aberbach, J.D., Putnam, R.D. and Rockman, B.A. (1981) *Bureaucrats and politicians in Western democracies*. Massachusetts: Harvard University Press.

Ackoff, R.L. (1981) *Creating the Corporate Future*. New York.

Administrationsudvalget af 1960 (1962) *Betænkning nr. 301*. København: Statens Trykningskontor.

Ahonen, P. (1987) Politiikan kautta politiikan yli: politiikan merkitysten tulkinnan paradokseista ja mahdollisuuksista. *Paradoksi 7*.

Alestalo, M. and Uusitalo, H. (1972) 'Eliittien sosiaalinen tausta ja yhteiskunnan muutokset Suomessa', *Sosiologa* 9(5): 193-207.

Allison, G.T. (1971) *Essence of decision*. Boston: Little Brown.

Antikainen, A. (1990) 'The Rise and Change of Comprehensive Planning: The Finnish Experience', *European Journal of Education* 25(1): 75-82.

Aristotle (1912) *The Politics*. Ed. A.D. Lindsay, 1943 ed. London: J.M. Dent.

Arvidsson, G. (1986) 'Performance Evaluation', in F.X. Kaufmann et al.

Ashby, R.W. (1957) *An Introduction to cybernetics*. New York: Wiley and Sons.

Ashby, R.W. (1960) *Design for a Brain*. London: Chapman & Hall.

Ashford, D. (1989) 'British Dogmatism and French Pragmatism revisited', in Marquand and Crouch *The New centralism. Britain out of step in Europe.*

Atkinson, J.W. and Birch, D. (1970) *The dynamics of action*. New York: Wiley.

Baakman, N.A.A. (1990) *Kritiek van het openbare bestuur*. Amsterdam: Thesis Publishers.

Bacharach, S.B. and E.J. Lawler (1980) *Power and Politics in Organizations*. San Francisco: Jossey-Bass.

Barbour, G. (1980) 'Law Enforcement' in G. Washnis *Productivity Improvement Handbook for State & Local Government*. New York: John Wiley & Sons.

Barrington, T. (1980) *The Irish Administration System*. Dublin: Institute of Public Administration.

Bateson, G. (1972) *The Logical Categories of Learning and Communication, Steps to an Ecology of Mind*. New York: Ballantine.

Bennett, C. (1992) *Regulating Privacy*. Ithaca and London: Cornell University Press.

Berg, J. v.d. en Molleman, H. (1974) *Crisis in de Nederlandse politiek*. Leiden and Alphen a/d Rijn.

Blau, P.M. and W.R. Scott (1963) *Formal organizations. A comparative approach*. London: Routledge and Kegan Paul.

Blume, P. (1992) 'European Data Protection' and 'Data Protection and the EEC', in P. Blume *3 Lectures on Data Protection*. Paper no. 45, University of Copenhagen: Institute of Legal Science.

Bogason, P. (1991) 'Control for whom? recent advances in research on governmental guidance and control', *European Journal of Political Research* 20: 189-208.

Bouckaert, G. (1990) *Productiviteit in de overheid*. Leuven: VCOB.

Bouckaert, G. (1990) 'The History of the Productivity Movement', *Public Productivity and Management Review* XIV(1): 53-89.

Bouckaert, G. (1992) 'A Productivity Analysis in the Public Sector: The Case of the Fire Service', in *International Review of Administrative Sciences* 2 (forthcoming).

Bouckaert, G. (1992) 'Public Productivity in Retrospective', in M. Holzer (ed.) *Public Productivity Handbook*. New York: Marcel Dekker Inc.

Boulding, K.E. (1970) *A primer on social dynamics*. New York: Free Press.

Boulding, K.E. (1978) *Ecodynamics*. Beverly Hills: Sage Publications.

Bourricaud, F. (1977) 'A quelles conditions les sociétés post-industrielles sont-elles gouvernables?', *International Conference on Les Démocraties occidentales, craintes et espérances*. Fondation Internationale des Sciences Humaines.

Bozeman, B. (1987) *All organizations are Public: Bridging Public and Private Organization Theories*. San Francisco: Jossey Bass.

Bradley, J. et al. (1992) *The Role of the Structural Funds: Analysis of Consequences for Ireland in the Context of 1992*. Dublin: Economic and Social Research Institute.

Braun, D. and Keman, H. (1986) 'Politikstrategien und Konfliktreguliering in den Niederlanden', *Politische Vierteljahresschrift* 27/1: 78-99.

Breuillard, M. (1991) 'Le Nouveau Conservate britannique à l'épreuve des réalités de Kent', *Les Cahiers du CRAPS 'Regards sur la Décentralisation et l'Aménagement du territoire en Europe'* no14, septembre 1991, 22:39.

Breuillard, M. (1992) 'La Dynamique du Tunnel', in R. Vickerman, Y. Luchaire and G. Marcou (eds) *Le Tunnel entre Etats et Marchés*. Presses Universitaires de Lille.

Brudney, J. (1986) 'The SBA and SCORE: Coproducing Management Assistance Services', *Public Productivity Review* 40: 57-67.

Brudney, J. (1990a) *Fostering Volunteer Programs in the Public Sector*. San Francisco: Jossey-Bass.

Brundtland commission (1987) *Our Common Future*. Oxford: Oxford UP.

Brunsson, N. (1989) *The Organization of Hypocrisy. Talk, Decisions and Actions in Organizations*. New York: John Wiley and Sons.

Buckley, W., Burns, T.R. and Meeker, D. (1974) 'Structural Resolutions of Collective Action Problems', *Behavioural Science* 19: 277-97.

Burkert, H. (1984) 'Information law problems for the eighties', *Transnational Data Report* 7: 331-36.

Burns, T.R., Th. Baumgarter and Ph. DeVille (1985) *Man, Decisions, Society*. New York: G & B Science Publishers.

Callon, M. and Law, J. (1982) 'On Interests and their Transformation: Enrolment and Counter-Enrolment', *Social Studies of Science* 12(4): 615-624.

Cameron, D.R. (1982) *Social Democracy, Corporation, and Labor Quiescence: The Representation of Economic Interest in Advanced Capitalist Society (Manuscript)*. Yale University.

Chubb, B. (1982) *The Government and Politics of Ireland (second edition)*. London: Longman.

Clegg, S.R. (1990) *Modern Organizations: Organization Studies in the Postmodern World*. London: Sage.

Commisariat général du plan (1988) *École de la deuxième chance, deuxième chance de l'école*. La Documentation Française.

Commission of the European Communities (1988a) 'Council regulation #2052/88 on the Task of the Structural Funds', *Official Journal* L185/9, 15 July.

Commission of the European Communities (1988b) 'Council regulation #4253/88 on the Coordination of the Activities of the Structural Funds', *Official Journal* L374, 31 December.

Commission of the European Communities (1990) 'Proposal for a council directive concerning the protection of individuals in relation to the processing of personal data' *COM(90) 314 Final--SYN 287*, 13 September, Brussels.

Conant, R.C. and Ashby, W.R. (1970) 'Every Good Regulator of a System Must Be a Model of that System', *International Journal of Systems Science* 1: 89-97.

Coombes, D., Rees, N. and Stapleton, J. (1991) *Economic Development Networks: Consultation of Economic and Social Interests for Purposes of Local Economic Strategy.* Brussels: LEDA.

Council of Europe (1981) *Explanatory Report on the Convention for the Protection of Individuals with regard to Automatic Processing of Personal Data.* Includes Treaty No. 108, Strasbourg: Council of Europe.

Crick, B. (1962) *In Defense of Politics.* Harmondsworth: Penguin Books Ltd.

Crozier, M. (1964) *The Bureaucratic Phenomenon.* Chicago: University of Chicago Press.

Crozier, M., Huntingdon, S. and Watanuki, J. (1975) *The Crisis of Democracy.* New York University Press.

Culliton, J. (1992) *A Time for Change: Industrial Policy of the 1990s.* Dublin: Stationery Office.

Dahl, A. (1961) *Who governs.* New Haven: Yale University Press.

Dahl, R. (1982) *Dilemmas of Pluralist Democracy, Autonomy vs. Control.* New Haven: Yale University Press.

Dale, R. et al. (1990) *The TVEI Story.* Open University Press.

Danaher, G. Frein, P. and Sexton, J. (1985) *Manpower Policy in Ireland.* Report #82, Dublin: NESC.

Denhardt, A.B. (1984) *Theories on Public Organisations.* Berkeley: University of California Press.

Denhardt, R. (1984) *Theories of public organizations.* Monterey, Cal.: Brooks/Cole Publishing.

Deutsch, K. (1963/1966) *The Nerves of Government.* New York: Free Press.

Developments in Education 1988-1990 Finland (1990) *Reference Publication.* Helsinki: Ministry of Education.

Dijkum, C. van, Tombe, D. de et al. (1992) *Gamma Chaos.* Bloemendaal: Aramith.

Dineen, D. and Wallace, J. (1987) *Labour market segmentation in Ireland.* Report prepared for PA Cambridge Economic Consultants Limited.

Dineen, D. (1989) *Changing employment patterns in Ireland: Recent trends and future prospects.* Paper prepared for the Irish National Pension Board.

Djupsund, G. (1984) 'The Futile Quest for Local Control', in H. Paloheimo (ed.) *Politics in the Era of Corporatism and Planning.* Tampere: The Finnish Political Association.

Downing, P.B. and K.I. Hanf, eds (1983) *International Comparisons in Implementing Pollution Laws.* Boston: Kluwer-Nijhoff.

Doxiadis, C.A. (1968) *Ekistics: an Introduction to the Science of Human Settlement.* London: Hutchinson.

Dörner, D., Kreuzig, H.W., Reither, F. and Stäudel, T. (1983) *Lohhausen - Vom Umgang mit Unbestimmtheit und Komplexität.* Bern: Huber.

Dror, Y. (1984) 'Facing Momentous Choices', *International Review of Administrative Sciences* 2: 97-106.

Dror, Y. (1988) 'Visionary Political Leadership, On Improving a Risky Requisite', *International Political Science Review* 9(1): 7-22.

Dror, Y. (1990) *Democratic Reformcraft*. Working Paper, European Institute of Public Administration.

Dryzek, John, S. (1987) 'Complexity and Rationality in Public Life', *Political Studies* 35: 424-42.

Dunleavy, P. and O'Leary, B. (1987) *Theories of the state. The politics of liberal democracy*. London: MacMillan.

Dunsire, A. (1978) *Control in a Bureaucracy*. Oxford: Martin Robertson.

Dunsire, A. (1986) 'A cybernetic view of guidance, control and evaluation in the public sector', in F.-X. Kaufmann et al.

Easton, D. (1953) *The Political System*. New York: Knopf.

Edelman, M. (1964) *The symbolic uses of politics*. Urbana: University of Illinois Press.

Edelman, M. (1977) *Political Language. Words that succeed and politics that fail*. New York: Academic Press.

Emery, F.E. and Trist, E.L. (1965) 'The Causal Texture of Organizational Environments', *Human Relations* 18: 21-32.

Etzioni, A. (1968) *The active society*. New York: Free Press.

Feldman, M.S. and March, J.G. (1981) 'Information in organizations as signal and symbol', *Administrative Science Quarterly* 26: 171-86.

Ferris, J. (1984) 'Coprovision: Citizen Time and Money Donations in Public Service Provision', *Public Administration Review* 44(4): 324-33.

Fitzgerald, M. and Durant, R. (1980) 'Citizen Evaluations and Urban Management: Service Delivery in an Era of Protest', *Public Administration Review* 40(6): 585-94.

Flaherty, D. (1989) *Protecting Privacy in Surveillance Societies*. Chapel Hill, N.C.: University of North Carolina Press.

Flynn, N. (1990) *Public Sector Management*.London: Harvester Wheatsheaf.

Foerster, H. von (1984) 'On Self-Organizing Systems and their Environments', in H. von Foerster *Observing Systems*. 2nd edition, Seaside (CA): Intersystems Publ.

Geary, P. (1988) *The Nature and Functioning of Labour Markets: A Survey of International and Irish Literature and a Statement of Research Priorities in Ireland*. Dublin: NESC.

Gersick, C.J.G. (1991) 'Revolutionary Change Theories: a Multilevel Exploration of the Punctuated Equilibrium Paradigm', *Academy of Management Review* (1): 10-36.

Giddens, A. (1979) *Central Problems in Social Theory*. London: Macmillan.

Gleick, J. (1988) *Chaos, Making a New Science*. Harmondsworth: Penguin Books Ltd.

Green, T.H. (1895) *Principles of Political Obligation*. London: Longman.

Goodman, P.S. and Pennings, J.M., (1977) *New Perspectives on Organizational Effectiveness*. San Francisco: Jossey Bass.

Goudt, M. and Dorsman, W. (1990) *Vrouwen en politieke strategieën*. Leiden: Stichting Burgerschapskunde.

Gough, I. (1979) *The Political Economy of the Welfare State*. London: The Macmillan Press Ltd.

Gretschmann, K. (1981) *Steuerungsprobleme der Staatswirtschaft*. Berlin: Duncker & Humblot.

Gunn, L.A. (1987) 'Perspectives on Public Management', in J. Kooiman and K.A. Eliassen (eds) *Managing Public Organizations*. Sage Publications: London & Beverly Hills.

Habermas, J. (1989) *De nieuwe onoverzichtelijkheid en andere opstellen*. Meppel: Boom.

Hall, P. (1972) 'A symbolic interactionist analysis of politics', *Sociological Inquiry* 42: 35-76.

Hall, P. (1980) *Great Planning Disasters*. London: Weidenfeld and Nicholson.

Hancher, L. & Moran, M. (1989) 'Organizing regulatory space', in Flynn, N. (1990) *Public sector management*. London: Harvester Wheatsheaf.

Hanf, K. (1982) 'Regulatory structures: enforcement as implementation', *European Journal of Political Research* 10: 159-72.

Hanf, K. and O'Toole, L. (1992) 'Revisiting old friends: networks, implementation structures and the management of inter-organizational relations', *European Journal of Political Research* 21: 163-80.

Hanf, K. and Scharpf, F. (eds) (1978) *Interorganizational Policymaking*. London: Sage.

Hardin, G. (1968) 'The Tragedy of the Commons', *Science* 162: 1243-48.

Harmon, M.M. and Mayer, R.T. (1986) *Organization Theory for Public Administration*. New York: Scott Foresman.

Hart, H.L.A. (1961) *The Concept of Law*. Oxford: Clarendon Press.

Haveman, R. and Margolis, J. (eds) (1970) *Public Expenditures and Policy Analysis*. Chicago: Markham.

Heffron, F. (1989) *Organization Theory and Public Organizations*. Englewood Cliffs: Prentice Hall.

Hegner, F. (1986) 'Solidarity and Hierarchy: Institutional Arrangements for the Coordination of Actions', in F.X. Kaufmann et al.

Henry, N. (1975) 'Paradigms of Public Administration', *Public Administration Review* July-August 35: 378-86.

Hernes, G. (1978) *Forhandlingsøkonomi og blandingsadministrasjon*. Bergen: Universitetsforlaget.

Hirsch, F. (1977) *Social Limits to Growth*. London: Routledge and Keegan Paul.

Hirschman, A.O. (1991) *The Rhetoric of Reaction. Perversity, Futility, Jeopardy*. Cambridge, Massachusetts and London: The Belknap Press of Harvard University.

Hjern, B. and Hull, C. (1982) 'Implementation research as empirical constitutionalism', *European Journal of Political Research* 10: 105-15.

HMSO (1985,'88,'89,'90) *Reports of the Data Protection Registrar*. London: HMSO.

Hoed, P. den, Salet, W. and Sluis, H. van der (1983) *Planning als onderneming*. The Hague: WRR.

Holliday, I., Marcou, G. and Vickerman, R. (1991) *Channel Tunnel, Public Policy, Regional Development and European Integration*. London: Belhaven Press.

Hood, C.C. (1983a) *The Tools of Government*. London: Macmillan.

Hood, C.C. (1983b) 'Using Bureaucracy Sparingly', *Public Administration* 61(2): 197-208.

Hood, C.C. (1986) 'Concepts of Control over Public Bureaucracies: "Comptrol" and "Interpolable Balance", in F.-X. Kaufmann et al.

Hood, C.C. (1990) *Beyond the Public Bureaucracy State? Public Administration in the 1990s*. London: London School of Economics.

Hood, C.C. (1990) 'Public Administration: lost an empire, not yet found a role?', in Adrian Leftwich (ed.), *New developments in political science.* London: Edward Elgar.

Hood, C.C. (1991) *Administrative Argument.* Hampshire: Dartmouth Publishing Company.

Hood, C.C. and Schuppert, G.F. (eds) (1988) *Delivering Public Services in Western Europe.* London: Sage.

Hovi, R., Kivinen, O. and Rinne, R. (1989) 'Komitealaitos, koulutusmietinnöt ja koulutuspolitiikan oikeutus. Koulutuskomiteoiden kehityslinjat ja oikeutusperustelut Suomessa', *Turun yliopiston julkaisuja* Sarja C osa 73. Turku.

House of Commons (1990) *Annual Report of the Data Protection Registrar.* First Report of the Home Affairs Committee, London: HMSO.

Ireland (1988) *The government policy on the maximisation of the benefits to Ireland of a revitalised Regional Policy in the European Community.* 23 September, Dublin: Government Information Office.

Jantsch, E. (1980) *The Self-organizing Universe.* New York: Pergamon.

Jarillo, J.C. and Ricart, J.E. (1986) *Sustaining Networks.* Research Paper. IESE.

Järvelä, M. (1991) 'Palkkatyö ja koulutustarve.', *Tutkijaliiton julkaisusarja* 68. Helsinki: Tutkijaliitto.

Jones, K. (1989) *Right-turn: the conservative revolution in education.* Radius.

Jordan, A.G. and Schubert, K. (eds) (1992) *European Journal of Political Research* 21, Special Issue: Policy Networks.

Jørgensen, B.T. and Larsen, B. (1987) 'Control - an attempt at forming a theory', *Scandinavian Political Studies* 10: 279-99.

Kapil, R. and Kekkonen, S. (1990) *Public Management Developments Survey 1990.* Paris: OECD.

Kelman, S. (1992) 'Adversary and Cooperationist Institutions for Conflict Resolution in Public Policymaking', *Journal of Policy Analysis and Management* 11(2): 178-206.

Kaufman, H. (1976) *Are Government Organizations Immortal.* Washington: Brookings Institution.

Kaufmann, F.X., Majone, G. and Ostrom, V. (eds) (1986) *Guidance, Control and Evaluation in the Public Sector.* New York: De Gruyter.

Kehittyvä koulutus (1990) *KM 1990:49.* Helsinki.

Kickert, W.J.M. (1985) 'The magic word flexibility', *International Studies of Management and Organisation.*

Kickert, W.J.M. (1991) 'Autopoiesis and the Science of Administration', in R.J. in 't Veld et al.

Kickert, W.J.M. (1992/1993) 'Steering at a distance', *Governance*, forthcoming

Kivinen, O. (1988) 'Koulutuksen järjestelmäkehitys. Peruskoulutus ja valtiollinen kouludoktriini Suomessa 1800- ja 1900-luvuilla', *Turun yliopiston julkaisuja* C:67. Turku.

Kivinen, O. and Rinne, R. (eds) (1992) *Educational Strategies in Finland in the 1990s.* Research Unit for the Sociology of education. Turku: University of Turku.

Klitzsch, W. (1986) *Behörden und Betriebe. Eine Analyse ihres Verhältnisses im Prozeß der Implementation politischer Programme.* Bielefeld: Kleine.

Knoke, D. and Laumann, E.O. (1982) 'The Social Organization of National Policy Domains' in P.V. Marsden and N. Lin (eds.) *Social Structure and Network Analysis.* Beverly Hills: Sage.

Kogan, M. (1975) *Educational Policy-Making. A Study of Interest Groups and Parliament.* London: George Allen and Unwin Ltd.

Komiteanmietintö 22 (1978) *Valtion keskushallintokomitean II osamietintö. Nide 1 ja 2.* Helsinki: Valtion painatuskeskus.

Kooiman, J. and Eliassen, K. (eds) (1987) *Managing Public Organizations, Lessons from Contemporary European Experience.* London: Sage.

Kooiman, J. (1988) *Besturen: overheid en maatschappij in wisselwerking.* Assen/Maastricht: Van Gorcum.

Kooiman, J. (1990) *Governance: new patterns of interaction between government and society.* ECPR Workshop Prospectus.

Kooiman, J. (1990) 'Sturen, besturen of (be)sturen', *Bestuurswetenschappen* 6: 408-425.

Kooiman, J. (1991) *Governance: the interaction between government and society.* Paper presented to the ECPR Joint Sessions Conference, 22-28 March, Essex: University of Essex.

Koppenjan, J.F.M. and J.A.M. Hufen (1990) *Learning and Public Policy.* Paper Conference Steering, Autopoiesis, Configuration. Rotterdam, 21-11-90.

Korsbækudvalget (1971) *Betænkning nr. 629.* København: Statens Trykningskontor.

Kouwenhoven, V.P. (1991) *Publiek-Private Samenwerking: Mode of Model?* Ph.D. series in General Management, Delft: Eburon.

Kreukels, A.M.J. (1989) 'Naar nieuwe besturingsconcepties', in A.B. Ringeling en I.Th.M. Snellen (eds) *Overheid: op de (terug)tocht of naar een nieuw profiel.* The Hague: VUGA.

Kuhn, T.S. (1962) *The Structure of Scientific Revolutions.* Chicago: University of Chicago Press.

Laegreid, P. and Olsen, J. (1978) *Byråkrati og beslutninger. En studie av norske departement.* Oslo.

Laffan, B. (1986) *The Operation of the European Social Fund in Ireland and Belgium.* Ph.D. Thesis, Dublin: Trinity College.

Laffan, B. (1989) 'While you're over there get us a grant: the management of structural funds in Ireland', *Irish Political Studies* 4: 43-57.

Landau, M. (1973) 'On the Concept of a Self-Correcting Organization', *Public Administration Review* 33: 533-42.

La Porte, T.R. (ed.) (1975/1979) *Organized Social Complexity. Challenge to Politics and Policy.* Princeton, NJ: Princeton University Press.

Lash, S. (1988) 'Postmodernism as a Regime of Signification', *Theory, Culture and Society* 5(2 & 3): 311-36.

Latour, B. (1987) *Science in Action. How to Follow Scientists and Engineers through Society.* Milton Keynes: Open University Press.

Legrand, L. (1982) *Pour un collège democratique.* La Documentation Française.

Lehning, P.B. (1986) *Politieke orde en Rawliaanse rechtvaardigheid.* Delft: Eburon.

Levine, S. and White, P.E. (1961) 'Exchange as a Conceptual Framework for the Study of Interorganizational Relationships', *ASQ* 5: 583-601.

Levine, Ch. (1984) 'Citizenship and Service Delivery: The Promise of Coproduction', *Public Administration Review* Vol. 44, special issue: 178-187.

Lijphart, A. (1975) *Politics of accommodation, pluralism and democracy in the Netherlands.* Berkeley: University of California Press.

Lindblom, C.E. (1959) 'The Science of Muddling Through', *Public Administration Review* 19: 79-88.

Lindblom, C.E. (1965) *The Intelligence of Democracy.* New York: Free Press.

Lindblom, C.E. (1977) *Politics and Markets. The World's Political-Economic System.* New York: Basic Books.

Loye, D. and Eisler, R. (1987) 'Chaos and Transformation, Implications of Nonequilibrium Theory for Social Sciences and Society', *Behavioral Science* 32: 53-65.

Luhmann, N. (1970) *Soziologische Aufklärung.* Köln/Opladen: Westdeutscher Verlag.

Luhmann, N. (1981) *Politische Theorie im Wohlfahrtsstaat.* München: Olzog.

Luhmann, N. (1984) *Soziale Systemen.* Frankfurt: Suhrkampf.

Lundgren, U.P. (1979) 'Educational Evaluation. A Basis for, or a Legitimation of, Educational Policy', *Scandinavian Journal of Educational Research* 32(1): 31-45.

Lyotard, J.-F. (1984) *The Postmodern Condition.* Manchester: Manchester University Press.

Majone, G. (1986) 'Mutual Adjustment by Debate and Persuasion', in F-X Kaufman et al. (eds)

Malkin, J. and Wildavsky, A. (1991) 'Why the Traditional Distinction between Public and Private Goods should be Abandoned', *Journal of Theoretical Politics* 3(4): 355-78.

Mandell, M.P. (1990) 'Network Management', in R.W. Gage and M.P. Mandell, op. cit.

March, J.G. (1962) 'The Business Firm as a Political Coalition', *Journal of Politics* 24: 662-78.

March, J.G. (1974) 'The Technology of Foolishness', in H. Leavitt, L. Pinfield and E. Webb (eds) *Organizations of the Future.* Preager.

March, J.G. (1978) 'Bounded Rationality, Ambiguity, and the Engineering of Choice', *Bell Journal of Economics* 9(2): 587-608.

March, J.G. and Olsen, J.P. (1989) *Rediscovering institutions. The organizational basis of politics.* New York: The Free Press.

Marin, B. and Mayntz, R. (eds) (1991) *Policy Networks.* Frankfurt/Boulder: Campus/Westview.

Mattson, G. (1986) 'The Promise of Citizen Coproduction: Some Persistent Issues', *Public Administration* 40: 51-56.

Mayntz, R. (1978) 'Intergovernmental implementation of environmental policy', in K. Hanf & F. Scharpf (eds) *Interorganizational Policy Making.* London and Beverly Hills: Sage.

Mayntz, R. (1978) *Vollzugsprobleme der Umweltpolitik.* Stuttgart: Kohlhammer.

Mayntz, R. (1985) *Political Intentions and Legal Measures: The Determinants of Policy Decisions.* European University Institute.

Mayntz, R. and Edelmann, B. (1987) 'Eigendynamische Soziale Prozesse', *Kölner Zeitschrift* 39: 648-68.

Mayntz, R. (1988) 'Political Intensions and Legal Measures', in T. Daintith (ed.) *Law as an Instrument of Economic Policy: Comparative and Critical Approaches.* Berlin: De Gruyter.

Mayntz, R. (1990) *The influence of natural science theories on contemporary social science.* Discussion paper 90/7, Köln: Max Planck Institut für Gesellschaftsforschung.

Melucci, A. (1984) *Altri codici. Aree di movimento nella metropoli.* Bologna: Il Mulino.

Metcalfe, L. (1974) 'Systems Models, Economic Models and the Causal Texture of Organizational Environments: An Approach to Macro-organization Theory' *Human Relations* 27: 639-63.

Metcalfe, L. (1978) 'Policy making in turbulent environments', in K. Hanf and F. Scharpf (eds)

Metcalfe, L. (1981) 'Designing Precarious Partnerships', in P.C. Nyström and W.H. Starbuck (eds) *Handbook of Organizational Design*. Vol. 1.

Metcalfe, L. (1982) 'Self-Regulation, Crisis Management and Preventive Medicine: The Evolution of UK Bank Supervision', *Journal of Management Studies* 19(1): 75-90.

Metcalfe, L. and Richards, S. (1987) *Improving Public Management*. EIPA, Sage: London.

Metcalfe, L. (1989) *Accountability and Effectiveness, A Meta-Power Perspective*. IPSA Round Table.

Meyer, J.W. and Rowan, B. (1977) 'Institutionalized organizations: formal structure as myth and ceremony', *American Journal of Sociology* 83: 340-363.

Miles, R.E. and Snow, C.C. (1984) 'Fit Failure and the Hall of Fame', *California Management Review* 3, Spring: 10-28.

Miller, P. and Rose, N. (1990) 'Governing Economic Life', *Economy and Society* 19(1): 1-31.

Mintz, A. (1951) 'Nonadaptive Group Behavior', *Journal of Abnormal and Social Psychology* 46: 150-59.

Mintzberg, H. (1983) *Structure in fives*. Englewood Cliffs, N.J.: Prentice-Hall.

Montesquieu, Baron C.L. de S. (1748) *De l'Esprit des Lois*. Nugent (trans.), Neumann (ed.) (1949) *The Spirit of the Laws*. New York: Hafner Publishing.

Morgan, G. (1986) *Images of Organizations*. London: Sage.

Mueller, A. (ed.) (1968) *Encyclopaedia of Cybernetics*. G. Gilbertson (trans.). Manchester: Manchester University Press.

Mushkin, S. and Sandifer, F. (1980) 'Personnel Management', in G. Washnis *Productivity Improvement Handbook for State & Local Government*. New York: John Wiley & Sons.

Nystrom, P.C. and Starbuck, W.H. (eds) (1981) *Handbook of Organizational Design*. Vol. 1 & 2, Oxford: Oxford University Press.

O'Riordan, T. (1983) *Environmentalism*. London: Pion.

Offe, C. (1984) *Contradictions in the Welfare State*. London: Hutchinson.

Offe, C. (1989) *Disorganized Capitalism*. London: Polity Press.

Olsen, J.P. (1986) 'Foran en ny offentlig revolusjon', *Nytt Norsk Tidsskrift* 3: 3-15.

Olson, M. (1965) *The Logic of Collective Action*. Harvard University Press: Cambridge.

Ostrom, E. (1990) *Governing the Commons*. Cambridge: Cambridge UP.

Ouchi, W.G. (1981) *Theory Z*. Philippines: Addison-Wesley.

Panhelainen, M. (1992) 'Work organizations and the expansion of continuing professional education in universities', in M. Parjanen (ed.) *Legitimation in Adult Education*. Tampere: University of Tampere.

Pateman, C. (1970) *Participation and democratic theory*. Cambridge: Cambridge University Press.

Pekonen, K. (1983) 'Byrokratia politiikan näkökulmasta', *Jyväskylä Studies in Education, Psychology and Social Research* 51.

Pekonen, K. (1985) 'Policy-making and the relationship between politics and bureaucracy', *International Review of Administrative Sciences* LI(3): 207-20.

Percy, S. (1987) 'Citizen Involvement in Coproducing Safety and Security in the Community', *Public Productivity Review* 42: 83-93.

Perelman, Ch. (1982) *The realm of rhetoric*. Indiana: University of Notre Dame Press.

Perrier, R. (1991) *Organisation et gestion de l'éducation national*. Berger-lavrault.

Perry, J.L. and K.L. Kraemer (1983) *Public Management: Public and Private Perspectives*. Palo Alto: Mayfield Publishing Co.

Pfeffer, J. and Salancik, G.R. (1978) *The External Control of Organizations. A Resource-dependence Perspective*. New York.

Pickvance, C.G. (1990) 'Economic intervention and political conflict in a declining resort', in M. Harloe et al. (eds) *Place, Policy and Politics; Do localities matter?* London: Unwin Hyman.

Pollitt, C. (1987) 'Performance measurement and the consumer: hijacking a bandwagon?', *Performance measurement and the consumer*. London: National Consumer Council.

Pollitt, C. (1990) *Managerialism and the Public Services*. Oxford: Basil Blackwell.

Pondy, L.R. (1977) *Effectiveness: A Thick Description*, in Goodman and Pennings.

Poulsen, J. (1992) 'EC support of regional development', in *The Regions: Partnership and Planning*. Mimeo, Dublin: Chambers of Commerce of Ireland.

Prigogine, I. and Stengers, I. (1984/1985) *Order out of chaos. Man's new dialogue with Nature*. New York: Bantam.

Prins, M.C.J. (1989) *Women's emancipation in Motion: Emancipation policy-making as a problem of governance, 1974-1989*. Groningen: Prins Productions & Styx Publications.

Prost, A. (1983) *Les lycées et leurs étude au seuil du 21ème siècle*. La Documentation Française.

Raab, C. (1991) *Can data protection be measured?* Paper presented at the International Institute of Administrative Sciences, Working Group on Public Sector Productivity, Brussels.

Raab, C. (1992a) 'Taking networks seriously: education policy in Britain', *European Journal of Political Research* 21: 69-90.

Raab, C. (1992b) 'Information and communication technology, government transparency and data protection', *Informatization and the Public Sector* 2: 75-91.

Raab, C. (1992c) *Data protection: the European dimension*. Paper presented at the ECPR, Joint Sessions of Workshops, Workshop on Police Co-operation in Europe after 1992, University of Limerick.

Raab, C. (1993) 'Data protection in Britain: governance and learning', *Governance* 6, forthcoming.

Rainey, H.G. (1984) 'Organization theory and political science: organizational typologies, political variables and policy studies', *Policy Studies Journal* 13: 5-22.

Rainey, H.G. (1991) *Understanding and Managing Public Organisations*. San Francisco: Jossey-Bass.

Rainey H.G. and H.B. Milward (1983) 'Public Organizations, Policy Networks and Environments', in R.H. Hall et al (ed.) *Organizational Theory and Public Policy*. Beverly Hills: Sage.

Ranson, S. (1980) 'Changing relation between centre and locality in education', *Local Government Studies* Vol. 6.

Reich, R.B. (1985) 'Public Administration and Public Deliberation: An Interpretive Essay', *The Yale Law Journal* 94: 1617-41.

Reidenberg, J. (1992) 'Privacy in the information economy: a fortress or frontier for individual rights?', *Federal Communications Law Journal* 44: 195-243.

Rhodes, R.A.W. (1987) 'Developing the public service orientation, or let's add a soupcon of political theory', *Local Government Studies* May/June: 63-73.

Richardson, J.J. and Jordan, A.G. (1979) *Governing Under Pressure*. London: Martin Robertson.

Richardson, J.J. and Jordan, A.G. (1983) 'Overcrowded Policymaking: Some British and European Reflections', *Policy Sciences* 15(3): 247-68.

Ringeling, A.B. and Hufen, J. (eds) (1990) *Beleidsnetwerken*. The Hague: VUGA.

Romein, J. (1967) *Op het breukvlak van twee eeuwen*. Amsterdam: E.M. Querido.

Rorty, R. (1989) *Contingency, irony and solidarity*. New York: Cambridge University Press.

Rose, R. and Page, E. (1990) 'Actions in adversity: responses to unemployment in Britain and Germany', *West European Politics* 13(4): 66-85.

Rothstein, B. 1987. 'Välfärdsstat, implementering och effektivitet', *Statsvetenskapligt Tidsskrift* 1: 21-37.

Sabatier, P. (1986) 'Top-down and bottom-up approaches to implementation research: a critical analysis and suggested synthesis', *Journal of Public Policy* 6: 21-48.

Salter, B. and Tapper, T. (1985) *Power and Policy in education: the case of independent schooling*. Falmer Press.

Sarjala, J. (1982) *Suomalainen koulutuspolitiikka*. Juva: WSOY.

Sartori, G. (1970) 'Concept Misformation in Comparative Politics', *American Political Science Review* 64: 1033-53.

Sartori, G. (1991) 'Comparing and Miscomparing', *Journal of Theoretical Politics* 3(3): 243-57.

Scharpf, F.W. (1978) 'Conclusions', in K. Hanf and F.W. Scharpf (eds).

Scharpf, F.W. (1987) 'A Game-Theoretical Interpretation of Inflation and Unemployment in Western Europe', *Journal of Public Policy* 7: 227-58.

Schelling, Th. (1978) *Micromotives and Macrobehavior*. New York: Norton.

Schendelen, M. van (1984) 'Consociationalism, pillarization and conflict management in the Low Countries, *Acta Politica* special issue, January.

Schmidt, M.G. (1987) 'The Politics of Labour Market Policy', in F. Castles et al. *Managing Mixed Economies*. Berlin: De Gruyter.

Schmitter, P.C. (1982) 'Interest Intermediation and Regime Governability in Contemporary Western Europe and North America', in S. Berger (ed.) *Organizing Interests in Western Europe*. Cambridge: Cambridge University Press.

Schon, Donald (1971) *Beyond the Stable State*. Temple Smith. Harmondsworth: Penguin Books.

Schuyt, C. (1989) 'De verzorgingsstaat als object van pars-pro-toto-generalisaties', *Beleid en Maatschappij* 3: 119-32.

Schwartz, P. (1992) 'Data processing and government administration: the failure of the American legal response to the computer', *Hastings Law Journal* 43: 1321-89.

Scott, W.R. (1987) *Organizations. Rational, Natural and Open Systems*. Englewood Cliffs: Prentice Hall.

Scott, W.R. and Meyer, J.W. (1982) *The Organization of Institutional Sectors*. Stanford University.

Selznick, P. (1947) *TVA and Grassroots*. New York: Harper and Row.

Sharpe, L.J. (1985) 'Central Coordination and the Policy Network', in *Political Studies* 33: 361-81.

Sherbourne, D.W. (ed.) (1966) *A key to Whitehead's Process and Reality*. New York: Mac Millan.

Siegel, G. and Sundeen, R. (1986) 'Volunteering in Municipal Police Departments: Some Hypotheses on Performance Impacts', *Public Productivity Review* 40: 77-92.

Simon, H.A. (1969) 'The architecture of complexity', *Proceedings of the American Philosophical Society* 106: 467-82.

Sorokin, P.A. (1941) *Social and cultural dynamics*. 4 Vol., New York: American Book Company.

Spinoza, B. de (1677) 'Tractatus Politicus', in A.G. Wernham (ed. and trans.) (1958) *Spinoza The Political Works*. Oxford: Clarendon Press.

Steiner, P. (1970) 'The Public sector and the Public Interest', in Haveman and Margolis, op. cit.

Streeck, W. and Schmitter, P.C. (1984) *Community, Market, State - and Associations? The prospective contribution of interest governance to social order*. Florence: EUI Working Paper 94.

Streeck, W. and Schmitter, P. (1985) 'Community, marlet, state - and associations?', in W. Streeck and P. Schmitter (eds) *Private Interest Government: beyond market and the state*. London: Sage.

Summa, H. (1989) *Hyvinvointipolitiikka ja suunnitteluretoriikka: Tapaus asuntopolitiikka*. Espoo: Yhdyskuntasuunnittelun täydennyskoulutuskeskuksen julkaisuja A 17.

Summa, H. (1990) 'Ethos, Pathos and Logos in Central Government Planning Texts', in S. Hänninen and K. Palonen (ed.) *Texts, Contexts, Concepts. Studies on Politics and Power in Language*. Jyväskylä: The Finnish Political Science Association.

Taylor, W. (ed.) (1984) *Metaphors of Education*. London: Heineman.

Taylor, J. and Williams, H. (1991) 'Public administration and the information polity', *Public Administration* 69: 171-90.

Teague, P. (1989) 'European Community labour market harmonisation', *Journal of Public Policy* 9(1): 1-33.

Teubner, G. (1982) 'Reflexives Recht. Entwicklungsmodelle des Rechts in vergleichender Perspektive', in *Archiv für Rechts- und Sozialphilosophie* 68: 13.

Teubner, G. and Willke, H. (1984) 'Kontext und Autonomie: Gesellschaftliche Selbststeuerung durch reflexives Recht', *Zeitschrift für Rechtssoziologie* 6: 4-35.

Traxler, F. and Vobruba, G. (1986) *Funktionale Äquivalente zum Recht durch neokorporatistische Steuerung?*. Lecture held at the Conference on 'Limitations of Law', Bielefeld.

Turner, B.S. (1986) *Citizenship and Capitalism: The Debate over Reformism*. London: Allen and Unwin.

Tyrell, H. (1979) 'Familie und gesellschaftliche Differenzierung' in H. Groß (ed.) *Familie -wohin?* Reinbek b. Hamburg: Rowohlt.

Varela, F.G., Maturana, H.K. and Uribe, R. (1974) 'Autopoiesis,the Organizing of Living Systems', *Biosystems* 5: 187-196.

Väestön koulutus 2000 (1988) *KM 1988:28*. Koulutussuunnittelun neuvottelukunta. Helsinki.

Veld, R.J. in 't, Schaap, L., Termeer, C. and Twist, M. van (eds) (1991) *Autopoiesis and Configuration Theory*. Dordrecht: Kluwer.

Vermeulen, W.J.V. (1989) 'Het economische en communicatieve sturingsmodel', in P. Glasbergen (ed.) *Milieubeleid: theorie en praktijk*. Den Haag: VUGA.

Vester, F. (1983) *Unsere Welt - ein vernetztes System*. München: Deutscher Taschenbuch Verlag.

Vickers, G. (1973) 'Values, Norms and Policies', *Policy Sciences* 4: 103-11.

Vogel, D. (1986) *National Styles of Regulation*. Ithaca: Cornell UP.

Vree, J.K. de (1991) 'Chaos in Europe: an Inquiry into the Nature of Social Systems and the Methodology of the Behavioral Sciences', *Acta Politica* 6(1): 25-65.

Waddock, S.A. (1986) 'Public-private Partnership as Social Product and Process, *Research in Corporate Social*.

Wamsley, G.L. and Bruce, R.R. (1991) *Policy subsystem and policy developments; learning to live with chaos*. Blacksburgh, VA: Virginia Polytechnic and State University.

Wassenberg, A.F.P. and Kooiman, J. (1980) 'Advice and the reduction of overload', in R.Rose (ed.) *Challenge to governance. Studies in overloaded politics*. London: Sage.

Watzlawick, P., Weakland, J.H., and Fisch, R. (1974) *Change: Principles of Problem Formation and Resolution*. New York: Norton.

Weick, K.E. (1977) 'Repunctuating the Problem', in P.S. Goodman, J.M. Pennings and Associates *New Perspectives on Organizational Effectiveness*. San Francisco: Jossey-Bass.

Weisbrod, B. (1988) *The nonprofit economy*. Cambridge Massachusetts: Harvard University Press.

Werlin, H.H. (1988) 'The theory of political elasticity', *Administration and Society* 20(1), May: 46-70.

Whelan, R. and Dupont, R. (1986) 'Some Political Costs of Coprovision: The Case of the New Orleans Zoo', *Public Productivity Review* 40: 69-75.

White, J.D. (1990) 'Images of administrative reason and rationality', in H.D. Kass and B.L. Catron (eds) *Image and identities in public administration*. London: Sage.

Wiethölter, R. (1982) 'Entwicklung des Rechtsbegriffs', in V. Geßner and G. Winter (eds.) *Rechtsformen der Verflechtung von Staat und Wirtschaft*. Opladen: Westdeutscher Verlag.

Wildavsky, A. (1979) *The Art and Craft of Policy Analysis*. London: Macmillan.

Wilden, A. (1987) *The rules are no game*. London: Routledge and Kegan.

Wilensky, H.L. (1976) *The 'New Corporatism', Centralization, and the Welfare State*. London: Sage.

Wilensky, H.L. (1983) 'Political Legitimacy and Consensus', in S.E. Spirow and E. Yuchtman-Yaar (eds.) *Evaluating the Welfare State: Social and Political Perspectives*. New York.

Willke, H. (1983) *Entzauberung des Staates. Überlegungen zu einer sozietalen Steuerungstheorie*. Königstein/Taunus: Athenäum.

Winsemius, P. (1986) *Gast in eigen huis*. Alphen a.d. Rijn: Samson.

Wittgenstein, L. (1981) *Filosofisia tutkimuksia*. Juva: WSOY.

Wittrock, B. (1989) 'Social science and state development: transformations of the discourse of modernity', *International Social Science Journal* 122. 497-507.

Wright, M. (1988) 'Policy Community, Policy Network and Comparative Industrial Policies', *Political Studies* 36: 593-612.

Wyatt, R. (1989) *Intelligent Planning. Meaningful Methods for Sensitive Situations.* London: Unwin Hyman.

Ziegler-Jung, B. (1991) *Self-regulation in data protection law?* Paper for the European Group of Public Administration Conference on Informatization, The Hague.

Zijderveld, A.C. (1985) *De dynamiek van macht en gezag.* Den Haag: VUGA.

Zouwen, J. van der and Geyer, F. (1986) 'Epilogue', in F. Geyer and J. van der Zouwen (eds) *Sociocybernetic Paradoxes: Observation, Control and Evolution of Self-steering Systems.* London: Sage.